Universities and Empire

MONEY AND POLITICS IN THE SOCIAL SCIENCES DURING THE COLD WAR

**Edited and Introduced by
Christopher Simpson**

THE NEW PRESS ★ NEW YORK
1998

© 1998 by Christopher Simpson. Epigraph © 1976 by Michael Dibdin.
All rights reserved. No part of this book may be reproduced, in any
form, without writter permission from the publisher.

ISBN 1-56584-387-8

Published in the United States by The New Press, New York
Distributed by W.W. Norton & Company, Inc., New York

The New Press was established in 1990 as a not-for-profit alternative to
the large, commercial publishing houses currently dominating the
book publishing industry. The New Press operates in the public interest rather than for private gain, and is committed to publishing, in
innovative ways, works of educational, cultural, and community value
that might not be considered sufficiently profitable. The New Press's
editorial offices are located at the City University of New York.

PRINTED IN THE UNITED STATES OF AMERICA

9 8 7 6 5 4 3 2 1

Contents

Acknowledgments

My special thanks to New Press publisher André Schiffrin, who made this book possible, and to editors Grace Farrell and Matt Weiland, who wrestled this manuscript to the ground and dragged it out the door in spite of every obstacle known to the publishing trade. Thanks also to the School of Communication at American University, which provided gainful employment for me that made my work on this book financially possible.

Particular recognition should go to Anabel Dwyer, John Kelly and Jeff McConnell for their valuable early contributions to this project, and to David Price for his discovery of the Millikan & Rostow manuscript and other work on Cold War anthropology.

Christopher Simpson
Washington DC, 1998

". . . A ratking is something that happens when too many rats have to live in too small a space under too much pressure. Their tails become entwined and the more they strain and stretch to free themselves the tighter grows the knot binding them, until at last it becomes a solid mass of embedded tissue. And the creature thus formed, as many as thirty rats tied together by the tail, is called a ratking. You wouldn't expect such a living contradiction to survive, would you? That's the most amazing thing of all. Most of the rat-kings that are discovered, in the plaster of old houses or beneath the floorboards of a barn, are healthy and flourishing. Evidently the creatures have evolved some way of coming to terms with the situation. That's not to say they like it! In fact the reason they're discovered is because of their diabolical squealing. Not much fun, being chained to each other for life. How much sweeter it would be to run free! Nevertheless, they do survive, somehow. The wonders of nature, eh?"

—Michael Dibdin, *Ratking* (1989)

(Christopher Simpson)

Universities, Empire, and the Production of Knowledge: An Introduction

The essays in this book examine the interplay between power and knowledge amid the rapid and sometimes violent social changes that took place during the cold war. They catalog the influence of military, intelligence, and propaganda agencies in setting the tacitly accepted boundaries that separated "legitimate" from "unreasonable" points of view among prominent social scientists in the United States and the former USSR.

Few readers today would argue with the proposition that the ideology or Zeitgeist of, say, twelfth-century Confucianism or nineteenth-century British imperialism profoundly shaped the methods used by intellectuals of those epochs to view events, and determined much of what they took to be literally and certainly true about the world around them. Today's social science is often said to be relatively immune from such encompassing illusions because, it is argued, the scientific method provides Western industrialized societies with the tools necessary to test our assumptions and eventually transcend the blinders they impose on us.

Yet if that is so—and the jury is still out on that question—we must at a minimum investigate the means by which social systems—especially one's own—give rise to corresponding sets of blinders.[1] To put the idea slightly differently, the claims made by social scientists during the Cold War are, I hope, sufficiently close at hand to be at once familiar and strange, so that they may provide a Rorschach test of sorts revealing some of the underlying patterns and evasions characteristic of contemporary intellectual life.

By now it is clear that military, intelligence, and propaganda agencies provided the by far the largest part of the funds for large research projects in the social sciences in the United States from World War II until well into the 1960s, and that such funding was designed to support the full range of national security projects of the day, from the benign to the horrific. The favored scholars most active in these affairs frequently formed tight, self-reinforcing networks—"reference groups," sociologists would call them—that came to have great influence over scholarly societies, foundation grants committees, tenure decisions, the contents of academic journals, and other levers of power in the academy.[2] The interweaving of social scientists with the national security apparatus was at least as pervasive and suffocating in the USSR as in the United States.

In some cases, the security agencies' intervention proved decisive in the "scientific" evolution of an academic field, which is to say, in the establishment of the institutions, texts, methodologies, and body of knowledge regarded as central to that academic enterprise. This has been true particularly in the interdisciplinary fields that have grown up since about 1945, such as development studies, area studies, communication research, and operations research, among others.[3] In the case of communication research, for example, it is unlikely that the field could have evolved in anything like its present form without early infusions of funds and contracts from intelligence, propaganda, and military agencies, or from foundations working closely with them. At least six of the most important U.S. centers of post-World War II communication studies grew up as de facto adjuncts of government psychological warfare programs. For years, government money—frequently without public acknowledgment—made up more than 75 percent of the annual budgets of Paul Lazarsfeld's Bureau of Applied Social Research (BASR) at Columbia University, Hadley Cantril's Institute for International Social Research (IISR) at Princeton, Ithiel de Sola Pool's Center for International Studies (CENIS) at MIT, and similar institutions.[4] The U.S. State Department secretly financed studies of U.S. public opinion by the National Opinion Research Center (NORC), at the University of Chicago, as part of the department's cold war lobbying campaigns on Capitol Hill, thus making NORC's ostensibly private, independent surveys financially viable for the first time.[5] In another case, the CIA clandestinely underwrote American University's Bureau of Social Science Research (BSSR), studies of torture of prisoners of war—though of course it was called by a different name—reasoning that interrogation of captives could be understood as simply another application of the social-psychological principles articulated in communication studies.[6] Taken as a whole, many of the key methodologies and preconceptions characteristic of modern university teaching in public opinion, international communication, persuasion, and related areas emerged primarily through large-scale projects and leading institutions dependent on money and political backing from security agencies specializing in foreign affairs.[7]

Money and political backing alone could not create a sustainable scientific paradigm, of course. But they did play an important role in determining the "authoritative" experts on a given topic and in shunting aside scholars who had fallen from favor. The loss of political/academic legitimacy could carry quite serious consequences, particularly during the first two decades of the Cold War: aborted careers, public humiliation, exile, and in some instances imprisonment. Not surprisingly, then, most scholars first sought to align themselves with the academic power structure of the moment, and only later attempted to negotiate a bit of intellectual freedom for themselves within its confines. The result in the social sciences in the United States and the USSR, at least, was that the most exciting intellectual work frequently took place *in spite* of official "encouragement" of selected scholars, not because of it.

A popular argument concerning the relationship between the social sciences and national security organizations during the Cold War has been that, however imperfect things may have been in practice, the latter *followed* the former. As academic polemicist par excellence Ithiel de Sola Pool contended, "the mandarins of the future"—Pool's term of praise for the decision-making elite—need a "way of perceiving the consequences of what they do if [their] actions are not to be brutal, stupid and bureaucratic but rather intelligent and humane. The only hope for humane government in the future," he continued, "is through extensive use of the social sciences by the government."[8] Thus, presumably enlightened social scientists were to educate the "mandarins," in a manner not so different from the inculcation of students in a graduate seminar.

As the essays in this book document, however, state and corporate security agencies frequently *initiated* social science concepts and projects, and the campus experts *followed*—not the other way around. Again, this has been true especially in the emerging, relatively influential interdisciplinary initiatives in the social sciences, such as development studies and area studies. As Alan Needell, Irene Gendzier, Bruce Cumings, and other contributors to this volume demonstrate, interdisciplinary programs at the pace-setting academic institutions often came *after* government security initiatives, and in some instances emerged primarily as a means of implementing policy decisions taken at the level of the National Security Council or similar elite bodies.

Several of the essays here focus on two overlapping, interdisciplinary academic enterprises—one is tempted to call them a paradigm, in the full sense of that word—known in the West as development studies and area studies. In their simplest form, university-based development studies and overlapping projects at area studies centers in the United States, both *predicted* and *required* the worldwide triumph of modernity and contemporary forms of global capitalism, or at least their extension to every part of the globe that had markets, resources, or a geo-strategic location of interest to the United States.

"Predicted," that is, because without the anticipated, ineluctable advance of capitalist-style modernity, there was little point in funding the study of the practical questions raised by its march forward. Further, as Irene L. Gendzier's essay demonstrates, many development theorists advocated the obverse proposition as well: failure to create a manageable, worldwide, "developed" economic system would entail not only a loss of resources, markets, and trade routes, but also fundamental political and cultural challenges in the United States as well. The precise character of the devil figure conjured up by the possibility of failure remained murky, but included various admixtures of Stalinist communism, deeper currents of racism, fear of the loss of the "good" aspects of imperial traditions (Christianity, rationalism, and so on), or the collapse of white world supremacy and patriarchy, with the implied threats of castration that entailed.

Among economists, political scientists, and international relations specialists in the West, the term "development" usually meant large-scale investment in the infrastructure necessary to bring to international markets the resources located in "developing" countries. Thus "development" entailed the construction of strategic railroads, highways, pipelines, and shipyards; upgraded electric power grids and telephone networks for those portions of the target country most closely tied to foreign investment; capital investment in large-scale mining and agriculture projects, and so on—the panoply of projects characteristic of the International Monetary Fund, Alliance for Progress, and many similar institutions. These investments would result in foreign private investment in the target economy, the specialists predicted, as well as various forms of trickle-down prosperity that were to nurture an emerging, local middle class (not to mention the careers of various aspiring academic entrepreneurs in the United States who would help keep things on track).

Meanwhile, anthropologists, sociologists, and even psychologists in certain subdisciplines found in development projects a well-funded laboratory—frequently the only well-funded laboratory during the early Cold War years—for the study of displaced and disappearing cultures, the diffusion of messages and shifts in socio-political attitudes, linkages between gender roles and economic forms, and scores of other intriguing questions pushed to the fore by the vast disruption of traditional societies that often followed in the wake of development projects.

For obvious reasons, experts in counterinsurgency, insurgency, political warfare, and police training also prospered both as academics (typically situated in schools of public administration or international service) and as private consultants. Supplanting traditional ways of life by development—which is to say, by cultural penetration, the expansion of international markets, and changes in property relations—required what was euphemistically known as a period of "transition" to the new and presumably better society. In many cases, such transitions spurred the democratic election of a local government suspicious of the march of progress; in other cases it led to armed insurrections. That, in turn, proffered opportunities for specialists in managing this sort of resistance.

The submerged history of the Cold War is to a large extent the story of American and Soviet efforts to contain local resistance to foreign-directed "development" and to the East-West scramble for regional spheres of influence. Each superpower sought in its own fashion to employ scientifically-informed methods of coercion and brutality, which have gone by such names as "the ideological offensive," "psychological warfare," "political warfare," "low-intensity warfare," "special warfare," "the minds race," "nation building," and a half-dozen other euphemisms. The common element among these tactics has been an effort—particularly at the level of the (purportedly) "best and brightest" civilian mandarins of East and West—to combine the techniques and insights of the social sciences (intelligence on demographic and cultural trends, public opinion data, media manipulation, and so on) with advanced engineering (in command and control, weapons, transport, and so on) to manage, defuse or in some cases obliterate local challenges to superpower influence.

Thus, certain applications of the social sciences were often at the heart of the real Cold War as it was experienced by people around the world.[9] Contrary to common assumptions, the "ideological offensive" has been at least as central to U.S. national security strategy since 1945 as the atomic bomb. For one thing, one could actually use ideological offensives on a day-to-day basis, as distinct from atomic warfare. They remained a far more intimate and personal demonstration of the strength of a government. Similarly, ideological offensives were adaptable for use against one's own population and that of allied (but rival) countries with whom one was officially at peace. The social sciences did not *create* ideological offensives, of course. But at the leading academic institutions, prominent social scientists built much of their claim to leadership, and their bid for government funding and political support, on promises that deft applications of sociology, anthropology, psychology, and social psychology would improve state-sponsored ideological offensives, make them cheaper, more effective, and more certain of victory.[10]

In American universities, development studies programs that accompanied and legitimated ideological offensives typically presented themselves as mildly innovative, interdisciplinary subsets of traditional disciplines, on the one hand, or as area studies centers and international studies programs, on the other. The former attempted to deduce rules for introduction of capitalist modernity as a general phenomenon;[11] the later focused on the exploration and management of challenges within particular geographic or cultural groups viewed as special problems. Thus, Russian and Soviet studies emerged as the first full scale area studies programs in the U.S. (founded at Harvard, Columbia, and MIT and underwritten largely by the U.S. Air Force, the CIA, and cooperative foundations), followed by Asian studies and Middle Eastern studies. In time these new disciplines were joined by country- and culture-specific specialties, which attempted to sort out the gross, and in many respects misleading, divisions that had been created by dividing the world up into these "areas" in the first place. MIT's well-known experiment, the Center for International Studies, emerged early on as an archetypal attempt to institutionalize development, international communication and operations research, area-specific programs, and several forms of police and counterinsurgency consulting into a de facto social science service bureau for U.S. security agencies and for the foreign regimes that happened to be in favor at the moment.

From the standpoint of the social scientist or area studies specialist, management of the "transition" crises associated with Cold War era development provided a spectrum of opportunities for academic entrepreneurship, ranging from seemingly innocuous population surveys and mapping, to cultural analysis of persuasive tactics suitable for particular cultures, to consulting on the design and operation of the special machinery of repression and terror.

For a time, there seemed to be plenty of money to go around. Funds for "Centers for . . ." and "Institutes on . . ." interdisciplinary projects flowed from the network of foundations well known to every academic of the era: the Ford Foundation, Carnegie Corporation, the various Rockefeller brothers funds, the Social Science Research Council, and so on. A network of social science funding foundations were subsequently revealed as beards for the CIA—that is, as cover organizations. These were employed to diffuse and disguise government interest in less savory tasks, such as the physical and psychological responses to prolonged sensory deprivation,[12] improved police interrogation, "scientific" studies of radiation's effects on prisoners and the corpses of paupers,[13] and other forms of scientific abuse presented to the world as medical or social science studies.

The history of the Bureau of Applied Social Research at Columbia University provides an instructive example. Even at this widely respected institution, Cold War projects included inquiries into the "Social versus the Physical Effects of Nuclear Bombing" and other studies on tactical management of nuclear war (by Fred Iklé and others, from 1951 through the end of the decade); psychological warfare in the Middle East and the USSR (by Benjamin Ringer, David Sills, Edmund Brunner, Daniel Lerner, and others, from 1951 through at least 1962); LSD studies—including use of LSD in interrogation and recruitment of political defectors—underwritten in part by CIA front foundations (by Henry Lennard and others, from 1956 through the early 1960s).[14]

This system worked reasonably well in the universities throughout the 1950s and 1960s. MIT's CENIS program—where sociologists and anthropologists such as Harold Isaacs and Clifford Geertz worked cheek-by-jowl with men whom many people would consider to be professional terrorists specializing in the suppression of indigenous democracy, such as Lucian Pye[15]—provided an archetype for government-funded, interdisciplinary imitators at the University of Washington, the University of Illinois, Columbia, Princeton, American University, George Washington University, the University of Michigan, and dozens of other centers.

The institutionalization within universities of these interdisciplinary initiatives proved to be more complex and more contested than might appear at first glance. That is, the creation of interdisciplinary teaching programs, academic journals and societies, and especially the authority to grant degrees, required negotiation and compromise with existing power structures in the academy, and these were not necessarily cooperative. Similarly, the growing resistance to the war in Vietnam and emerging popular awareness of the brutality of some social science projects—awareness brought into the universities by new generations of students, by the way, and only rarely by their professors—led to new rounds of student protests and erosion of the secrecy surrounding some of the less savory programs. As the essays in this book explain, CENIS and a number of its on-campus imitators failed to survive the social upheavals of the 1960s and early 1970s.

Since that time, the tasks of CENIS-type social science service bureaus often have been assumed by lower-profile, Ph.D.-heavy, high-security government contractors operating off campus, such as Abt Associates, the RAND Corporation, the MITRE Corporation, the Center for Naval Analysis and a dozen others. The CIA also remains a major employer of newly minted social scientists and international studies Ph.D.'s, at least for the moment. Doctoral candidates in relevant fields learn early on where the jobs can be found. Sympathetic professors, who once might have enjoyed an institute of their own, now often have to make do with consulting projects and incentives for recommending promising recruits.

The essays in this book reexamine through new lenses part of what is known today of this submerged history of the social sciences throughout these years of change. They trace the emergence and maturation of interdisciplinary forms such as development studies and area studies. They examine the interplay between ideology and academic discourse in both the United States and the USSR and provide an unusual glimpse of the Cold War's impact on African American intellectuals in search of a strategy and tactics for liberation. The text also includes a previously unpublished, early essay on development strategy and tactics prepared by Max Millikan and Walt W. Rostow for the CIA.

The essays appear in rough chronological order, beginning at the close of World War I, then continuing through the emergence and consolidation of what might be called the academic–national security complex of the early and middle Cold War years. The final chapters consider Soviet *perestroika* and the accelerating corporate penetration of American universities today.

Our intention has been to make the role that power plays *in* knowledge more visible; to bring the dynamics of the power-in-knowledge relationship forward as a tangible subject for study; and to make research into these questions as concrete as presently available information permits. As I have argued elsewhere, the Zeitgeist or "dominant paradigm" of the mainstream social sciences throughout the cold war is better understood as a *paradigm of domination*, one in which social scientists studied the experience of power and hegemonic relations in order to rationalize the exercise of that power—that is, to improve its efficiency and effectiveness.[16]

Yet there was a time when leading U.S. social scientists regarded cooperation with the government's military and intelligence agencies as disreputable, and even as hostile to science per se. At the close of World War I, the anthropologist Franz Boas—a self-described socialist who was among the most influential social scientists of his day—wrote in shocked terms to *The Nation* that a group of anthropologists' wartime undercover work for U.S. military intelligence agencies had "prostituted science in an unpardonable way," forcing them to forfeit any claim to be regarded as scientists at all. Political espionage, Boas continued, does "the greatest possible disservice to scientific inquiry."[17]

Within a few decades, attitudes on such cooperation among mainstream social scientists had changed dramatically in both East and West. Spurred by World War II, the Holocaust, and Stalin's purges; fed by the grants and status associated with giant government research projects; and encouraged by the promises of reformist political administrations, many of the world's most sophisticated social scientists made "ideological offensives" and military and intelligence projects integral to their day-to-day work.

Project Troy at MIT during 1950–51 provides a vivid example of this process at work. The historian and curator Allan Needell uses newly declassified federal records to trace the steps from Truman-era national security directives such as NSC 59 and NSC 68 to the creation of Project Troy and similar government-sponsored gatherings of senior scientists at MIT. Project Troy in turn provided much of the impetus for the establishment of the Center for International Studies and the relatively stable, ongoing intelligence and national security work by prominent U.S. social scientists that CENIS came to exemplify. Equally important in the present context, Needell contends, is that Project Troy and its offspring "powerfully reinforced postwar efforts to associate the social with the natural sciences, not only in terms of the assumed reliability and objectivity of the research methodologies they employed, but also in terms of the potential contributions they could make to promoting American interests around the globe."

The model of "big" social science crystallized in Project Troy

CHRISTOPHER SIMPSON

and, shortly thereafter, in CENIS proved remarkably useful and resilient for a half-dozen social science disciplines for at least twenty years. The CENIS recipe—academic prestige, government and foundation funding, assertion of precise scientific authority on social questions and selective purges of dissenting academics—operated within the context of the relative stability of American power at home and abroad. Together, they gave birth to an academic regime in the social sciences that functioned for two decades in the West with little effective challenge.

Max Millikan and Walt W. Rostow's previously unpublished 1954 essay, "Notes on Foreign Economic Policy," captures the enthusiasm and the claims of sophistication characteristic of this academic structure and practice in its early years. Rostow and Millikan each found a roost at CENIS during the mid-1950s, where they became influential advisers on international affairs to the Department of State and the CIA throughout the Eisenhower administration. Both later emerged among John F. Kennedy's "best and brightest" brain trust, which devised American strategy for Vietnam and Latin America. "Notes on Foreign Economic Policy" provides an idealized yet relatively frank statement of the preconceptions of liberal anticommunist intellectuals of the day with respect to America's political and economic mission in world affairs and the corresponding tasks of Western intellectuals in the cold war.

Originally prepared as a government-financed report to CIA Director Allen Dulles, "Notes on Foreign Economic Policy" is of special interest here because it sketches out the rationale for the particular forms of "development" and "modernization" that set much of the agenda for the interdisciplinary projects that dominated a generation's academic work in anthropology, area studies, international studies, communication research, and in significant subfields of economics, sociology, political science, military studies, and even psychology.[18] As that essay demonstrates, whether the academics involved preferred to recognize it or not, U.S. national security strategy was at the heart of this initiative, particularly in studies of Third World countries that became the focus of regional competition between the two super-powers.

Contrary to modern stereotypes about the supposedly naive but well-intentioned intellectuals of the 1950s, Millikan and Rostow unambiguously subordinated respect for democracy or human rights to the imperatives of exporting U.S. capital and extending Western ideological and military campaigns, especially in Southeast Asia. They argued that the United States should promote a mix of economic incentives and internal security measures intended to modernize local elites and create "an environment in which societies which directly or indirectly menace ours will not evolve." The readily apparent tension between the altruistic and the selfish characteristics of the American initiatives was a "false . . . dichotomy," Rostow and Millikan contended, because "we believe our long-run objectives to be in fact identical with those of others."

The next two essays in this collection—from Irene L. Gendzier and Ellen Herman—examine the origins of this form of international economic and political development and its impact on the production of knowledge in the United States. Gendzier brings to the surface new understandings of the intellectual origins of development theory on American campuses during the 1940s and 1950s, and demonstrates a modern-day revival of much of the same theory and rhetoric in investment schemes presently promoted by former Secretary of the Treasury Lloyd Bentsen and others.

Gendzier helps document that National Security Council decisions initiated certain aspects of interdisciplinary social science projects which are often assumed to have sprung more or less spontaneously from the minds of the leading intellectuals and private foundation executives of the day. For example, NSC 129/1 of April 1952 "bluntly stated concerns echoed in the thematic content of development studies," Gendzier writes. Quoting from the declassified document, she shows that U.S. concessions to "nationalistic demands," as the NSC put it, in areas such as improved health and education, land reform and so on, were to be linked to and dependent on the enlistment of "leadership groups in the area which offer the greatest prospect of establishing political stability oriented toward the free world," which is to say, toward the United States. Thus, the task of U.S. programs was not to prevent change in local regimes but rather "to guide them into channels that will offer the least threat to Western interests and the maximum assurance of independent regimes friendly to the West."

Project Camelot became perhaps the best documented of a series of national-security state-sponsored interdisciplinary initiatives to create the information base needed for the social engineering projects discussed by Gendzier—and for the counterinsurgency and psychological warfare operations undertaken when these projects failed. According to the historian of psychology Ellen Herman, Camelot also marked psychology's "rise to public power" as an instrument of government, in somewhat the same manner that CENIS-type projects earlier established the legitimacy of interdisciplinary development and area studies programs as elements of Cold War strategy.

Camelot was conceived by the U.S. Army's Special Operations Research Office in 1963 as a means of bringing social science to bear on the task of managing national liberation movements in Latin America, sub-Saharan Africa, and the Middle East, Herman writes. Its object was creation of "a general social systems model," as its principal sponsor put it, "which would make it possible to predict and influence politically significant aspects of social change in the developing nations of the world." Camelot became the focus of bitter academic and political controversy when Chilean academics protested its methods and ideological agenda, and the project was nominally shut down in 1965.

Herman's reconsideration of the Camelot affair sheds new light on the project and on the effects of its cancellation. Importantly, the behavioral and social sciences emerged from the Camelot controversy with greater influence than ever within intelligence and security agencies in the United States. True, some funding conduits for national security–oriented social science projects temporarily closed. Nevertheless, CIA support for "psychological" and political operations abroad expanded significantly during the decade following the cancellation of Camelot. Virtually all of the original Camelot-style projects in Latin American went ahead under new project names, Herman reports, and a Camelot-inspired computer model created by Abt Associates eventually became the testbed for CIA scenarios for the overthrow of the democratically elected Allende government in Chile in September 1973.

In the essay following Herman's, Kevin Gaines provides a dramatic, yet little known example of the impact of Cold War-era academic politics on events and intellectual trends inside the United States. Unlike the academics discussed thus far, African American scholars were to a large degree excluded from university life of the 1950s and 1960s, and frequently limited to adjunct professorships on white campuses, occasional lectures, or service at the historically African American universities that left them tacitly excluded from many academic debates. Others were driven into exile. Nevertheless, African American scholars and intellectuals—W.E.B Du Bois, Paul Robeson, James Baldwin, Malcolm X, Martin Luther King and an extraordinarily broad range of others—helped shape African American consciousness, and in that way had an impact on certain aspects of U.S. domestic and foreign affairs greater than that of many of the most prominent white academics of the era.

Ghana, the first African state to achieve independence from colonial rule, became during the early 1960s a refuge for hundreds of African American scholars, writers and political activists exiled from the United States. Under the charismatic Pan-African socialist Kwame Nkruma, radical African and African American intellectuals sought to build 'Black Power' in Ghana in the truest sense of the term. A central premise of their work was that black liberation was necessarily interwoven with other international struggles, including resistance to the war in Vietnam.

Gaines examines the often bitter debate among African American intellectuals of this period over a strategy and tactics for

African American liberation. By contrasting the well known work of Harold Cruse to the relatively obscure writings of the African American exile in Ghana Julian Mayfield, Gaines contends that Cruse proved useful to Cold War liberals anxious to channel civil rights struggles onto politically palatable paths.

For Gaines, "Black Power—understood as the rise of militant black nationalism and separatism—was not the undoing of civil rights liberalism" in the United States, as is frequently argued. "Rather, it was the impact of Cold War ideology and politics, in defining a narrowed civil rights agenda, that proved the undoing of Black Power" in the mid-1960s. The experience of the black expatriate intellectuals is instructive, he contends, "precisely because they defied pressure from Cold War liberals to confine black politics within the domestic realm of civil rights. . . . [T]hey resisted anticommunist propaganda [characteristic of Cold War liberalism] that portrayed domestic struggles against segregation and African nation-building projects as spearheaded by Soviet 'outside agitators.'"

Several important "ideological" or "psychological" aspects of the tactics described by Gendzier, Herman, and Gaines can be readily identified in the modern history of area studies centers. Bruce Cumings of the University of Chicago traces the manner in which Western national security policies played themselves out at the level of university departments, textbooks, and academic disciplines—where the broad arteries of power became "capillary," as he puts it. The political economy of the Cold War shaped the content of disciplines in his field to a remarkable degree, he contends. By examining the ways in which the boundaries of academic disciplines such as area studies and international studies were set and shifted during the Cold War, Cumings provides a number of examples supporting his argument that the production of academic knowledge has generally followed changes in world power and world markets rather than the other way around. A good recent example is found in the abrupt attempts at realignment by certain university area studies programs following the unanticipated dissolution of the USSR. "Scholars caught up in one historical system and one discourse that defined discipline, [academic] department, area and subject, suddenly found themselves in another emerging field of inquiry, well in advance of imagining or discovering the subject themselves," he writes. "To put a subtle relationship all too crudely, power and money had found their subject first, and shaped fields of inquiry accordingly."

Like Cumings, Slava Gerovitch of MIT focuses on the political and ideological aspects of academic discourse during the Cold War. Gerovitch's subject, however, is the sociology of knowledge in a key discipline in the Soviet Union and in post-communist Russia. Changes in academic discourse on the history of science and technology long have been a particularly clear barometer of the intellectual shifts in Soviet and post-Soviet Russian society, he writes, and can be used to trace the interplay of influence between the state and the academy over time.

Gerovitch stresses another point as well: simplistic explanations that paint scientists as mere tools (or victims) of the political regime in power fail to account for the complexity of relationships among academics, their financial and political sponsors, and the ideological orthodoxy of the Cold War years. In the case of Soviet and post-Soviet Russia, a debate continues today among those who attribute scientific and academic developments to "external" factors such as social context; those who attribute change largely to discoveries "internal" to the various disciplines; and those who point to organizational and administrative structures of academic organizations as the determinative factors in change. Gerovitch demonstrates that these views are often linked to the historical experiences of various generations of Russian scientists and to their experience of the political/academic conditions that prevailed as each generation came into its prime.

Readers in the United States may find some parts of Gerovitch's description of modern Russian academic life eerily familiar. His carefully documented work indicates that many Western preconceptions about Russian academic life since at least the

1950s have been at best half-true. In reality, the tight, dynamic linkages among the academy's prevailing ideological framework, its choice of research method, and its research results have had much more in common in East and West than either side generally has been willing to admit.

In the final essay in this collection, Larry Soley contends that a reconstruction of important parts of the U.S. academy is underway today. The era of the national-security-state/university relationship epitomized by Projects Troy and Camelot has today been supplanted by new forms of corporate-sponsored "scholarship" and "knowledge," Soley contends. University-based entrepreneurs today market named professorships, sports licensing agreements, and the services of transparently biased research centers to corporate customers and foreign governments seeking a gloss of academic respectability for what are at heart often little more than public relations projects tailored to produce predictable results. Some of the new generation of sponsors seek low-cost access to university research and development capabilities, particularly in the physical sciences. Conservative foundations meanwhile are pursuing their own "ideological offensive" in the social sciences and law schools aimed at selecting and nurturing future judges, international affairs experts, social scientists, and news editors who they hope can be depended on to be sympathetic, Soley writes.

This latter tactic has deeper roots than most people realize. In fact, it is much the same method that intelligence organizations have used for years to attempt to influence or recruit future leaders from around the world, to create "an environment," as Millikan and Rostow prescribed, "in which societies which directly or indirectly menace ours will not evolve."

In sum, then, the social and behavioral sciences in East and West since at least 1945 only rarely focused on a direct quest for knowledge about the world as we find it. The far more pressing issue in academic life consistently has been the battle over what *types* of questions may be asked and *whose* results will be taken to be legitimate and responsible. That contest, in turn, has had relatively consistent social dynamics that show up on both sides of the ideological and cultural divide that separated the United States and the USSR. Such dynamics, or patterns of behavior, are often officially non-existent, yet in reality have been well-entrenched aspects of the social sciences since the dawn of the Cold War. These patterns include the pervasive inbreeding between the academy and intelligence and propaganda agencies, for example; the role of ambitious scholars who legitimize state and corporate brutality, the political characteristics of debates among "externalist" and "internalist" theorists of scientific change; and several paradoxes of ideology and negotiation of ideology; to name only a few. Almost without exception, institutions and individuals with power or money have nurtured the academic initiatives they regard as likely to protect their status, and avoided or actively suppressed those seen as threatening. One result has been that in the short term, power typically *selects* ideas, as anthropologist David Price has put it, while in the long term ideas tend to *conform* to the realities of power.[19]

The modest essays in this collection cannot tell the full story of their respective disciplines. Commercial interests, university bureaucracies, shifts in the technological infrastructure of society, outside economic and political developments, sheer chance, and many other factors sometimes proved pivotal in intellectual affairs during the Cold War. Nevertheless, these essays sketch out many of the subtle and complex relationships between professional intellectuals and the national security state in the United States and other countries. The essays demonstrate some of the means by which the dominant institutional mechanisms of the Cold War set academic agendas, and show how politically liberal intellectuals articulated and rationalized development and area studies strategies that pervaded U.S. academic activities abroad, frequently at considerable cost to scientific integrity and to the peoples being "developed."

Such aspects of the intellectual life of the United States and the USSR typically have been overlooked or intentionally obscured in the semiofficial histories of the social sciences available thus far. The new insights offered in the texts collected here help fill important gaps in our understanding of the way social science develops and operates. More fundamentally, they challenge us to reconsider the nature of "knowledge" as such in the United States and the USSR during the years the leaders of those two societies presumed to hold the fate of humanity in their hands.

Notes

1. For a recent and provocative overview of the epistemological issues involved, see James A. Anderson, *Communication Theory: Epistemological Foundations* (New York: Guilford, 1996).

2. For earlier accounts of the social sciences' dependency on funds from military, intelligence, and propaganda agencies see Pio Uliassi, "Government-Sponsored Research on International and Foreign Affairs," in Irving Louis Horowitz, ed., *The Use and Abuse of Social Science* (New Brunswick, N.J.: Transaction, 1971), pp. 309–42; Albert Biderman and Elisabeth Crawford, *Political Economics of Social Research: The Case of Sociology,* (Springfield, Va.: Clearinghouse for Federal Scientific and Technical Information, 1968); Elisabeth Crawford and Albert Biderman, *Social Scientists and International Affairs* (New York: John Wiley & Sons, 1969), esp. Appendix III, "The Organization of Policy-Oriented Research" (pp. 298–306), and Appendix V, "The Substance of Social Science Knowledge and Policy Concerns in International and Military Affairs" (pp. 312–17). For more recent scholarship, see Fred Kaplan, *The Wizards of Armageddon* (New York: Simon & Schuster, 1983) (particularly his discussion of the social science division of the RAND Corporation); Irene Gendzier, *Managing Social Change: Social Scientists and the Third World* (Boulder, Co: Westview, 1985); John Trumpbour, ed.,*How Harvard Rules: Reason in the Service of Empire,* (Boston: South End Press, 1989); Jonathan Feldman, *Universities in the Business of Repression* (Boston: South End Press, 1989); Sigmund Diamond, *Compromised Campus: The Collaboration of Universities with the Intelligence Community* (New York: Oxford University Press, 1992); the special issue of *Radical History Review* no. 63 (fall 1995), eds., Michael Bernstein and Allan Hunter, with work by Michael Bernstein (on economics), Stephen Waring (on operations research), Ellen Herman (on psychology), Deborah Welch Larson (on nuclear deterrence, game theory, and related social science), and Daniel Kleinmann and Mark Solovey (on the Na-

tional Science Foundation); Christopher Simpson, *Science of Coercion: Communication Research and Psychological Warfare, 1945–1960* (New York: Oxford University Press, 1994); and of course the first volume in this New Press series, Noam Chomsky et al., *The Cold War and the University: Toward an Intellectual History of the Postwar Years* (New York: The New Press, 1997).

3. On development studies and area studies, see the essays by Irene L. Gendzier and Bruce Cumings in this volume. On communication research, see Simpson, *Science of Coercion*. On operations research, see Stephen Waring, "Cold Calculus: The Cold War and Operations Research," *Radical History Review*, no. 63 (fall 1995), pp. 28–51.

4. On BASR, see Jean Converse, *Survey Research in the United States* (Berkeley: University of California Press, 1987), pp. 269, 275–76, 500–7 n. 37 and 42. On Cantril's IISR, see John Crewdson and Joseph Treaster, "The CIA's 3-Decade Effort to Mold the World's Views," *New York Times*, Dec. 25, 26, and 27, 1977, with discussion of Cantril and IISR on December 26. For Cantril's version, which conceals the true source of his funds, see Hadley Cantril, *The Human Dimension: Experiences in Policy Research* (New Brunswick, N.J.: Rutgers University Press, 1967). For discussion of evidence concerning CENIS funding and associations with the CIA, see Simpson, *Science*

of Coercion, pp. 81–84; Massachusetts Institute of Technology, Center for International Studies, *The Center for International Studies; A Description* (Cambridge, Mass: MIT, July 1955); Ithiel de Sola Pool, "The Necessity for Social Scientists Doing Research for Governments," *Background* 10, no. 2 (August 1966). On CIA funding of CENIS, see Victor Marchetti and John Marks, *The CIA and the Cult of Intelligence* (New York: Dell, 1974) p. 181; David Wise and Thomas Ross, *The Invisible Government* (New York: Vintage, 1974) p. 244. For an example of a major study reported to have been underwritten by the CIA, see W. W. Rostow and Alfred Levin, *The Dynamics of Soviet Society* (New York: Norton, 1952).

5. For details on the Department of State contracts, which produced a scandal when they were uncovered in 1957, see House Committee on Government Operations, *State Department Opinion Polls*, 85th Congress, 1st sess., June–July 1957 (Washington, D.C.: USGPO, 1957).

6. Albert Biderman, "Social-Psychological Needs and 'Involuntary' Behavior as Illustrated by Compliance in Interrogation," *Sociometry* 23, no. 2 (June 1960), pp. 120–47; Louis Gottshalk, *The Use of Drugs in Information-seeking Interviews*, Bureau of Social Science Research report 322, December 1958, BSSR Archives, series II, box 11, University of Maryland Libraries Special Collections,

College Park, Md.; and Albert Biderman, Barbara Heller, and Paula Epstein, *A Selected Bibliography on Captivity Behavior,* Bureau of Social Science Research report 339–1, February 1961, BSSR Archives, series II, box 14, also at the University of Maryland Libraries. Biderman acknowledges the Human Ecology Fund—later revealed to have been a conduit for CIA funds—and U.S. Air Force contract no. AF49 (638)727 as the source of his finding for this work. For more on the CIA's use of the Human Ecology Fund and the related Society for the Investigation of Human Ecology, see John Marks, *The Search for the 'Manchurian Candidate': The CIA and Mind Control* (New York: Times Books, 1979), pp. 147–63.

7. Explored in Simpson, *Science of Coercion,* esp. pp. 107–17.

8. Ithiel de Sola Pool, "The Necessity for Social Scientists Doing Research for Governments," pp. 114–15.

9. The U.S. House of Representatives held a series of relatively frank hearings on the concept of an "ideological offensive," which succeeded in boosting the uses of social science as a weapon in the cold war in the wake of the controversy over the Camelot project; see Committee on Foreign Affairs; Subcommittee on International Organizations and Movements, *Winning the Cold War: The U.S. Ideological Offensive; Behavioral Sciences and National Security* (Washington, D.C.: USGPO, 1965, 1966).

10. For examples, see ibid. or William Lybrand, *The U.S. Army's Limited-war Mission and Social Science Research: Proceedings of the Symposium* (Washington, D.C.: American University/Special Operations Research Office, June 1962), with contributions on the topic from Paul Linebarger (Johns Hopkins), John W. Riley (then of the Equitable Life Insurance Company and a longtime member of the Rutgers faculty), W. Phillips Davison (Council on Foreign Relations, RAND Corporation), Ithiel de Sola Pool (CENIS), Klaus Knorr (director of Princeton's Center of International Studies), Harry Eckstein (also of the Princeton center), Guy Pauker (RAND Corporation), and Lucian Pye (CENIS), among others.

11. See the discussion of Project Camelot, below.

12. For descriptions of thirteen relevant HumRRO studies, see Human Resources Research Organization, *Bibliography of Publications as of June 1969* (Alexandria, Va.: HumRRO, 1969), pp. 48–50.

13. U.S. Government, Advisory Committee on Human Radiation Experiments (ACHRE), *Final Report,* (Washington, D.C.: USGPO, October 1995). Most of these tests were organized by medical doctors, many of them affiliated with highly regarded teaching hospitals at the University of California, University of Massachusetts, Vanderbilt University, and similar institutions. Social scientists' role in these affairs

appears to have focused on efforts to measure the morale of U.S. soldiers exposed to atomic explosions and to "indoctrinate" the troops (as the Department of Defense put it) against their " 'mystical' fear of radiation." See esp. chap. 10, "Atomic Veterans: Human Experimentation in Connection with Atomic Bomb Tests," and its discussion of HumRRO for background on the role of psychologists and social scientists, at pp. 459–65, 489–92. HumRRO was at the time affiliated with George Washington University and the Operations Research Office at Johns Hopkins University. See also Peter Bordes et al., DESERT ROCK I: A Psychological Study of Troop Reactions to an Atomic Explosion," February 1953, HumRRO-TR-1, available as ACHRE doc. no. CORP. 111694-A. For a table of related Desert Rock and psychological warfare studies, see HumRRO, *Bibliography of Publications as of June 1969*, entry under "Psychological," p. 298.

14. For BASR studies designed to enhance U.S. tactics for nuclear warfare, see BASR studies B-0390-1, B-0390-2, B-0390-3 (Iklé on World War II conventional bombing as an analog for study of the effects of nuclear destruction of cities, 1951); study B-0390-4 (Eleanor Bernet and Iklé, on evacuation of cities under nuclear attack, 1952); B-0390-5 (Iklé on destruction of communication and transport utilities, 1952); B-0390-6 (Iklé, published as *The Social Impact of Bomb Destruction*, 1958);

B-0484 (Iklé and Harry Kincaid, on evacuation of cities under nuclear attack, 1954, 1956); B-1018 (Gene Levine and John Modell, on U.S. public opinion about the threat of war, 1964); B-0540-1 (Margaret Rowan and Takuya Maruyama, on identifying 'essential personnel' for selective protection during atomic war, 1956); and B-0540-2 (Margaret Rowan and Harry Kincaid, on views of corporate executives on maintaining production in the wake of atomic war, 1956). Apparently there were at least 25 BASR studies, reports, and papers in this series, which was underwritten by the U.S. Air Force; see Judith Barton, ed., *Guide to the Bureau of Applied Social Research* (New York: Clearwater, 1984), p. 164. See also BASR project B-1018 (Levine, Model, Gerwitz, et al. on popular attitudes toward fallout shelters, 1962, 1964).

The list of BASR reports, books and monographs concerning psychological warfare in the Middle East, Soviet periphery, and the USSR is too lengthy to reproduce here. For examples, see Judith Barton, Ibid., pp. 21–27, 30, 31, 44, 46, 47, 74, 92, 94, 96, 99, 135–36, 141, 163, 174.

On BASR's role in LSD studies, see H. A. Abramson, et al., "The Stablemate Concept of Therapy as Affected by LSD in Schizophrenia," *Journal of Psychology* 45 (1958), pp. 75–84; BASR project B-0582 (Henry Lennard and Molly Hewitt on interpersonal communication processes under large doses of LSD, 1960); B-0582 [sic] (Lennard, Abramson and Hewitt on social interaction and LSD, 1959); B-1008 (Lennard's proposal for studying LSD, other drugs, and their impact on social systems, 1964). The LSD work was underwritten at least in part by the Josiah Macy Jr. Foundation, which was later revealed to have been a frequent conduit for CIA funds. See Barton, pp. 99, for acknowledgment of the Macy Foundation role.

Also of interest in this context was BASR's work for tobacco interests: project B-0675 (Paul Lazarsfeld and Robert Mitchell, on point of purchase advertising for the "Model Twenty-700 Cigarette Vending Machine," 1959); and project B-0637 (Lennard, on cigarettes, 1958). No copies of the tobacco reports are known to have survived in BASR records, according to Barton (see pp. 172 and 173).

15. For one example among many of Pye's activities, see Lucian Pye, *Lessons from the Malayan Struggle Against Communism* (Cambridge, Mass.: CENIS, n.d. [1956?]).

16. Simpson, *Science of Coercion* esp. p. 62.

17. The quotes that follow in this introductory essay from Boas, Needell, Millikan & Rostow, Gendzier, Herman, Gaines, Cumings, Gerovitch, and Soley—are drawn from the essays published in this collection.

18. The essay was eventually absorbed into Millikan and Rostow's the widely circulated *A Proposal: Key to an Effective Foreign Policy*, New York: Harper Brothers, 1957. There, the authors cite the Ford Foundation and the Rockefeller Foundation as the source of the funds that underwrote CENIS and, through that channel, their own work. In reality, both foundations are today known to have extended grants to CENIS specifically to serve as financial "covers" for the CIA's large scale entry into academic affairs and domestic politics in the United States—an activity that appears to have violated both the CIA's legal charter and the fiduciary responsibilities of the foundations' executives and trustees. See Note 4, above, for citations. For Millikan and Rostow's assertion (as of 1957) regarding foundation funding and the origin of their project, see Millikan and Rostow, *A Proposal*, p. vii, ix.

19. David Price, "Cold War Funding and the Evolution of Academic Anthropology," unpublished paper, 1997.

(**Franz Boas**)

Scientists as Spies

In his war address to Congress, President Wilson dwelt at great length on the theory that only autocracies maintain spies; that these are not needed in democracies. At the time that the President made this statement, the Government of the United States had in its employ spies of an unknown number. I am not concerned here with the familiar discrepancies between the President's words and the actual facts, although we may perhaps have to accept his statement as meaning correctly that we live under an autocracy; that our democracy is a fiction. The point against which I wish to enter a vigorous protest is that a number of men who follow science as their profession, men whom I refuse to designate any longer as scientists, have prostituted science by using it as a cover for their activities as spies.

A soldier whose business is murder as a fine art, a diplomat whose calling is based on deception and secretiveness, a politician whose very life consists in compromises with his conscience, a businessman whose aim is personal profit within the

This essay was originally published as a letter to the editor of *The Nation*, December 20, 1919.

limits allowed by a lenient law—such may be excused if they set patriotic devotion above common everyday decency and perform services as spies. They merely accept the code of morality to which modern society still conforms. Not so the scientist. The very essence of his life is the service of truth. We all know scientists who in private life do not come up to the standard of truthfulness, but who, nevertheless, would not consciously falsify the results of their researches. It is bad enough if we have to put up with these, because they reveal a lack of strength of character that is liable to distort the results of their work. A person, however, who uses science as a cover for political spying, who demeans himself to pose before a foreign government as an investigator and asks for assistance in his alleged researches in order to carry on, under this cloak, his political machinations, prostitutes science in an unpardonable way and forfeits the right to be classed as a scientist.

By accident, incontrovertible proof has come into my hands that at least four men who carry on anthropological work, while employed as government agents, introduced themselves to foreign governments as representatives of scientific institutions in the United States, and as sent out for the purpose of carrying on scientific researches. They have not only shaken the belief in the truthfulness of science, but they have also done the greatest possible disservice to scientific inquiry. In consequence of their acts every nation will look with distrust upon the visiting foreign investigator who wants to do honest work, suspecting sinister designs. Such action has raised a new barrier against the development of international friendly cooperation.

(**Allan A. Needell**)

Project Troy and the Cold War Annexation of the Social Sciences

Project Troy was, in the words of the television and radio executive Justin Miller, conceived in 1950 as a way to "bring together the best brains in the country" to point the way toward solution of the vexing problem of "getting the truth behind the Iron Curtain."[1] Underwritten by the Office of Naval Research, Project Troy enlisted prominent social scientists regarded as reliable by the military and the CIA to develop psychological warfare tactics for use throughout the world. Organized as a highly classified summer session gathering at the Massachusetts Institute of Technology, the project was one of at least three structured brainstorming councils at MIT during 1950–51, focusing on strategy, tactics, and military hardware for the Cold War.[2] Project Troy proved to be the most influential of these projects in many respects, for it provided a model and many personnel for a series of large-scale, classified consultancies between leading social scientists and U.S. military, intelligence, and propaganda agencies which have persisted in one form or another since that time. Perhaps most importantly in the present context, Project Troy also served to powerfully reinforce postwar efforts to associate the social with the natural sciences, not only in terms of the

3

assumed reliability and objectivity of the research methodologies they employed, but also in terms of the potential contributions they could make to promoting American interests around the globe.[3]

The Project Troy final report, delivered to the secretary of state in February 1951, was intended by its authors both to help provide the technical wherewithal and the intellectual framework for fighting the nonmilitary aspects of the Cold War. "Invited by the Department of State to try to defeat Russian jamming of the Voice of America," explained the Troy participants, "we soon realized that no such isolated study of radio would meet the real issue. The technical problem constitutes only one of a collection of inseparable conditions. What is the nature of the people to whom the United States' messages are and ought to be directed? What ultimate effects are to be desired? What sort of messages ought to be sent?"[4]

Equally important, the report was crafted to help cement lasting relations between American academics (specifically, natural scientists, social scientists, and historians) and the American foreign relations and intelligence bureaucracies. The Project Troy report suggested that, much as the continued participation of academic scientists and engineers in the development of new weapons and tactics for the U.S. military, academic scientists, social scientists, and historians had an essential contribution to make, outside the military, ensuring the survival of freedom, democracy, and the American way of life in the postwar world.

In one of the Project Troy report annexes the historian participants pointed out that the United States, in war, had always relied on "logistical mastery, the piling up of men and material for one overwhelming blow." By 1950, they claimed, technological advances had "put in our hands logistical weapons of such power that we find ourselves literally unable to use them for limited objectives." Military confrontation, in their words, had become "not only all-out but all-or-none."[5] The report writers insisted that the United States urgently needed to develop alternative means to prevail in the struggle against world communism, and that the skill and the determination with which the United States engaged communists, nonmilitarily, around the world would ultimately determine whether the United States could ultimately avoid having to chose between the almost unspeakable alternatives of capitulation to totalitarian domination or all-out nuclear war.

The Origins of Project Troy

During World War II, American social scientists served the war effort in a number of capacities.[6] For example, psychologists served in special military units devoted to the conduct of psychological warfare operations. General propaganda broadcasts overseas, in contrast, were coordinated by the Office of War Information (OWI), one of the many special civilian agencies created by the Roosevelt administration during the early years of the war. The OWI also made use of a number of academically trained experts.[7] Significantly, with the war ended, President Truman ratified Roosevelt's commitment to civilian control of American propaganda efforts, transferring the operations of the OWI to an Interim International Information Service (IIS) created within the Department of State. The mission of IIS, as publicly described by Truman, was to give others "a full and fair picture of American life and the aims and policies of the United States Government."[8] To fulfill this mission the IIS operated the so-called Voice of America radio network with the stated goal of providing information overseas about American life, aspirations, and official policies.

Meanwhile, the military established a number of postwar programs related to psychological warfare. For the most part, these programs focused on preparing for future wars, although it was taken for granted that such preparations had to be closely coordinated with the normal conduct of peacetime foreign relations. At first, coordination was promoted primarily as a means to ensure that, in time of war or in case the president determined the threat of war was sufficient, psychological operations by the military could be begun much more quickly and effectively than had been the case at the start of World War II.[9] As time went on, however, and as the Cold War took shape, distinctions between emergency, war- and peacetime operations became less and less clear.

The originally relatively low-key State Department information programs received increasing attention as a direct result of the period's major foreign policy initiatives. Secretary of State George C. Marshall's announcement of economic assistance to the war-ravaged states of Europe in 1947 had more than a minor psychological component.[10] So, too, did the later provision of direct military assistance to those countries willing and able to face up to the threat of world communism.[11] In March 1949, persuaded by a series of studies conducted by the new National Security Council, the president formally approved an expanded propaganda and psychological warfare effort to go along with these measures. The State Department was designated as the home of the special interdepartmental organization created for oversight and coordination.[12]

When Dean Acheson became secretary of state in January 1949, he faced many seemingly intractable administrative problems, not the least of which were those associated with the coordination of government propaganda and psychological warfare programs. James E. Webb was director of the Bureau of the Budget and was known in Washington, D.C., as a master of administration and management reform.[13] Thus, when Truman requested that Acheson accept Webb as his undersecretary, Acheson readily agreed.[14] Webb accepted the new assignment and from the start concerned himself directly with the problem of overseeing the nation's psychological warfare effort.

Webb also had long been interested in improving relations between government and academic experts. A personal friend of Lloyd V. Berkner, the man who in 1946 had accepted the job of setting up formal links between the military's Joint Research and Development Board (which would become the Research and Development Board [RDB] following passage of the National Security Act of 1947) and the nation's academic and industrial scientific and engineering research communities, Webb supported the military's attempt to make permanent the close relations that had been established with academic scientists during the war.[15]

When in the spring of 1949 the Soviet Union significantly increased its efforts to jam Russian-language broadcasts by the Voice of America (VOA),[16] Webb turned to Lloyd Berkner, who was by training a radio engineer and, as Webb knew, uniquely positioned to help him tap into the military's network of academic advisers and fabricate a similar set of relationships between private experts and the nonmilitary agencies of the federal government.

The technical jamming problem arose at the same time that books and articles in popular magazines began to tout the political, economic, and social vulnerability of the Soviet Union to overt information programs. These articles brought increased attention (much of it negative) to the Voice of America.[17] The president queried Acheson about the subject, and Acheson turned to Webb and to William Barrett, who had recently been selected to lead the expanded State Department Public Affairs Office.[18] Barrett proposed to create a government-wide review committee on radio propaganda and to incorporate that committee into his own plans for "taking the propaganda offensive."[19] He also expressed the hope that such a committee might help the department get higher priority assistance from the military and the CIA than was being obtained through ongoing informal contacts.[20]

There was, as Barrett well knew, long-simmering discontent within the State Department over the way the military and the CIA tended to protect their own intelligence and research activities. Barrett knew that their reluctance to share intelligence and expertise was fostered in part by long standing distrust of the State Department and the Foreign Service within the national security bureaucracy and in Congress, but that it also reflected a profound struggle for influence and for access to experts among the various military and civilian agencies of the executive branch.[21] Webb and Barrett wanted the State Department to compete more successfully in that arena.

In March 1950 the president approved a National Security Council report (NSC 59) that called once again for increasing psychological warfare planning and for placing the responsibility for coordinating such activities squarely on the secretary of state.[22] In April, Barrett pressed ahead by convening a symposium on propaganda and political warfare.[23] Later in the month he helped President Truman prepare an address to be delivered before the American Society of Newspaper Editors. In his address the president commented on the "powerful Communist campaign aimed at swaying peoples around the world in favor of Communism." He singled out for praise the activities of the Voice of America and concluded that "we must make ourselves known as we really are, not as Communist propaganda pictures us. We must pool our efforts with those of other free peoples in a sustained, intensified program to promote the cause of freedom against the propaganda of slavery. We must make ourselves heard round the world in a great campaign of truth."[24]

Afterward, the State Department submitted to Congress a supplemental budget request asking for a substantial increase in funding for foreign information programs.[25] Senate hearings on President Truman's request for funds for his "campaign of truth" brought forth a parade of supporting witnesses. Referred to as a "contest for the minds and loyalties of men" and as "a Marshall plan in the field of ideas," the campaign elicited support from, among others, Dwight D. Eisenhower, John Foster Dulles, Walter Bedell Smith, Bernard Baruch, and the president of RCA, David Sarnoff.[26]

Meanwhile, the military continued to pursue its own interests in related areas. In May 1950 the Joint Chiefs of Staff formally requested the Research and Development Board examine the technical, sociological, and psychological aspects of the Cold War.[27] The RDB asked Donald Marquis, a University of Michigan psychologist and chairman of the RDB's Human Resources Committee, to call together a conference of academic experts.[28] The conference, which took place August 10–11, 1950, covered much of the same ground that the State Department symposium had in April. Persuaded that there was a need for much more basic research on the psychology of propaganda, on the nature of various national targets, and on various social groups within nations, the conference participants recommended further study by a select group of scholars. With earlier air force– and navy-sponsored study projects in mind, they suggested that the study be undertaken through a contract with a prestigious university, arranged by the RDB and funded by the Office of Naval Research.[29]

Unbeknownst to the RDB experts, however, Lloyd Berkner had already informally approached James Killian, president of MIT, with news about recent developments at the State Department and specific information about the problems facing the propaganda efforts it directed.[30] At the end of the month Webb invited Killian and John E. Burchard, dean of humanities and social studies at MIT, to lunch with him in Washington; the next day they were provided a classified briefing on the problems facing the Voice of America. Just one week later, Killian wrote to Webb to "confirm the intent of the [Massachusetts] Institute [of Technology] to proceed with the study suggested by the State Department of the broad problem of how to get information into Russia." "We are," Killian continued, "prepared to undertake this project as an intensive study and investigation by a group of competent scientists and other scholars and to make a report to the State Department as near as possible to January 1, 1951."[31]

To administer the State Department–funded project Killian chose Burchard, who, in addition to his long term service to MIT, had been an active division chief of the Office of Scientific Research and Development under Vannevar Bush during the war. Killian also promised that he and the MIT provost, Julius A. Stratton, would give the State Department their "full collaboration and support." As for the organizational and administrative details, Killian suggested that "we have an admirable precedent in the study [Project Hartwell] we are completing this month for the Navy." On August 16, Webb acknowledged Killian's commitment and reiterated that he could not "emphasize enough the tremendous importance of the problems we face in this field."[32]

Killian immediately turned to Harvard University for help in staffing the State Department study group. He told Harvard provost Paul H. Buck that the State Department had "requested the Institute to undertake an exceedingly important project on ways of getting information behind the iron curtain. This involves difficult and complex technical problems, particularly an effort to find ways of preventing jamming operations of the Russians. It involves the broad problems of information theory, psychology, and other aspects having to do with the effectiveness of the kind of information we transmit. The project will also have great importance to the National Defense Establishment and the progress towards the objectives set up by the State Department could yield important military benefits." The MIT president concluded by writing that he was "convinced that the problem posed by the State Department is an exceedingly important one, perhaps one of the most important in our total national defense planning. I believe, too, that this kind of project may provide a pilot program for the study and review of many different kinds of important problems in government."[33]

At first the project participants approached their task cautiously. While Killian and his science and engineering colleagues at MIT and Harvard had grown quite comfortable working with the military, the State Department seemed strange and potentially dangerous territory. Senator Joseph R. McCarthy's (R–Wisc.) extended attack on Acheson and other employees of the State Department reinforced their caution.[34] As Burchard wrote to Killian, "I do not suppose it is possible to predict how [the attack is] going to come out. . . . But regardless of where it comes out, I think we have to recognize that there is more difference of opinion about the State Department in Washington than about most agencies and that there are plenty of people in positions of influence on the Joint Chiefs and elsewhere who might not accept the findings of our group if they were attached to the exclusive label of the State Department."[35]

In that same letter Burchard voiced the hope that "either the RDB or the Joint Chiefs of Staff" might cosponsor the project. Killian was sympathetic to Burchard's concern and hoped that the State Department would of its own accord bring in the Joint Chiefs. But he was more concerned that the project conform to the successful model of earlier military summer studies. "I would be hesitant about any kind of joint sponsorship that would result in dual responsibility. Long experience has indicated that we can work best with one agency taking the major responsibility and others being associated."[36]

Burchard soon turned his attention to costs and contractual matters. The State Department contract officers had no idea what they were getting into, but because of Webb's enthusiasm they were committed to work out the details. Yet even Webb, who had been thinking of spending about $50,000 for the study, was a little taken aback by the $150,000 estimate (approximately $830,000 in 1990 dollars) that the MIT contracting officer came up with. Nevertheless, he agreed to find the money. For him, at least, it was very important to keep the study wholly within the department.[37]

With the MIT administrators working out the contractual details, Burchard next turned his attention to staffing the project. In mid-August Paul Buck wrote back to Killian that Harvard would do all it could to make its personnel available; he would see to their temporary release from teaching and other university responsibilities. He listed several desirable participants: Edward M. Purcell, a Harvard-trained physicist and electronics expert, veteran of the wartime MIT Radiation (Radar) Laboratory and leading participant in the Hartwell study; Jerome S. Bruner, a Harvard-trained psychologist and OWI veteran; and Clyde K. M. Kluckhohn, a Harvard-trained anthropologist, OWI veteran, consultant to Gen. Douglas MacArthur and to the Human Resources Committee of the RDB, and director of the recently established Harvard Russian Research Center, a research organization separately funded by the Carnegie Corporation.[38]

Purcell had already indicated to Burchard that he was willing to play a leading role in the study. The two discussed several potential outside participants and drew heavily on the existing group of advisers and committee members working for the military's Research and Development Board. Burchard listed several MIT professors: Alex Bavelas (psychologist), Elting Morison (historian), Burnham Kelly (law professor, city planner, and former wartime associate of Burchard), and Max Millikan, the economist son of the Nobel Prize–winning Caltech physicist, Robert A. Millikan. Burchard also included on his list Donald Marquis and Robert Morison, the director of medical sciences at the Rockefeller Foundation. Over the course of August and September, Burchard and Purcell added several more experts to the group, including Dana K. Bailey, a radio expert at the National Bureau of Standards; John A. Morrison, a geographer at the University of Maryland and former consultant to the State Department's policy planning staff; John R. Pierce, a multitalented Bell Telephone Laboratory electronics expert; Hans Speier, chief of the RAND Corporation's Social Science Division; Jerome Wiesner, associate director of the MIT Research Laboratory of Electronics; and finally, Lloyd Berkner. Among those who were considered or who were asked to participate but could not escape prior commitments were McGeorge Bundy, Robert Merton, and George Kennan.[39]

Typifying the attitude of many toward the project were comments made by the physicist Edward Purcell just prior to his being named, at Killian's request, deputy director of the entire effort. "I am glad to be in this thing myself," he wrote, "because it is so important an experiment that I would rather make even a small contribution to it than a big contribution to anything else I can think of."[40]

By early October arrangements had been made with all of the participants' home institutions to pay their salaries and benefits, and detailed plans and a schedule of activities had begun to take shape. Briefings were scheduled for the last week of the month at the State Department, with attendance to be tightly controlled. During the evenings team members were encouraged to stay in one of a block of adjoining hotel rooms to facilitate informal discussion.[41] Beginning on Monday, November 6, the intensive study sessions began, using the same facilities at MIT's Lexington Field Station outside of Boston that had been used earlier by the Hartwell group. The agenda for these sessions was left largely up to the participants and was interrupted only by a group sojourn to Washington to meet with Dean Acheson. In Lexington the group called in a raft of consultants for briefings and discussions of specific issues.[42]

To do the bulk of their work the project team divided up into cross-disciplinary panels. Each panel developed outlines of approaches to specific problems or problem areas. The outlines were then discussed and critiqued by the whole group and turned over to working groups composed primarily of specialists but including one or more nonspecialists. These working groups prepared reports, which were again reviewed and critiqued by the entire group. The results were turned over to an editorial committee, which prepared drafts of the various sections of the final report for another group review. The process took most of three months.[43]

Published, firsthand accounts by both Barrett and Jerome Bruner suggest that the project was a rather heady experience. "There was, as well [as the team members and consultants]," wrote Bruner, "a salting of this assistant secretary or that, and we had a faithful attendant for a week in the person of that remarkable man James Webb. . . . For all the gravity of the proceedings, Project TROY was the best club I ever belonged to, so much so that a handful of its 'old boys' set up a Supper Club that dined together at the St. Botolph's Club in Boston the first Friday evening of each month for the next fifteen years."[44]

The final report from Project Troy, classified top secret, was eighty-one pages long. It was sent to the State Department on February 15, 1951, for duplication. Twenty-six annexes in three additional volumes were forwarded piecemeal over the next few weeks.

The foreword to the report was written by Burchard, who reviewed the charge to the team members and related how, "by general agreement," the project had been expanded to go beyond the problem of overcoming Soviet attempts to jam Voice of America broadcasts to "look at other methods of perforating the iron curtain." He stated that everyone agreed that the effectiveness of the VOA "was inevitably tied to the target and to the content of the material to be conveyed and finally to the effect that was ultimately desired." He then turned to a discussion of "political warfare," which was the concept around which the team constructed the entire report. He noted that neither the concept nor the elements associated with it were new. "The newness of our idea, if any," he wrote, "lies in the understanding of the strategic power of the several elements when combined as a well rounded and coordinated whole."[45]

The team members credited earlier policy makers with making a start. "The Marshall plan, the Point Four program, and some of the operations of the Economic Cooperation Administration in the Far East are examples of American efforts." But in a declaration that reflected the rhetoric that was then coursing through the American political establishment—rhetoric reinforced by the recently approved NSC 68 and the crisis atmosphere generated by events in Korea—they described these measures as "essentially defensive."[46] "If we now go over to the offensive in an aggressive, integrated, and comprehensive political warfare program," they wrote, "we may yet achieve our purposes without armed combat."[47]

With definitions and generalities out of the way, the main report proceeded to analyze components of the problem of conducting effective political warfare. The group had been asked to concentrate its attention on the potential of radio and balloons. Nevertheless, it began by looking into other possibilities: motion pictures, intelligent travelers, library services, student exchanges, and the like. It also noted that information already penetrated the Iron Curtain through "direct mail, professional journals, and industrial and commercial publications." And it noted that much about the United States was communicated abroad through the export of certain commodities: pharmaceuticals, flashlights, fountain pens, and small radio receivers.[48]

The chapter on radio was the longest, the most self-confident, and the most technically detailed. It identified two possible approaches to piercing the Iron Curtain: (1) advances that would enable the Voice of America to broadcast to selected regions a signal so powerful as to be able to overcome current jamming capabilities and (2) the development of "a tiny, cheap, self-contained, durable receiver that could eventually be distributed in large numbers over the world."[49]

The experts recognized that the new techniques they proposed could eventually be countered, but they insisted that even so they were worth pursuing. It could be demonstrated, they claimed, that the Soviet Union would have to devote far more scarce financial and technical resources to countermeasures than the measures themselves would cost. That, they pointed out, had distinct political warfare advantages extending well beyond the information programs themselves. Technicians and industrial resources devoted to countering American propaganda initiatives would be unavailable to address critical problems of far more immediate concern to national security—that is, to the full-scale "electromagnetic war" that the scientist members of the team predicted was imminent. The team was concerned about and sought technical solutions for the extreme vulnerability of communications with the people, governments, and armed forces in Europe. They noted that "if our high-frequency transmissions were jammed (they could be jammed tomorrow) and the Atlantic cables cut by submarine action, air mail would be our only means of communication."[50]

The other technical area the team concentrated on was balloons, which could drop millions of propaganda leaflets on selected targets. As the report pointed out, "balloons provide a cheap, expendable device for carrying loads to otherwise inaccessible regions." They could, indicated the experts, saturate an area of a million square miles "with a billion propaganda sheets in a single balloon operation costing a few million dollars." That would mean, they explained, that in the target area "a man would have better than an even chance of seeing at least one leaflet within 10 feet of his path while walking 1000 feet."[51]

With summaries of the technical matters complete, the scientists and the engineers retreated to the background, and the social scientists and historians took center stage. The report turned to the subject of target populations (which were not limited to enemy—or even foreign—national, ethnic, and social groups). Once again the team broke the problem down into components, devoting sections of the main report to Russia, Europe, China, and the defector. In these areas especially, the authors made it clear that they felt it was their job to point out the kinds of questions that should be asked and to recommend areas in desperate need of further research, rather than to make definitive statements.[52] They implied that social science research, if supported in the manner technical research had been supported by the military since World War II, would eventually pay powerful dividends.

The team members made some preliminary suggestions about each of the targets listed above. Those concerning the Soviet Union and defectors, many of which remain classified, turned out to be among the most controversial. For example, the report advised patience and at least some degree of tolerance. "We should avoid the position, expressed or implied, that communism is bad, or any implication of contempt for communism," warned the authors. "Our line should rather be that Stalinism has betrayed certain ideals of Marxism which have actually had a peaceful evolution in the West. There should be no appearance of an all out overt attack upon the intellectual foundations of Soviet Society." In a similar vein, the report warned against directly emphasizing the materialistic accomplishments of the West. "They impress the Russians," stated the report, "and this awareness must be maintained without antagonizing them by the contrast and without conveying the stereotype that all Americans care about is first rate plumbing."[53]

The experts warned that other things should be avoided too. The United States should not emphasize the isolation of the Soviet Union or the forces arrayed against the Soviets; it should not encourage hopeless acts of rebellion; and it should "not advocate Ukrainian or other separatist movements because they will rally far more people to the unity of Mother Russia."[54]

European target audiences received a great deal of attention. The team members concluded that "the purpose of our political warfare in Europe is to align the European countries with us as an effective force in our opposition to the USSR. A program to achieve this purpose must take into account the historical, racial, and political heterogeneity of Europe. Yet, in spite of the obvious wisdom of tailoring particular programs to fit the needs of special regions, the political warfare effort as a whole must emphasize the essential unity of Europe." With that in mind the team devoted considerable attention to Germany and to the issue of integrating German forces into a unified European defense force.[55]

The team members did not shrink from advocating policies designed to reform European economies and society. "France, Germany, Italy, and Greece need an enforceable and steeply graduated income tax," they declared. "While the great majority of the population still is inadequately fed and clothed, owners and managers have returned to a life of conspicuous consumption which arouses increasing resentment. This life is unfortunately identified by the underprivileged with the American free enterprise system." The team rejected this linkage and painted a remarkably rosy picture of American class relations. As to the methods to be used to accomplish European reform, they stated baldly that "if we propose to support the Adenauers and the de Gasperis we should press them to make fiscal and social reforms. If they do not, we should find politicians who will."[56]

When they came to consider China and Southeast Asia, the team identified three separate circumstances that had to be taken into account. First, the United States currently had very little access to China, which was the major player in Asia. Second, Asians identified the United States with Western imperialism. Third, the region was technologically backward. With these circumstances in mind, the team declared that only long-term initiatives would be effective. "Communism in China and Southeast Asia does not constitute a simple extension of Soviet power. Mao in China and Ho in Vietnam are not automatic tools of the Kremlin, but men with aspirations for their own countries who have embraced Communist doctrine as a formula for achieving progress in their own countries and who rely on Moscow for moral and military support."[57]

One concrete suggestion on how to proceed in that region was made in an annex printed in volume 3 of the Troy final report. Signed by the University of Maryland geographer Robert S. Morison, the annex suggested that the region's backwardness precluded most traditional means of communications, leaving only communications via "face to face contact on a wide scale." He proposed "the recruiting of a group of American youth willing and able to spend two or four years of their lives in intimate personal contact with the village people of Asia. Their primary task would be the demonstration of suitably modified western techniques of public health and agriculture. If they were the right sort of representative Americans they would also make use of their position to transmit almost automatically American ideas of cooperation in the common job, respect for individual dignity, and the free play of individual initiative."[58]

Characteristically, the entire Asia section concluded with an appeal for more research. The team advised the State Department to strengthen its research capability and called for "special private university-sponsored Institutes or programs . . . to carry out research on economic, social, psychological, and technical problems" in Asia.[59]

The additional areas of focus of the Troy report—an organized research and operational effort involving defectors from the Eastern bloc and an aggressive covert program to "overload and delay" the functioning of the Soviet state apparatus—remain largely classified.

The main report concluded with a series of general discussions. The first dealt with planning, which, the team concluded, "is not at present in a highly developed stage, probably because no specific agency in the government is now charged with this overall planning function." The second general discussion was on American public opinion. "The present situation," stated the report, "calls for a thorough and continuing study of the fundamental attitudes and values of the American people as a factor in the formulation, presentation, and acceptance of foreign policy decisions."[60] The final discussion was devoted to administration and echoed many of the conclusions of the earlier section on planning. The team members reminded their readers that as they prepared their report, there was "no single authority . . . strong enough to direct with certainty the several elements that claim an interest in the prosecution of political warfare. The parts are there—in separate agencies and departments—but the whole is not there." They concluded that "until these parts, contributed by the economic, military, diplomatic and information services, are brought into a coherent relationship under central direction, our political warfare will lack the striking power it needs today."[61]

The State Department praised the Troy report for its thoroughness and for the new ideas it contained, although some officials were slightly defensive about some of its suggestions. Even before William Barrett had completed a thorough reading, he told Burchard that he thought the project had "blazed important new paths, not only in helping to solve the major problems we face but in showing the way that we might go about getting solutions to other problems in the future."[62] One State Department analyst within the Economic Affairs Division wrote that the main report was "really quite an extraordinary piece of work." He characterized the chapter on Russia as "one of the most thoughtful and penetrating treatments of this subject I have seen recently" and declared that it would have "important implications in the economic as well as the political and psychological fields." He considered the report strong in its economic considerations regarding Europe but weak on Asia. Overall his impression was that the study "clearly shows that a group of outside experts can make a distinct contribution in foreign policy planning." In fact,

19

he thought that a parallel study focusing "on the economic defense field" (including labor issues) might be worth convening.[63]

Not all of the internal reactions were positive. Especially defensive was the existing State Department intelligence organization, which believed that its own work, especially with defectors, had not been described fully to the Project Troy participants. W. Park Armstrong Jr., within the Research and Intelligence office, also objected to certain of the report's analyses, believing that the report writers were, in places, overly defensive. He believed, further, that the report placed insufficient emphasis on American strengths. According to Armstrong, the Troy participants tended to "concede too much to the enemy" in that they seemed to be calling for an acknowledgment of the "basic correctness of the Kremlin's program and world outlook and for centering our efforts on persuading people that contrary to the Kremlin's contention we actually are not opponents of the essential aspects of the Bolshevik system."[64]

Armstrong's discomfort with the ideological bent he perceived among the academic participants in Project Troy are worth mentioning, if only as a precursor of sentiments that would later surface. In the spring of 1951, however, they were apparently not yet a matter of serious concern within the narrow circle of policy makers privy to the top secret study. Webb's reaction was more typical. He was essentially positive in his initial evaluation and had no objections to the ideological tone the report recommended for American propaganda broadcasts. He did have some doubts, but they were all organizational. Most of all, he was not convinced that a "single authority" outside of the State Department was consistent with the "basic principle that political warfare must, of necessity, conform to the foreign policy of the U.S. thus requiring that the role of the Department of State be predominant in this type of activity."[65]

Paul Nitze, director of the State Department's policy and planning staff also expressed preliminary agreement with most of the report's recommendations. But he too objected to several of the conclusions made in the section on "administration." Nitze, like

Webb, did not believe that a single external authority could or should be established to oversee political warfare. In that regard, in April, writing to Webb concerning recent proposals on how a strengthened Psychological Strategies Board might function, Nitze charged that Project Troy, in making its institutional recommendations, had "vastly overstepped its terms of reference and its area of competence."[66]

Regardless of any internal reservations, the State Department found a way to use Project Troy even before its final report was at hand.[67] Early in 1951, Senator William Benton, a Connecticut Democrat who had served in Barrett's position in the State Department from 1945 to 1947, proposed to remove the entire propaganda effort from State Department control. With Project Troy in mind, Secretary of State Acheson, in a move typical of bureaucratic politics, tried to convince Benton that the State Department had already gone a long way toward establishing the effective and comprehensive program he was seeking. Writing on January 24, 1951, Acheson emphasized that the department had used the increases in appropriations that had followed Truman's "campaign of truth" initiative in part "to secure the advice of the best brains we can find in this country on more effective techniques for getting the truth into areas where it is now largely excluded, and to develop the content which will in fact have the impact you are looking for."[68]

Running parallel to the struggle for operational control of the Voice of America was the struggle over which agency would set strategy for and control the planning of propaganda and psychological warfare operations. The main report issued by Project Troy had recommended a "single authority for political warfare." Max Millikan, who after Project Troy went on to serve for a year as assistant to the director of the CIA, was especially concerned with the issue of centralized planning and accountability. From his position within the CIA he urged Killian to call the president's attention to the conclusions of the Troy study. Apparently, Project Troy recommendations had a direct influence on the form of the president's April 4 directive establishing the Psychological Strategy Board (PSB).[69] In addition, as the PSB organized itself, Project Troy was touted by the State Department as the "principal research undertaken with reference to penetration of the Iron Curtain" and as having "vast implications for the overt propaganda program."[70]

Perhaps the most fruitful of all the Project Troy recommendations, however, especially given that bureaucratic infighting over psychological warfare continued almost unabated after the creation of the PSB,[71] were those on recruiting competent researchers. In one of the annexes to the main report, five of Troy's social scientists and historians wrote that "careful planning of basic research requirements carried out jointly by policy makers, government research officers, and university scholars implemented by a flexible policy of contractual grants to university centers can be of immense help in assuring a backlog of vital basic research." The group added that it was "desirable that as much research as possible be allocated by contract to private research centers and universities in order that a wide array of talent outside of the Government may be brought to bear on the critical problems of political warfare." An "added advantage" to that strategy was that "specialists in the various phases of political warfare can be trained in their tasks by assisting at universities in political warfare research." The group also proposed that a new kind of research institute be created on university campuses. "These institutes could carry out government research programs in the field of political warfare utilizing university personnel either on a part-time basis or by the use of a rotation plan which would permit university specialists to remain in their 'home atmospheres' during leaves of absence from university duties."[72]

Even before the final annexes of the Troy report were delivered to the State Department, Killian reported to Webb on progress in organizing a "second phase" of Project Troy. He wrote that Harvard and MIT would undertake a joint follow-on program (with MIT serving as the contractor) and that the two university provosts, Paul Buck and Julius A. Stratton, would serve on a small policy board along with John Burchard. Further, he announced that various staff members of both Harvard and MIT had agreed to participate and that Richard M. Bissell, assistant administrator of the Economic Cooperation Administration, had agreed to direct the effort.[73]

The Troy follow-on project was to involve four nontechnical research initiatives. The first was an intense scholarly study of "the dynamics of Soviet society." The second was a research and interview program designed to glean as much information as possible from Soviet and Eastern Bloc defectors. The third was the "overload and delay" research and planning effort, and the fourth was the establishment at MIT of a permanent model research institute of the sort described in the original Troy report. In addition, the scientists and engineers planned to carry forward research on radio propagation, the development of inexpensive radio receivers for possible distribution behind the Iron Curtain, and other technical matters in conjunction with the Army Signal Corps, the National Bureau of Standards, and several private contractors.[74]

The task of conducting the study of Soviet society fell to Walt Whitman Rostow, who was a close friend of Max Millikan. Rostow turned the completed study over to the State Department and the CIA in August 1952.[75] The follow-on defector interview and research program, later funded by the air force, was undertaken by a group led by Clyde Kluckhohn at the Harvard Russian Research Center.[76] The "overload and delay" program was conducted by the MIT psychologist Alex Bavelas.[77]

The final initiative of the follow-on to Project Troy led directly to the creation of the present-day MIT Center for International Studies. In January 1952, after serving with the CIA, Max Millikan returned to MIT, established CENIS, and became its first director.[78] Funded by the Ford Foundation and the CIA (not the State Department), CENIS was created, in the words of Center member Walt Rostow, "to bring to bear academic research on issues of public policy." Ford Foundation involvement is a powerful indication of the hidden influence of Project Troy. Ford's behavioral sciences program had been initiated only in February 1951, when H. Rowan Gaither agreed to organize the effort. Gaither immediately appointed as consultants Han Speier and Donald Marquis, both of whom were just completing the final review of the Troy report.[79]

CIA funding of CENIS would lead to controversy later, when people began to question whether academic freedom could exist at a CIA-funded institution.[80] But at least through the 1950s CENIS served exactly the function outlined for such institutes in the Troy report. It was a place where a wide variety of academic specialists could come together in academic surroundings to participate full- or part-time in classified research and discussions. CENIS served as a model for similar programs at several other universities and, as the Troy team members had hoped, gave additional impetus to the whole area studies movement already becoming prevalent within many American universities.[81]

The State Department eventually gave up control to the military of the technical suggestions made by Project Troy of ways to increase the security and effectiveness of long-distance communications.[82] And in 1953, following the recommendation of a panel chaired by W. H. Jackson and charged with investigating government information programs, Eisenhower established the United States Information Agency (USIA) outside of the State Department to manage the VOA's operations.[83]

Although the State Department failed to retain direct control over the VOA and was not very successful in its bureaucratic struggles with the military and the CIA, the overarching national security apparatus within the executive branch did succeed in institutionalizing—outside of the military—its own special relations with private expertise.[84] The military's earlier acceptance of radical new weapons as the key to postwar preparedness had already significantly transformed the ways in which university-based scientific research was funded and organized.[85] Using the military program to take advantage of private scientific expertise as a model, academic administrators and professors wanted to bring to bear the additional capabilities located within the university on the broader problems of national security and, not incidentally, to have the humanities and social science disciplines share in some measure the bounty of federal support.

Military security requirements had dominated many of the arrangements that already had been made between the armed services and universities. The high level of classification and obvious international and domestic sensitivity of political warfare made security a fact of life for the social science programs as well. Consequently there was no open discussion of the academic community's growing commitment to serve the needs of the state. Government support of research quickly began to move beyond the sciences and engineering, to include the academic disciplines of anthropology, economics, psychology, sociology, political science, and history, yet the potential impact of such support—direct or indirect—on the quality and independence of research and on the teaching of these subjects remained largely unevaluated.

In the 1960s, when circumstances were very different, the secrecy surrounding arrangements such as those between the CIA and CENIS did (at least temporarily) lead to resentment and a sense of betrayal on the part of antiwar students and faculty at MIT, as at other universities.[86] There is an irony to the disruptions that resulted, if only because the Project Troy report—which helped originate those relations—also warned explicitly against the potentially corrosive effects of secrecy on the university and more generally of the Cold War on American society.

In one of the report's annexes, Elting Morison (the MIT historian of technology and editor of the letters of Theodore Roosevelt) asked how values "created by our relatively free society in a past that was, for the most part serene," could be "perpetuated within a relatively controlled society during an ominous present? or how, more simply, in the words of the Under Secretary of State, can we maintain democracy in a garrison?"[87] Morison's reflections on those questions provide a fitting conclusion to this study.

Morison feared the vastly expanded government machinery established to cope with the looming international crises. This governmental "authority to control large sections of the environment presents at least a threat to some of the historic qualities that we have heretofore assumed to be an inherent part of our way of life," he wrote. He listed several aspects of American life as at least partially threatened by government intervention: the "quality of diversity"; the "quality of mobility"; the "quality of affection or sympathy"; and, most relevant here, "the quality of curiosity." As he wrote, "the single purpose of the garrison state tends, naturally, to absorb the attention of all intelligences—whether in industry, government, or university. This concentration on a single problem or set of problems will tend to reduce not only the variety of intellectual work, but will tend also to reduce . . . the American bump of curiosity."[88]

One of Morison's specific concerns was secrecy, "or the classified idea." "In the long run," he wrote, secrecy might "prove to be more dangerous to free communication than any other single thing." He went on to explain that "at the moment, to be sure, the influence of the classified idea has not been much felt [clearly he meant outside of the hard and engineering sciences]; it has been extended only with great caution and, almost exclusively, to the few universities that have secret projects for the government. There is pause in the thought, however, that universities are, in this society, one of the great wellsprings of ideas and that the source of supply for these springs is the unobstructed flow of information and ideas."[89]

Morison was optimistic that damage to the American university and to American values could be minimized. On behalf of his colleagues he called for, in addition to the programmatic research on political warfare, simultaneous research on the impact of the Cold War on American society and on ways of mitigating its negative effects. "We earnestly recommend," he wrote, "a research program that will pool the energy and wisdom of historians, anthropologists, economists and psychologists to analyze the possible effects of a prolonged preparedness upon this society and to provide us with a basis for dealing intelligently with the life that lies immediately before us."[90]

Morison was perhaps too optimistic both about what government agencies and Congress would be willing to fund and about the capacity of academic researchers to look beyond the immediate, short-term requirements of their new patrons. It was also optimistic to assume that long-term analysis by scholars would somehow have a meaningful effect in a nation at cold war. Most importantly, although the acute sense of emergency that pervaded the winter of 1950–51 would pass, many of the institutions, habits, and relationships born in crisis would long endure. What Morison could not have known was that, emergency or not, the nation would remain at war (sometimes cold, sometimes hot) for upward of forty years. Perhaps now that the Cold War is finally over, Morison's issues will be addressed fully, openly, and in detail—if not prospectively as applied social science, at least retrospectively as history.

Notes

1. Justin Miller served as president of the National Association of Broadcasters and, earlier, as chairman of the U.S. Advisory Commission on International Information. His comments on Project Troy are cited in Edward W. Barrett, *Truth Is Our Weapon* (New York: Funk & Wagnalls Co., 1953), p. 115.

2. Project Troy actually took place in the fall and winter of 1950–51. It was called a "summer study" because the earliest examples (an air force study, code-named Project Lexington, to determine the feasibility of a nuclear-powered airplane; and a navy study, Project Hartwell, of means to assure uninterrupted overseas transport in the face of a large and sophisticated fleet of Soviet submarines) were all scheduled with the academic calendar and its summer recess in mind. The "summer study" was quickly seen as a convenient way to arrange for outside experts to devote concentrated effort to solve important military problems. See J. R. Marvin, and F. J. Weyl, "The Summer Study," *Naval Research Reviews*, (August 1966), pp. cover–7 and 24–28.

3. For a review of this tendency to impose a natural science model on the social sciences, see Mark Solovey, "The Politics of Intellectual Identity and American Social Science, 1945–1970," dissertation, University of Wisconsin, Madison, 1996.

4. Massachusetts Institute of Technology, "Project Troy Report to the Secretary of State," vol. 1, pt. 1, p. 3, General

Records of the Department of State, Record Group 59, lot file 52-283, National Archives, Washington, D.C. (hereafter, *Troy Report* with volume, part or annex no., and pages).

5. *Troy Report*, vol. 2, annex 1, p. 3.

6. Peter Buck, "Adjusting to Military Life: The Social Sciences Go to War, 1941–50," in Merritt Roe Smith, ed., *Military Enterprise and Technological Change* (Cambridge, Mass.: MIT Press, 1985), pp. 203–252.

7. Allan A. Winkler, *The Politics of Propaganda: The Office of War Information, 1942–45* (New Haven: Yale University Press, 1978).

8. For Truman's speech published in full, see Department of State *Bulletin* 2 (September 1945). The excerpt cited here is reprinted in [U.S. Department of State, *Foreign Relations of the United States* (hereafter cited as FRUS), 1951 (Washington, D.C.: GPO, 1979)], vol. 1, p. 958, n. 2.

9. "Review of SANACC Studies Pertaining to Psychological Warfare," SANACC 304/15, July 21, 1948, which summarizes the series of documents beginning in March 1946 on this topic generated by the State-War-Navy Coordinating Committee (later the State-Army-Navy-Air Force Coordinating Committee). Copy in Research and Development Board files, RG 330, entry 341, subject-numeric series, box 103, "SANACC" folder (hereafter, RDB Papers, subject-numeric series, with filing information).

10. John Lewis Gaddis, *Strategies of Containment: A Critical Appraisal of Postwar American National Security Policy* (New York: Oxford Univ. Press, 1982), pp. 36–51.

11. NSC 7, *FRUS 1948*, vol. 1, pp. 546–48. See also SANACC 360/11, "Military Aid Priorities," appendix 5, August 18, 1949, *FRUS 1949*, vol. 1, p. 259; and the NSC report, "Governmental Programs in National Security and International Affairs for the Fiscal Year 1951," September 29, 1949, *FRUS 1949*, vol. 1, p. 387, which justify the military assistance program.

12. NSC draft report (NSC-43), "Measures Required to Achieve U.S. Objectives with Respect to the U.S.S.R.," March 30, 1949, *FRUS 1949*, vol. 1, p. 276; John Prados, *Keeper of the Keys: A History of the National Security Council from Truman to Bush* (New York: William Morrow and Company, Inc., 1991), 50–56.

13. W. Henry Lambright, *Powering Apollo, James E. Webb of NASA* (Baltimore: Johns Hopkins University Press, 1995), pp. 30–47, On Webb's role at the Bureau of the Budget in national security matters, see Anna Kaston Nelson, "President Truman and the Evolution of the National Security Council," *Journal of American History* 72 (September 1985), pp. 365–66.

14. Dean Acheson, *Present at the Creation: My Years in the State Department* (New York: W. W. Norton, 1969), p. 250.

15. Lloyd V. Berkner (executive secretary, Joint Research and Development Board)

memorandum for the files, "Points to be covered in conference with Dr. Bush [chairman, JRDB] - September 20, 1946," September 19, 1946, detailing discussions with James Webb, RDB Papers subject-numeric series, box 156, folder "117 - Organization 1947." The pre-unification military's Joint Research and Development Board was established in July 1946. Berkner served as its executive secretary under board chairman Vannevar Bush until July 1947. On the RDB, see Don K. Price, *Government and Science: Their Dynamic Relation in American Democracy* (New York, NYU Press, 1954), pp. 144–52; and Allan A. Needell, "From Military Research to Big Science: Lloyd Berkner and Science-Statesmanship in the Postwar Era," in *Big Science: The Growth of Large-Scale Research*, eds. Peter Galison and Bruce Hevly (Stanford, Stanford Univ. Press, 1992), pp. 290–311. Webb and Berkner served together in the naval reserves. From April 1949 until September 1949 Berkner served as special assistant to the secretary of state: coordinator for foreign military assistance programs. Later that year he headed another special advisory group as special consultant to the secretary of state on department responsibilities in international science, producing in April 1950 an important study on science and foreign relations. See Eugene Skolnikoff, *Science, Technology and American Foreign Policy* (Cam-

bridge, MIT Press, Mass., 1967), pp. 255–57.

16. Barrett, *Truth Is Our Weapon*, pp. 115–18; memorandum, "Support for the Voice of America in the Fields of Intelligence and Research and Development," undated, attached to James S. Lay (executive secretary, NSC), cover note to NSC 66, April 4, 1950, *FRUS 1950*, vol. 4, p. 287.

17. Stephen Marshall, "NSC 68 and the Vision of Soviet Vulnerabilities," unpublished manuscript. I am grateful to Stephen Marshall for providing me with a copy of his paper and for his permission to cite his work. Among other evidence he amasses of perceptions of Soviet vulnerabilities during the period are a *LIFE* Magazine article by Wallace Carroll, published on December 19, 1949, entitled, "It Takes a Russian to Beat a Russian"; and James Burnham, *The Coming Defeat of Communism*, which called for "offensive political-subversive warfare." On Burnham's background and influence see Bruce Cumings, *The Origins of the Korean War, Vol. 2, The Roaring of the Cataract: 1947–50* (Princeton, Princeton Univ. Press, 1990), 117–21.

18. Truman to Acheson, March 1, 1950, *FRUS 1950*, vol. 4, p. 271.

19. Barrett to Webb, March 6, 1950, *FRUS 1950*, vol. 4, pp. 274–75.

20. On Berkner's involvement, see Berkner to Howland Sargeant (State Department Office of Public Affairs), November 9, 1949, Lloyd V. Berkner Papers, box 10, Manuscript Division,

Library of Congress, Washington, D.C.

21. It was a common complaint among knowledgeable people in and out of government, then as later, that the State Department was incapable of leading required foreign policy initiatives. See Richard J. Barnet, *Roots of War: The Men and Institutions behind U.S. Foreign Policy* (Baltimore, Penguin Books, 1973), 24–35; and Charles E. Neu, "The Rise of the National Security Bureaucracy," in *The New American State: Bureaucracies and Policies since World War II*, ed. Louis Galambos (Baltimore, Johns Hopkins Univ. Press, 1987), pp. 85–90 and 96. For a slightly later private comment specifically on the State Department's inability to lead a political warfare campaign, see Bush to James B. Conant, January 8, 1951, Vannevar Bush Papers, box 27, folder 614, Manuscript Division, Library of Congress. On the struggle for influence among the various agencies of the executive branch, see Nelson, "President Truman and the Evolution of the National Security Council," pp. 363–66; and Prados, *Keeper of the Keys*, pp. 51–53.

22. Prados, *Keeper of the Keys*, pp. 51–52.

23. In addition to members of the department's International Information and Educational Exchange Program, the symposium featured several of Barrett's former OWI colleagues, including Hans Speier, chief of the RAND Corporation's Social Science Division, consultant to the RDB, and future member of Project TROY. An agenda and an outline of the symposium are filed in RDB Papers, subject-numeric series, box 103, folder "State Department."

24. *FRUS 1950*, vol. 4, p. 304.

25. Webb to Lay, May 26, 1950, *FRUS 1950*, vol. 4, pp. 311–12.

26. In July the president wrote to the Speaker of the House requesting $89 million (approximately $490 million in 1990 dollars) for information and education, with $41 million of that earmarked for the expansion of radio broadcasting facilities. In August, responding to Acheson's denunciation of a step-up in the Soviet Union's propaganda efforts, twenty-seven senators wrote to the president urging a "psychological and spiritual offensive against the Kremlin." Truman used the letter to buttress his own complaints about House attempts to cut funds for propaganda. The result was that the Supplemental Appropriations Act, signed by the president on September 27, 1950, contained $63.9 million for the information programs and an additional $15.2 million in so-called counterpart currencies. See editorial note, *FRUS 1950*, vol. 4, pp. 316–17. Here and hereafter, 1990 figures are based on the Consumer Price Indices 1950–1990.

27. JCS SM-1039-50, May 15, 1950, referred to in Edwin A. Speakman (executive director, Committee on Electronics, RDB)

memorandum to executive secretary, RDB, September 5, 1950, RDB Papers, subject-numeric series, box 15, folder "EL-Countermeasures."

28. The Human Resources Committee was established in January 1947 and was made up of knowledgeable military officers and academic social scientists with the responsibility of considering issues of manpower, troop morale, and training, as well as the organization and maintenance of psychological warfare capabilities. Its charter and activities are documented in RDB Papers, subject-numeric series, box 38, folder "Human Relations and Morale," especially Col. D. W. Johnson to E. F. Black (RDB Planning Division), "Research Pertaining to Psychological Warfare," January 13, 1947. Among the consultants to the Human Resources Committee were Hans Speier, Elting Morison, and Clyde Kluckkohn, all of whom would later take part in Project Troy.

29. See Walker (executive secretary, RDB) to Webster (chairman, RDB), August 3, 1950, copy found in Compton/Killian Papers, designation AC 4, folder "Project TROY," Massachusetts Institute of Technology Archives and Special Collections (hereafter, Project Troy File, MIT Archives); and Speakman to executive secretary, RDB, September 5, 1950, RDB Papers, subject-numeric series, box 15, folder "El-100-ECM." On the earlier "summer studies," see note 5 above.

30. In May, Webb established an "Interdepartmental Foreign Information Staff," with Barrett as assistant secretary of state serving as chairman. On August 17 that staff was converted into the so-called National Psychological Strategy Board, consisting of representatives of the Department of Defense, the Joint Chiefs of Staff, and the CIA. Barrett's formal board would be "responsible for coordinating foreign information and psychological strategy in situations where joint action was required. See, Acheson to Embassies, May 4, 1950, reprinted in *FRUS 1950*, vol. 4, p. 305n. Also prepared was another NSC document (NSC 74), which contained provisions for the creation of an independent agency to treat strategic issues surrounding the integration of propaganda and psychological operations with overall national security goals. Apparently, disagreement over the relative strength to be given to the State Department relative to the other national security agencies resulted in a deadlock, one that would not be broken until the creation by the President in April 1951 of a formal Psychological Strategy Board. On Berkner's role initiating the State Department–MIT discussions, see W. J. Sheppard to W. Barrett, July 31, 1950, which states: "Dr. Berkner called on Friday in reference to the MIT contract which, as I understand it, he had talked about with Mr. Webb. Dr. Berkner said that he had taken this up with Messrs. Killian and Stratton at MIT and

felt that they were going to accept the contract." RG 59, Records of the Executive Secretariat (Dean Acheson), "William J. Sheppard" file, NARA.

31. Killian to Webb, August 7, 1950, Project Troy File, MIT Archives, Cambridge, Mass.

32. Killian to Webb, August 7, 1950, Webb to Killian, August 16, 1950, both in Project Troy File, MIT Archives.

33. Killian to Buck, August 11, 1950, Project Troy File, MIT Archives.

34. Acheson, *Present at the Creation*, pp. 354–70.

35. Burchard to Killian, August 14, 1950, Project Troy File, MIT Archives.

36. Killian to Burchard, August 16, 1950, Project Troy File, MIT Archives.

37. Burchard to Sage, August 14, 1950, Project Troy File, MIT Archives.

38. Buck to Killian, August 15, 1950, Project Troy File, MIT Archives. On Kluckhohn and the creation of the Russian Research Center in 1948, see Charles Thomas O'Connell, "Social Structure and Science: Soviet Studies at Harvard" (Ph.D. diss., UCLA, 1990), pp. 163–96.

39. *Troy Report*, vol. 3, annex 16; Burchard to Purcell, August 14, 1950, and memorandum, "Status of Recruiting in Project Troy as of 9/21/50," Project Troy File, MIT Archives.

40. Purcell to Burchard, September 5, 1950, Project Troy File, MIT Archives. Similar remarks can be found elsewhere in this same collection in letters written by the chief executive officers of the universities and other institutions approached by Killian to release their employees for the project. See, for example, Frank R. McCoy (president, Roosevelt Memorial Association, and employer of Elting Morison) to Killian, October 2, 1950; Chester J. Bernard (president, Rockefeller Foundation, and employer of Robert Morison) to Killian, September 27, 1950; and James P. Adams (provost, University of Michigan, and employer of Donald Marquis) to Killian, September 27, 1950.

41. Burchard memorandum, October 6, 1950, AC 125, box 57, folder 9, "Project Troy," MIT Archives; *Troy Report*, vol. 3, annex 18, p. 1.

42. *Troy Report*, vol. 3, annex 17. The consultants listed are Frank Altschul, Edwin H. Armstrong, Ross Bateman, Richard M. Bissell, Henry G. Booker, Raymond V. Bowers, Gerald B. Brophy, Ralph Clark, Harlan Cleveland, R. M. Coquillette, B. R. Curtis, John Davies, John Devine, Henry V. Dicks, Harald T. Friis, George W. Gilman, Col. O. L. Grover (USAF), George Q. Herrick, Charles M. Hulten, Frank B. Jewett Jr., Mervin J. Kelly, George F. Kennan, Admiral Allan G. Kirk, Capt. Dennis W. Knoll (USN), Foy D. Kohler, Urner Liddel, Brig. Gen. Robert A. McClure (USAF), Charles B. Moore, Malia G. Natirbov, Paul H. Nitze, Todo M. Odarer, G. Hall Paxton, Charles H. Pease, A. J. Pote, Albert Ravenholt, Richard D. Robinson, Richard B. Roberts, Melville J. Ruggles, Col. R. S. Sleeper (USAF), Win-

trop M. Soutworth Jr., William T. Stone, Gail L. Stubbs, Davidson Taylor, Adam Watson, and A. H. Waynick.

43. Burchard to Acheson, February 19, 1951, RG 59, 611.00/2–1951, NARA.

44. Barrett, *Truth Is Our Weapon*, pp. 118–22; Jerome Bruner, *In Search of Mind: Essays in Autobiography* (New York, Harper & Row, 1983), p. 210.

45. *Troy Report*, vol. 1, pp. vii–ix.

46. NSC 68 was approved in September, during the Troy deliberations the Chinese entered the fighting in Korea, and on December 15 President Truman declared a "national emergency." See Cumings, *The Roaring of the Cataract*, pp. 745–47.

47. *Troy Report*, vol. 1, p. 4.

48. *Troy Report*, vol. 1, pp. 9–10; vol. 4, annex 26; Barrett, *Truth Is Our Weapon*, p. 116.

49. *Troy Report*, vol. 1, pp. 11 and 22–23.

50. *Troy Report*, vol. 1, pp. 24–27. With that possibility in mind, the project scientists expressed deep dissatisfaction with the quality of intelligence available to them on Soviet jamming equipment and made several suggestions on methods of gathering better intelligence (much of which remains classified and was blotted out in the report copy made available under the Freedom of Information Act). On a method of providing secure, high-frequency communication from point to point over distances of many hundreds of miles, the scientific experts of Project Troy actually approached an exciting, poten-

tially significant technical breakthrough—one that has since generally been referred to as ionospheric, or E-layer, scatter communications. The new technique of very high frequency (50–100 mHz) communications had many military and potential commercial applications as well as applications as a means of securely linking the European and other overseas VOA broadcasting stations with program sources in the United States. The scientific results of these investigations were published in D. K. Bailey et. al., "A New Kind of Radio Propagation at Very High Frequencies Observable over Long Distances," *Physical Review* 86 (April 1952), pp. 141–95. The story was broken by the *New York Times* prior to the official release date of the *Physical Review* article in a remarkably insightful and technically accurate piece of science journalism. See Jack Gold, "New Radio Signal Opens Door to Global Video," *New York Times*, 30 April 1952.

51. *Troy Report*, vol. 1, pp. 29–32 [pp. 33–36 being deleted].

52. *Troy Report*, vol. 1, p. 80.

53. *Troy Report*, vol. 1, p. 44. Such suggestions raised the eyebrows of some members of the State Department's own research and intelligence organization. On contemporary expressions by State Department officials about "pro-communist leanings" of members of the Harvard Russian Research Center and FBI surveillance of its activities, see

O'Connell, "Social Structure and Science," pp. 133–38. State Department officials were exquisitely sensitive lest the department's attitudes become grist for Senator McCarthy. See Acheson, *Present at the Creation*, pp. 362–70; and Cumings, *The Roaring of the Cataract*, pp. 35–121.

54. *Troy Report*, vol. 1, p. 48.
55. *Troy Report*, vol. 1, p. 51.
56. *Troy Report*, vol. 1, p. 55.
57. *Troy Report*, vol. 1, p. 65
58. *Troy Report*, vol. 3, annex 9, p. 1, "Personnel for Southeast Asia and other Backward Areas." Since many of the men associated with the Troy and follow-on projects were also involved with the Kennedy administration (James Killian, Max Millikan, and Walter Rostow chief among them), the similarity between Robert Morison's suggestion and the Peace Corps as it ultimately developed may be more than coincidental. Truman-era study programs are not generally cited by historians either as among the sources of the Peace Corps idea or as vehicles by which that idea attracted political support. (See, for example, Gerald T. Rice, *The Bold Experiment: JFK's Peace Corps*, South Bend, Ind., Univ. of Notre Dame Press, 1987). Interestingly, in his recent memoirs James Killian makes the otherwise logically suspect claim that Max Millikan, director of the MIT Center for International Studies (CENIS), which was a direct outgrowth of Project Troy, had "originated the idea

of a Peace Corps." (See Killian, *The Education of a College President*, Cambridge, Mass., The MIT Press, 1985, p. 68.) He cites as evidence a December 30, 1960, memorandum from Millikan to the president-elect, found in the files of the Kennedy Library. Yet the Peace Corps idea was bandied about and even proposed in Congress by Hubert Humphrey during the campaign. I think it plausible that Killian misremembered when Millikan first suggested a Peace Corps–like organization. After all, the Troy report has remained classified and largely unread since the early 1950s.

59. *Troy Report*, vol. 1, p. 70.
60. *Troy Report*, vol. 1, p. 79.
61. *Troy Report*, vol. 1, pp. 80–81. One of the nontechnical annexes deserves special mention, although the bulk of it remains classified (including the name of its author). The annex is titled "Stalin." It addresses the special political warfare opportunity that would present itself upon the death of the Soviet leader. "Since Stalin's death offers the best opportunity for exploiting the fear and self-interest of the Soviet elite," the section begins, "with the aim of weakening the regime to the point where it can no longer threaten our world objectives, and since the death of the dictator can occur at any time, it is of the utmost importance to initiate planning for this eventuality without delay." The few remaining segments that have been spared the de-

classification officer's scissors call for the creation of a special section "within the Political Warfare Executive to concentrate exclusively on this task," and list the special "competencies" required to staff it. *Troy Report*, vol. 3, annex 15, p. 1 [the remaining pages deleted].

62. Barrett to Burchard, March 3, 1951, RG 59, lot file 52–283, NARA.

63. Schaetzel memorandum, to Willard L. Thorp, "Comments on Project Troy Report," March 8, 1951, RG 59, 611.00/3-851, NARA.

64. Armstrong to Barrett, January 24, 1951, RG 59, lot file 52-283, NARA.

65. J. E. Webb to C. M. Hulten, March 7, 1951, Records Related to Project Troy, RG 59, lot file 52-283, NARA.

66. Nitze to Webb, April 9, 1951, Policy Planning Group, U.S. Department of State, RG 59, lot file 64 D 653, box 034: "Chronological 1951 (3)," NARA.

67. For example, while fleshing out the details and costs of the recommendations contained in NSC 68 (the new agressive Cold War planning document that had been approved by President Truman the previous fall), Barrett's organization in the State Department was called on to prepare an annex to the follow-on document, NSC 68/3, one which detailed the tasks and methods to be used by an expanded Foreign Information Program. Completed on December 8, 1950, the so-called Annex 5 contains a great deal of language that,

largely without attribution, mirrors that contained in the Project Troy final report. Furthermore, its own section on "Investigation and Research" boasts explicitly that "a group of social and natural scientists have [sic] already been engaged to investigate every possible method of getting information into the Soviet world." NSC 68/3, annex 5, reprinted in *FRUS 1950*, vol. 1, pp. 459–60.

68. Acheson to Benton, January 24, 1951, *FRUS 1951*, vol. 1, pp. 908–11. Benton was not convinced by these arguments and in February launched a "complete investigation" of the U.S. information program. See editorial notes, *FRUS 1951*, vol. 1, pp. 919 and 932–33. Another instance of State Department use of Project Troy to bolster the image of its own efforts is Barrett to Nitze, "JCS Memoranda of 15 January and 13 April 1951," dated May 2, 1951, *FRUS 1951*, vol. 1, pp. 919–21. Reference to Project Troy is on p. 921.

69. Millikan's suggestion to Killian is described in Burchard to Killian, February 21, 1951, Project Troy File, MIT Archives. Among the documents released from the State Department's Project Troy records (lot file 52-283) are two unsigned draft directives for creating a "Psychological Strategy Board." The first is dated February 19, 1951; the second was attached to a memorandum from Webb to the director of the Bureau of the Budget and dated March 12. (The cover memorandum was

not provided.) The wording of the later version is virtually identical to that of the directive actually signed by the president on April 4. The April 4 directive is reprinted in *FRUS 1951*, vol. 1, pp. 59–60.

70. NSC 114/1, Annex 5, "Study Prepared by the Department of State: The Information Program," August 8, 1951, *FRUS 1951*, vol. 1, pp. 923–32. Although not referred to by name, the description of Project Troy is item 28, p. 928.

71. Prados, *Keeper of the Keys*, pp. 53–56.

72. *Troy Report*, vol. 3, annex 11, p. 4. The authors were Jerome Bruner, Francis L. Friedman, Donald Marquis, Robert S. Morison, and Robert Wolff.

73. Killian to Webb, February 28, 1951, Killian to Stratton and Burchard, January 12, 1951, and Killian to Bissell, February 15, 1951, all in Project Troy File, MIT Archives. On Bissell, see Rhodri Jeffreys-Jones, *The CIA and American Democracy* (New Haven, Yale Univ. Press 1989), p. 107.

74. This account of the plans for what Killian called "TROY Plus" is drawn from Killian to Stratton, January 12, 1951, with attachment, "Organization of TROY Plus as an M.I.T. Project," Project Troy File, MIT Archives, and from statements in Killian, *The Education of a College President*, pp. 67–68; Marshall, "NSC 68 and the Vision of Soviet Vulnerabilities," pp. 16–18; and especially Walt Rostow, *Europe after Stalin: Eisenhower's Three Decisions of*

March 11, 1953 (Austin, Tex., Univ. of Texas Press, 1982), pp. 35–39.

75. It was as a result of this work that Rostow first became associated with C. D. Jackson, who in 1953 would be selected by President Eisenhower to be his special assistant for psychological warfare activities. Rostow, *Europe after Stalin*, p. 36.

76. O'Connell, "Social Structure and Science," pp. 332–76. On the extent of military and PSB involvement in defector interview programs, see HR 66/1, Dwight W. Chapman (executive director, Human Resources Committee) to executive secretary RDB, "Need for a Defector Policy from a Research and Development Viewpoint," February 9, 1951, and the closing lecture to a secret, ONR-sponsored psychological warfare seminar held at the University of North Carolina in August 1952, delivered by Raymond B. Allen, Gordon Gray's successor as director of the Psychological Strategy Board, both in RDB Papers, subject-numeric series, box 38, folder "RDB-HR-100." In his remarks Allen listed coordination plans already completed by the PSB in the approximately fifteen months it had been in existence. These plans included prominently a coordination effort for "Soviet Orbit Escapees."

77. J. A. Stratton [MIT provost and acting director of the Troy follow-on effort] memorandum to Max Millikan, "Continuation of Project TROY," March 30,

1951, (sanitized) State Department RG 59, lot file 58-D776, NARA. Almost all details of the "overload and delay" program remain classified.

78. Ibid.

79. On Gaither, Speier, and Marquis's role in the origins of the Ford behavioral Science program, see Mark Solovey, "The Politics of Intellectual Identity and American Social Science, 1945–1970," diss., University of Wisconsin, Madison, 1996, pp. 67–70.

80. See Killian, *The Education of a College President,* p. 67; and Rostow, *Europe after Stalin,* p. 35. Protests of CENIS are mentioned in Dorothy Nelkin, *The University and Military Research: Moral Politics at M.I.T.* (Ithaca, N.Y., Cornell Univ. Press 1972), 110.

81. L. S. Cotrell (group director) to chairman, RDB, "Summary of First Meeting [at CENIS] of Ad Hoc Working Group on Program Planning, Advisory Group on Psychological and Unconventional Warfare," March 12, 1953, RDB Papers, subject-numeric series, box 181, folder "Psychological Warfare and Cold War Operations." An account of the area studies movement, which emphasizes the role played after 1950 by the Ford Foundation, can be found in Robert A. McCaughey, *International Studies and Academic Enterprise: A Chapter in the Enclosure of American Learning* (New York, Columbia Univ. Press 1984). See also O'Connell, "Social Structure and Science," pp. 167–78. Be-

cause of the problem of classification, there is a dearth of public accounts of CIA involvement with the Ford and other private foundations or direct CIA support of social science research or of university area studies efforts. Records of military contracts for social science research from the period do indicate, however, that government interest and support was widespread. For example, see Aaron B. Nadel (executive director, Committee on Human Resources) to the assistant secretary of defense for R&D, "Status of Human Resources Research and Development as of 1 July 1953," with attachments, July 20, 1953, RDB Papers, subject-numeric series, box 38, folder "RDB-HR-100."

82. Of special importance was the discovery of VHF scatter communications. On the attempt to arrange with the military for its exploitation, see Barrett to Webb, August 9, 1951, with attached draft letter to the secretary of defense and the chairman of the FCC, RG 59, Records of the Executive Secretariat, box 29, folder "George C. Marshall, May–August 1951"; and H. Sargeant to Webb, December 10, 1951 with attachment, "Considerations of the Department of State in the Use of Scatter Transmission in the VHF Regions," RG 59, Records of the Executive Secretariat, box 28, folder: "Robert A. Lovett (Sec. of Defense) 1951." VHF scatter communications became an essential component of the DEW line radar system

for continental defense built by the air force later in the decade.

83. Wilson Compton, "Report by the Administrator of the United States International Information Administration to the Secretary of State," undated, *FRUS 1952–54* (Washington, D.C., 1984), vol. 2, p. 1636; the Jackson panel comments are in ibid., 1945. The establishment of the USIA was announced on July 31, 1953. See editorial note, ibid., p. 1735. On the subsequent development of the USIA and the many problems associated with it, see Julian Hale, *Radio Power: Propaganda and International Broadcasting* (Philadelphia, Temple Univ. Press 1975), pp. 31–48.

84. Barnet, *The Roots of War*, pp. 41–47; Samuel Z. Klausner and Victor M. Lidz, eds., *The Nationalization of the Social Sciences* (Philadelphia, 1986); Robin Winks, *Cloak & Gown: Scholars in the Secret War, 1939–1961* (New York, Morrow 1987).

85. See Paul Forman, "Behind Quantum Electronics: National Security as Basis for Physical Research in the United States, 1940–1960," *Historical Studies in the Physical and Biological Sciences*, vol. 18, p. 1 (1987), pp. 149–229; and Stuart W. Leslie, *The Cold War and American Science: The Military-Industrial-Academic Complex at MIT and Stanford* (New York: Columbia University Press, 1993).

86. Dorothy Nelkin, *The Military and the University*, p. 110; Irving Louis Horowitz, "Michigan State and the CIA: A Dilemma for Social Science," *Bulletin of the Atomic Scientists* 22 (September 1966), pp. 26–29.

87. *Troy Report*, vol. 3, annex 13, p. 3.

88. *Troy Report*, vol. 3, annex 13, p. 2.

89. *Troy Report*, vol. 3, annex 13, p. 3.

90. *Troy Report*, vol. 3, annex 13, p. 4.

(Max F. Millikan and Walt W. Rostow)

Notes on Foreign Economic Policy

I. What National Purposes Might a Foreign Economic Policy Serve

It is the immediate purpose of the foreign economic policy of the United States to participate in a partnership with the nations and peoples of the free world designed to promote the health and growth of the free world economy. By economic growth we mean a sustained increase in production per head, which gives or promises to give a higher real income to every free world citizen.

There is confusion both abroad and perhaps in our own minds as to why we want to do this. If the various specific measures this group agrees to be desirable are to receive firm support at home and understanding abroad, we must achieve clarity as to their interlocking purposes.

The growth of the free world economy is important to us for much more than economic reasons. We believe material progress to be a necessary foundation for more far reaching American aspirations for a civilization in which human dignity,

This essay was originally prepared as a report delivered to CIA Director Allen Dulles in early 1954.

MASSACHUSETTS INSTITUTE OF TECHNOLOGY
CENTER FOR INTERNATIONAL STUDIES
50 MEMORIAL DRIVE
CAMBRIDGE 39, MASSACHUSETTS

May 21, 1954

Mr. Allen W. Dulles
2430 E Street N.W.
Washington 25, D.C.

Dear Allen:

I am sending to you and Dick Bissell only an interim
revision of the document we emerged with on Saturday noon at
Princeton. It includes certain urgent minor revisions suggested
by the group; but we have been instructed to prepare a new and
developed version over the next month, embracing certain features
of substance and presentation not attempted here that we all agree
are badly needed. This interim revision is merely to let you see
roughly where we came out on the first go-round.

We have made this interim revision and are sending it to you
at C. D.'s suggestion. He thought that it might be useful as
background, should anything be launched in Asia as an economic
backstop to our proposed collective security arrangements. You
will note that Part IV of this document spells out briefly the
main points made in the discussion of Asia late Saturday afternoon.
Our feeling is that the situation in Asia represents not only an
urgent need to launch something like this, but also an opportunity
to launch it. If we do this, however, we should be prepared from
the beginning with the larger perspective and larger plans roughly
sketched out in this document.

Sincerely yours,

Max per WWR

Max F. Millikan
Director

MFM:peb
Enclosure

freedom, and respect for the individual can flourish, and in which societies based on these principles can effectively defend themselves. The concrete specifics of foreign economic policy must be related integrally to this American dream both in our own thinking and that of the rest of the world.

The multiple purposes we believe free world economic growth might serve are partly short term, partly long term. They can be described as follows:

1. Our immediate short-run concern is with our military security. The non-Communist areas of the world must have the economic resources to permit them to oppose immediate military threats with military force of their own without disastrous cost in lowered incomes.

2. Resistance to aggression is, however, only partly a matter of resources. As the last four years have demonstrated, it is a matter of will. The societies of the free world must have such vitality that men are prepared to make the sacrifices necessary to defend them from every kind of attack and encroachment. Economic growth is a necessary, though not a sufficient, condition for this vitality.

3. Taking a longer view, we, in common with virtually all the peoples of the world, have an overwhelming interest in the development of world conditions which will free security from dependence on military strength. Where men's energies can be turned constructively and with some prospect of success to the problems of expanding standards of living in a democratic framework we believe the attractions of totalitarian forms of government will be much reduced. In the short run communism must be contained militarily. In the long run we must rely on the development, in partnership with others, of an environment in which societies which directly or indirectly menace ours will not evolve. We believe the achievement of a degree of steady economic growth is an essential part of such an environment.

4. The growth of our own economy is related to an important extent to the growth of the world economy. Americans, who have from our nations's beginnings devoted a goodly share of their energies to the creation of an economy of expanding opportunity on this continent, are coming to realize that continued expan-

sion at home now requires growing incomes throughout the world.

This characterization of our purposes deserves several footnotes. First, it is emphatically not our purpose to attempt to mold other societies in our own image. Each society must find that form of growth appropriate to its own traditions, values, and aspirations. Indeed there may be societies in which economic growth is not yet a sufficiently widely felt need to make its satisfaction a condition of stability and of satisfaction for its citizens. Our purpose is to join in partnership with those who seek such a partnership rather than to impose our will or our resources on others.

Second, a characteristic of all but the first of these aims is that they are directed *against* nobody. We should make clear that we welcome into the partnership all those genuinely concerned with world economic growth and willing to contribute to it. Though present conditions force upon us a short-term military purpose, our long-term purpose is to find a constructive alternative to military build-up.

Third, these aims make clear how false is the dichotomy between selfish and altruistic considerations motivating our actions. Every one of the above objectives serves what is in the broad sense a selfish end. But we believe our long-run objectives to be in fact identical with those of others. Insofar as there are wellsprings of American energy seeking opportunities for world service, they can find no outlet in this set of policies. But our purposes will be clearer to our partners if they understand the depth of our conviction that our own national interest is fundamentally involved.

Finally, these purposes should be viewed in the light of the changed position and responsibilities of the United States. These have always been purposes important to us. Both our capacity to help achieve them and our responsibility to try have been enormously heightened, however, by the results of our own growth. We now produce half the free world's income. We should thus provide leadership diplomatically, militarily, economically, and ideologically. We have accepted this responsibility in the diplomatic and military field. We have not yet understood completely our responsibility for economic and ideological leadership.

II. The Shape of the Partnership for Growth

The central task of the free world is to grow at a sufficient rate and in such balance as to achieve the large purposes suggested in Section I. Investment and improvement of techniques, trade and currency arrangements are among the instruments for this basic purpose. They must be brought to bear upon the specific problems the free world now confronts so as to be mutually reinforcing.

In broadest terms the free world faces two problems. First, many underdeveloped countries are confronting the difficulties of the transition to self-sustaining growth. Second, U.K., Germany, Japan and other industrialized countries lack sufficient markets to purchase from their own resources the imports they need to support rising standards of living. At present levels of income and with present U.S. military aid the so-called dollar gap problem of the European countries has largely been solved. They have recovered from the extreme dislocations produced by the war and in some cases have begun to rebuild their financial reserves. Continued growth for them, however, requires expanding markets for their industrial output.

The two weaknesses in the free world economy, properly handled, could be converted into assets: the underdeveloped areas need the products and markets the industrialized areas can supply; the industrialized areas need the markets and products of the underdeveloped countries.

In order to grow, the underdeveloped areas need:

—capital;
—the spreading of appropriate existing techniques;
—the development of new techniques appropriate to their special problems and resources;
—reliable markets and steady incomes from their exported products.

In a democratic society the growth process can only be sustained if its purposes are understood and shared by the workers and peasants who must carry it through, and this demands an equitable distribution of the growing national income, as well as freedom to organize.

The transition to sustained growth involves complex and difficult changes that go deep into a society. The job must be done mainly within the country itself, on local initiative. The job takes time. But important help from outside is possible.

It is on an adequate rate of growth in the underdeveloped areas, conducted in proper balance as among agriculture, industry, and raw material production, that the industrialized areas of the world must depend for a solid solution to their own growth problem. It is a firm lesson of history that the growth and industrialization of underdeveloped societies, in proper balance, leads to an expansion not a contraction of world trade.

The United States has a major direct interest in bringing about this partnership and in sustaining it. This interest flows from the basic U.S. political and security interest in a free world.

There are, in addition, direct U.S. economic interests in balanced free world growth. First, specifically, the U.S. requires and will require increasingly a substantial flow of imported raw materials, both as strategic reserve and to sustain our rate of industrial growth. Second, in general, it is extremely doubtful that we can maintain in the United States a free and growing economy unless the free world economy of which we are a part is also growing.

The creation and maintenance of an effective free world economic partnership has a particular importance in the struggle against the Communist Bloc:

> First, free world success in seeing the underdeveloped
> countries through their difficult transition to self-sustaining
> growth would deny to Moscow and Peking the dangerous
> mystique that only Communism can transform underdevel-
> oped societies.
>
> Second, it would provide a foundation for pursuing East-

West trade on a basis of political safety, and even political advantage, which can only be provided if an alternative to such East-West trade is available for the Western trading partner.

Third, an effective free world economy would hold out to the Communist world an open-ended alternative to the present costly struggle, to be taken up whenever they are ready to join.

It cannot be too strongly emphasized that no one economic measure can in itself make and sustain the free world economic partnership. Economic growth needs capital and science, education and enterprise, technique and sustained hard work. It is a complex process, which can be advanced from many directions. The United States can, however, mightily assist in the free world partnership if its actions have three qualities:

—they are coordinated;
—they are on a sufficient scale;
—they are pursued with continuity.

III. Action and Continuity

The translation of a new conception of policy into practical operating programs does not so much require the invention of new proposals as it does a review and restatement of proposals already available. It requires that new priority, energy, and continuity of action be applied to these proposals; and above all, it requires that they be pursued on a sufficient scale to have the desired quantitative impact on the problem we confront.

This is not to rule out the possibility of new ideas. But our emphasis must be on organizing within the new framework—the new policy—the wealth of existing proposals and programs with which the free world is already familiar. These specific lines of action fall generally under five main headings:

1. the mobilization of capital;

2. the development of "know-how" (or the effective use of capital by management, labor, and farmers);

3. the development of new scientific possibilities;

45

4. the growth of trade along lines of mutual advantage; and

5. the growth of the sense of partnership arising out of our partnership for economic growth.

A. The mobilization of capital

Economic growth requires, in the first place, capital as a principal tool. The mobilization of capital for the underdeveloped countries of the world must *combine* in partnership a transfer of funds from the highly industrialized to the so-called backward areas with the progressive accumulation of savings within those areas themselves. With postwar reconstruction in Europe and Japan substantially accomplished, capital is now available from these countries for use in the underdeveloped countries. While private foreign investment can be brought to play a growing role in this process, it is likely that capital provided from governmental sources will play a very large part. We already have effective public agencies in the *International Bank,* which makes bankable loans for basic overhead investment that can be guaranteed by the local government, and the *U.S. Export-Import Bank,* which extends commercial credits to American exporters and the dollar requirements for certain types of bankable loans, chiefly in South America.

Fairly large potentials exist for increasing the flow of *private* capital both *to* and *in* the underdeveloped areas. Changes in the U.S. revenue code may help encourage more direct investment, as would a revitalization of the transfer guarantees by the Export-Import Bank. As expanded stockpiling commitment by the American Government (discussed below) may also encourage most foreign investment by American and other mining companies. However, there does seem need for a new type of international institution capable of providing *equity* capital for private projects which lie outside the competence of existing private capital markets. The projected International Finance Corporation, to be affiliated to the International Bank and capitalized with public funds intended to be used in cooperation with private capital, constitutes a new proposal deserving sympathetic consideration. Similar institutions designed to operate within individual countries (such as the proposed Indian Development Corporation) deserve equal support. It should not be overlooked, that the growth of private investment across national borders is important not only because it is private but because it often involves, when capital from a developed and an underdeveloped country participate jointly, a productive *use* of indigenous capital that would otherwise lie idle, plus a transfer of planning skill and "know-how" from one country to another.

Finally, there may exist a modest margin for increasing the sale of foreign securities in the U.S. and other capital-surplus countries if suitable transfer guarantees can be provided. Indeed, the extension of transfer guarantees is important regardless of the form private capital transfers assume.

It must be expected that government capital in the form of *grants* will be necessary in a small number of cases of essential but nonbankable projects or for emergency relief or reconstruction situations. But the number of such cases, and the amount of money involved, must be kept small.

The amount of foreign capital likely to be supplied to underdeveloped areas is not likely to constitute a large proportion of total capital formation in those areas. But the role played by foreign capital as a critical marginal supplement—and as an instrument for the transfer of know-how—must be understood in both the supplying and receiving countries.

Finally, it is probably wrong to think that the lack of success hitherto scored by American diplomats in negotiating more favorable investment climates should continue to discourage us. There is every reason to expect that a fresh attack on this problem in many countries would be well worth the effort, if it is sustained. International private capital flows have been held up by political and psychological blocks which have perceptibly diminished; although by no means disappeared. It may well be appropriate for the capital importing countries to explore now a free world code for capital movements, which would incorporate the best lessons of recent experience in protecting both the national sovereignty of the recipient and the legitimate economic interests of the lender.

B. Technical assistance, or the transfer of "know-how"

One of the most common failings of underdeveloped countries is that they do not know how to make the most productive possible use of the capital available to them. This is true with respect to both agriculture and industry, and indeed in the organization and operation of such public services as public health, vocational training, and government administration. Technical assistance has already made a commendable start in this direction, and should be continued.

However, this program has not been equally successful everywhere it has been used and it would probably help the future administration of the technical assistance program if a sympathetic review of its strengths and weaknesses could be conducted in the near future.

The U.N. program in this field should likewise be reviewed, strengthened, and continued. In general, an economic growth program of this kind requires the sustained participation of private as well as public authorities. This is nowhere more true than in the area of technical assistance where private firms—and universities—can make valuable contributions. The extension of the *management contract* device; of *licensing arrangements*; of the use of private engineering consultants; and of international collaboration between universities, management associations, medical societies, and trade unions for education, research, and training—all these can contribute to the more effective use of available resources. The exchange of training aids (such as vocational training films and T.W.I. programs) through the USIS and the International Labor Organization can well be expanded and the establishment of national *productivity centers* and *professional associations* will likewise add to the growth of "know-how." Finally, the role of *technical journals* in transferring technique should not be underrated: anything that can overcome the inability of underdeveloped countries to purchase such journals in large volume deserves strong support.

C. The development of new scientific possibilities

The concept enunciated in the President's proposal for the development of atomic energy for peacetime uses could be made the focal point for a more general cooperative scientific program. The President's proposal has now been turned down by Moscow. We must proceed, without the Russians if necessary, to implement this proposal—and perhaps others built upon it—in the free world, under the concept of partnership for growth.

It appears technically possible to establish the inspection safeguards which would be required to permit atomic power developments either in central jointly-sponsored laboratories or in national institutions provided the participating nations would permit the required inspection procedures. While it is unlikely that the Soviets would submit to the required examination, it is almost certain that such inspection would not be offensive to the nations of the free world. And it is now evident that the launching of an enterprise on a free world basis does not diminish but actually enhances the possibility of Soviet participation. The development of inspection procedures in the free world would in no way obstruct the pursuit of the larger objective.

Scientists generally agree that a practical inspection program could provide the necessary safeguards against improper use of atomic materials. It is much more difficult to keep account of the output of an atomic fuel production facility than it would be to control a small number of experimental power units having available only limited amounts of atomic fuels.

Peacetime use of atomic energy is only one of many exciting new technical developments which should be exploited in the battle to raise the living standards of the free world.

Fresh water can be made from sea water, rainfall can be controlled in some parts of the world, solar energy has been captured in the laboratory, algae food sources appear possible, chemical means of population control is in the offing. While science today, given time and money, can produce almost anything that society requests, no one of these developments is being pursued with a vigor approaching its importance to society.

Regional laboratories or institutes could be established to work on these problems, and scientists and engineers from the entire free world could be brought to them.

In addition to their scientific output such centers would also provide a training ground for badly needed technical staffs and a mechanism for rapid exchange of technical information.

Properly constituted, such centers would not only be the source of specialized technical know-how and of trained manpower, but would also provide an experiment in atomic cooperation and inspection which might be made so attractive that it would lead to a realization of the President's vision of a truly international cooperative atomic program.

D. The growth of trade and currency convertibility

The full potential of the free world's partnership will not be realized unless goods are able to move among countries more freely than is now the case. In particular, capital-exporting or creditor countries such as the U.S. must be willing to accept imports liberally if the debtor countries are to earn the currencies (chiefly dollars) needed to honor their debts. The U.S. has a particular responsibility in this regard in view of its twofold position as the largest creditor country and as leader of the free world partnership. Furthermore, trade liberalization is not something America should do only to help others: America has an important self-interest in larger imports—through the benefit of wider choices and lower prices for American consumers and through the expansion of export markets for important sections of agriculture and industry which larger imports would open up.

To this end, a strong case exists for the widespread further reduction of American tariffs for the elimination of the peril point and escape clause provisions of our Trade Agreements Act, for the elimination of cargo preference stipulations and "Buy American" requirements in government procurement policies, and for a more whole-hearted American participation in the multilateral approach to tariffs through the General Agreement on Tariffs and Trade.

This is also an appropriate occasion to reexamine and consolidate the free world policy on East-West trade. The present embargo yields the free world only a negative asset: might not an offer to supply the Soviets with consumer goods (which they now profess to want for their peoples) dramatically convert our negative asset into a positive asset for our friends and positive liability for the Russians? There are many indications that they are not really prepared to make good on their politically seductive offers of expanded trade. Provided we maintain a minimum list of strategic goods there may be little danger and much advantage in calling their bluff. More generally, only an effective free world growth program can eliminate the political dangers of East-West trade and permit its exploration for purposes of political advantage.

The potentialities for expanding America's foreign trade as a result of liberalizing our trade policies should not be overemphasized. But neither must we underestimate the symbolic importance of trade liberalizations as an earnest of America's leadership in doing what must be done. If we mean business, we must do business.

In this connection the government might well initiate a special study designed to establish the character and scale of the effect of increased imports on U.S. production and employment, so that the possibility and wisdom of compensatory action might be assessed on the basis of fact rather than vague speculation.

A further important area of trade policy—one likely to assume increasing importance—is the extension, on a longer-run basis, of America's stockpiling program. This device is particularly adapted to strategic minerals and metals, basic raw materials that will become progressively more costly as the easily got supplies become exhausted. These commodities suffer from price fluctuations which cause serious injury to the supplying countries, many of which are heavily dependent on this type of industry. While recognizing that problems of pricing, the use of stockpiles, and the timing of government purchases are not easy, the extension of our stockpile program offers a much more constructive method of closing the dollar gap than do outright grants. The use of this device would be additional to our military stockpile program and would need to be subject to a maximum liability. Purchases would have to be timed with phases when inventories were being run down in the American economy. The policy would have to avoid encroaching on the development and maintenance of economic U.S. resources. It is our view, however, that new policy and action in this area could play an important part in accelerating and stabilizing the growth process in the free world over an important transitional phase.

A gradual approach to greater convertibility, which is greatly to be desired as a means of regulating trade along economical lines, should be encouraged as the cumulative effect of more liberal trade among the free world countries makes this possible.

E. The growth of the sense of partnership

The growth of feelings of goodwill and respect among the peoples of the free world is both a condition and can be a result of economic partnership. This dimension of our relationship cannot stand on sentimentality. It can grow on specific action programs, but programs which lie primarily outside a cash nexus. The international exchange of persons (students, teachers, government officials, engineers, industrial managers, trade union leaders, farmers, etc.) can contribute largely to the understanding all partners have of each other. The contribution of such a program to the exchange of know-how is obvious; less obvious, but no less real, is the development of international private investment opportunities which international visits open up. The role of a more liberal U.S. passport and visa policy in this connection needs wider appreciation.

Finally, there exists a possibility for a much more imaginative use of America's chronic food surpluses. The potential use of these stocks could relieve the chronic food shortages of the underdeveloped areas until their own agricultural production suffices to meet their own needs more adequately. The economic leverage offered by the use of these stocks is considerable; the political and ideological leverage is no less so.

People familiar with America's attempts to mount an effective foreign economic policy will find much that is familiar in the foregoing proposals. They should also find some fresh suggestions—notably the development of new scientific possibilities. But the aim of this is not restatement, nor is it the addition of one or two new proposals. The aim is rather to demonstrate that there is already at hand a wealth of practical programs which can be added up to a new total—a total policy that meets the needs not only of the hour but also of the new times in which the free world finds itself, a policy executed on a sufficient scale and sustained with sufficient energy to yield the steady rise in per capita income we seek for ourselves and the free world. The particular facets of this total policy of partnership that will prove appropriate for particular times and places must be left flexible. What must not be left flexible is our sense of urgency concerning the world's crisis or our determination to do something about it on a sufficient scale—and to keep on operating on a sufficient scale for years to come.

IV. The Case of Asia

The lines of thought and action outlined in Sections I to III above have, of course, a particular urgency and relevance to the current position in Asia.

First, any possible salvage of all or part of Indo-China requires that the Indo-Chinese believe we are in Asia to stay, not merely in a military sense, but politically and economically as well. Some such program as that outlined above is an essential backdrop to wrestling the Indo-China problem to a tolerable solution.

Second, if India, Burma, and Indonesia are to be gradually

brought more effectively into the free world alliance they must believe that the U.S. interest in Asia is not confined merely to our top priority concern—military security—but authentically extends to their top priority concern—economic development. One way for instance of bringing to their attention their own concern with a non-Communist Indo-China is to focus their minds on how Indo-Chinese resources might be used in a cooperative free Asian economic development program.

Third, the peculiar and urgent economic problem of Japan—lacking markets in which it can earn what it must buy—is a major test of the concept of the free world partnership. Can we organize a pattern of markets and sources of supply for Japan which would both reinforce the process of growth in Asia and gradually make Japan independent of extraordinary American assistance?

Fourth, with its new General Line Peking has launched its bid to demonstrate that Communism holds the key to Asian industrialization. The comparative economic performance of Communist China and Free Asia over the next five years will be a major and perhaps decisive test of two ideologies, two civilizations, and their methods.

We may, therefore, wish to consider as a matter of urgency the following:

1. We indicate through appropriate channels that we are prepared to accept an invitation from all the free Asian countries to join in a special economic conference to consider both short-run and long-run measures to accelerate economic growth in the region as a whole with special regard to the interrelations among the free Asian economies. Emphasis on a trade and resource pattern for the region as a whole will force them to consider whether Indo-China is to be counted in or out.

2. We enter this conference prepared to back our play; that is, prepared to increase and enlarge our Asian economic effort along such specific lines as may be agreed.

3. We maintain the position that we are working here on the Asian problem as a whole, with a time horizon of a decade, although

the economic implications of the Indo-China situation must be taken into account.

4. For the time being, we keep separate our collective military measures in Asia from any regional economic program that may emerge.

5. We make sure that the measures we are prepared to agree in Asia are consistent with measures we may wish to pursue on a worldwide basis.

May 21, 1954

(Irene L. Gendzier)

Play It Again Sam:
The Practice and
Apology of Development

Development for Profit

The proposition that the more things change, the more they remain the same is a truism in the case of development policies. Indeed, a comparison of the 1960s and 1990s offers striking parallels in policy objectives as well as their public justification, in which universities played a major role. In the Cold War era academic development studies served the state in a double capacity: providing information and legitimation. Compliant scholars and research analysts accumulated information on Third World development and dissent in the interests of U.S. foreign policy, including for a number of counterinsurgency and destabilization programs.[1]

Inspite of the end of the Cold War, the logic driving development policies in the 1990s remains the extension of corporate liberalism, while the arguments used to justify it at present serve much the same function of legitimation that they did in the

---

I dedicate this essay to the memory of Martin Diskin, Professor at MIT, whose commitment to a humane and socially just development in Central America was his life's work. — I.L.G.

1960s. In this environment, the accumulation of information is no less vital than that of capital, and the containment of dissent no less critical to the legitimation of policy. Furthermore, the objectives of promoting democracy and increasing participation remain as they were in the 1960s: rhetorical props for policies supported by elites fearful of both. Hence, democracy and participation are encouraged in talk far more than in practice, while the informal understanding among policy makers is that development means economic growth for foreign capital.

As will be seen, today's relentless endorsement of privatization and globalization as correctives for the ills of statism is no startling initiative in the short history of development policies. Nor does the reliance on cultural explanations of economic and political failure offer a break with past practice, as the mainstream literature of development studies in the 1960s so vividly demonstrated.

There are, undeniably, major differences between the two periods. Among those relevant to development policies are the transformation of the states of Asia, Latin America, Africa, and the Middle East, and, notably, the emergence of Asian and European economic giants, which have challenged U.S. hegemony. And no consideration of this subject would be complete without recognizing the impact of the collapse of the Soviet Union and nearly the entire communist bloc, given that the Cold War was a major justification of development policies in the past. Inspite of this, the parallels between development policies and their justification in the 1960s and 1990s are compelling, and provide a guide to demystifying their past and present orthodoxies.

In my remarks on development in the 1990s, I will focus on the equation of development as economic growth, which is interpreted by international lending agencies and their private sector allies in terms of privatization. My emphasis is, rather, on the social cost of privatization and globalization—especially their detrimental effects on the more vulnerable elements in society. Attention is paid to the *cultural* apology for the current economic, political and social orthodoxy, an approach that is enjoying a more general revival in analyses of development and democracy. That theme provides a bridge to discussion of the legitimation of development policies in the 1960s and a reconsideration of post–World War II U.S. foreign policy, with its speical emphasis on the export of corporate liberalism to the emerging states of the Third World. The Cold War connection is unmistakable in this regard. Justification for development policies was rarely made in terms of profit seeking or even economic growth alone; it was far more often couched in terms of promoting democracy and containing communism and Soviet influence. The academic field of development studies, which emerged in the late 1950s and continues to thrive, has reflected the same interests and modes of justification. The following pages examine the role of those who have dominated that field. The true character of their role is spelled out in the very name of the 1965 congressional hearings on the contribution of behavioral and social science research in Fighting the Cold War: "Winning the Cold War: The U.S. Ideological Offensive."[2]

For the student of development in the 1990s, two tracks define the subject. The first focuses on the policies of international lending agencies and the practice of development as what is presented as economic growth. The second, which dominates the academic literature, deals with the so-called transition from authoritarian rule—though to what this transition actually leads is a moot point. It is, in any case, a process viewed through the prism of economic and political liberalism.[3] The study of civil society—a veritable growth industry—is closely related to this second approach. "Civil society" is seen as a key prerequisite to democracy, provided that it is understood in terms of the "leader-class," to use Benjamin DeMott's word.[4] In prevailing usage the term is synonymous with a depoliticized private sector compatible with the market. In short, it reflects the combined antistatist and antiwelfare sentiment of neoliberals and neoconservatives. It is hardly a surprise, then, that this approach is in harmony with the outlook of those who have defined the parameters of development policies in the 1990s. For graduate students in pursuit of research funding or junior professors in search of tenure, the direction to follow is clear. But for those who remain concerned with social inequality, political repression, and maldevelopment—and the structures of power that acount for their reproduction—the address differs.[5]

The following remarks provide a sampling of currents and criticisms of development policies in the 1990s. My first focus is on the effects of trade pacts engineered in the name of furthering the "liberating" trends of privatization and globalization but which in fact augment corporate profit at the expense of labor, whether in the U.S. or abroad. I also briefly examine the practices of the International Monetary Fund (IMF) and the critiques leveled at both the IMF and World Bank, which have consistently exposed the limits of their approach as well as their real beneficiaries.

As will be seen, there are important similarities in development policies and rhetoric between those used today and those of the 1950s and 1960s. In both eras, these policies have in truth 'maldeveloped' rather than developed much of the world, in part as a result of the pursuit of U.S. security interests at the expense of true economic and social development. This maldevelopment *necessarily* has carried with it brutal forms of counterinsurgency, destabilization and anti-democratic practices, which First World security agencies have long underwritten as a means of attempting to manage the social upheavals characteristic of the reorganization of national economies for the benefit of transnational capital. Universities and think tanks have been and remain deeply involved in producing apologetic covers for these processes, as well as in gathering intelligence and offering tactical advice on investments and managing crisis. Within that context "cultural" explanations for Third World political events are once again in vogue during the 1990s. In reality, though, "cultural" rationales for poverty and crisis in the Third World have long been used to blame the victim for what is in truth a product of the maldevelopment system itself.

Today's media exponents of globalization and privatization maintain that the differences between the critics and the exponents of these policies can be reduced to those between "winners" and "losers," between "safety-netters" and "let-them-eat-cakers."[6] Yet media coverage of NAFTA , the North American Free Trade Agreement among the United States, Canada, and Mexico, for example, suggests a more sober assessment of what is at stake. According to a report on the impact of NAFTA in Jamaica, the effect of the multilateral trade pact has been to shift trade dramatically away from the Caribbean basin to an even more impoverished location where labor cost is even more depressed. The consequences of NAFTA for Jamaica have been intensified unemployment and the undermining of an already meager manufacturing base. In Jamaica "more than 600 people, about 95 percent of them women, felt the effects of Nafta when the Youngone Garment factory on Marcus Garvey Drive here closed just before Christmas. The plant had been making T-shirts for export to the United States. But a Mexican factory took the business away with a lower bid, prompting the Korean company to shut down operations in Jamaica and send its employees home. The company then shipped its equipment off to Bangladesh."[7] As a result, unemployment increased from 9.5 to 16 percent, among women working in apparel manufacturing, unemployment reached 33 percent. With the reduction of U.S. investment in the region, such negative effects have been compounded. The impact of global trade policies on workers' wages has been stark. In the absence of protective measures, wages are stabilized at subsistence level.[8]

The globalization of labor has significantly affected industrialized societies as well. Assessing the effects of such policies in the United States, France, Germany, Belgium, and Sweden, Ethan Kapstein has argued that the "global economy is leaving millions of disaffected workers in its train. Inequality, unemployment, and

endemic poverty have become its handmaidens. Rapid technological change and heightening international competition are
fraying the job markets of the major industrialized countries. At
the same time systemic pressures are curtailing every government's ability to respond with new spending. Just when working
people most need the nation-state as a buffer from the world
economy, it is abandoning them."[9]

As for those who fear that the IMF's policies will lead to increasing immiseration, they are considered part of the problem
rather than the solution. For those in command of capital and
resources, the withdrawal of subsidies is worth the cost, since, as
was remarked in another context, "it may be unfashionable to say
so, but income differentials have their place."[10] Or, following the
logic of the Harvard economist Robert Barro, who has studied
Haiti and other developing states, given the Third World's condition, western governments should focus not on remedying the
political situation but on modifying the economic. That is they
should export "their economic systems, notably property rights
and free markets, [but] rather than their political systems, which
typically developed after reasonable standards of living had been
attained."[11] Note Barro's point well, because historically it reap-
pears in one form or another whenever maldevelopment strategies have turned particularly brutal.

Today's World Bank policies are hardly at odds with the current approach to development. "In Post-Cold-War Washington
Development Is a Hot Business," Jeff Gerth of the *New York
Times* reveals the financial combines at the root of the development business and leaves no doubt as to the political connec-
tions involved. "A cottage industry of consultants, business
executives and lobbyists are tapping into one of Washington's
least-known pools of money: international development banks.
Foreign aid budgets are shrinking, but these banks are growing.
Each year they generate some $30 billion in contracts."[12] Among
those involved are major figures in the corporate world and their
partners in international lending agencies. Such arrangements
are justified by the participants as uniquely appropriate to the

post—Cold War environment, in which the private sector is the preferred vehicle of economic policy. As Gerth notes, "big public works projects that were once undertaken by governments— from airports to water treatment plants—now are often being done by private entrepreneurs." In this transition to the private sector, the many unasked questions include, Who chooses the entrepreneurs and contractors, and who benefits from such choices? At present, the Inter-American Development Bank and a group of private investors guarantee their clients an unparalleled access to capital and profit.

This trend has been welcomed by such prominent figures as former U.S. Secretary of the Treasury Lloyd Bentsen, who is currently helping to "organize a billion-dollar investment fund backed by giant corporations and pension funds" with an annual profit pegged at 25 percent.[13] Among former officials of the World Bank now collaborating on such projects is Moeen Querishi, who in turn has brought along equally well placed colleagues. The objective of such collaboration is to invest in key Latin American power projects, including (according to Mr. Bentsen) "telecommunications systems and toll roads." Figures are instructive in this regard. According to Gerth, "last year [1995], the Inter-American Development Bank lent $7 billion while the World Bank lent $12.7 billion. The inter-American bank also began making riskier loans to private capital projects last year as part of a program to lend up to 5 percent of its capital without any official guarantee."[14] The marriage of big business and development agencies represents a dynamic convergence of the profit motive. In 1989, as Gerth notes, the Inter-American Development Bank "set up a separate investment corporation, the Inter-American Investment Corporation, to lend to and invest in Latin American businesses." The transfer of capital from banks to investors, according to Donald Strombom, is in the order of $4 billion to $5 billion, while in the reverse direction some $30 billion are awarded annually by "borrowers."

The approach has been applied elsewhere, with meaningful results for contemporary engineers of economic growth who do

not question its uneven results. Nor do they consider sociopolitical factors, let alone economic ones, as sufficient to account for
success or failure. Among noneconomists who have dealt with
such issues, culture offers a convincing explanation. According
to James Bradford de Long, "it appears highly likely that a correct
explanation of comparative growth performance will have to incorporate something like the accumulative ethic at a fundamental level."[15] For Francis Fukuyama, the relationship of culture,
morality, and economic policies is beyond question. Fukuyama's
"Social Capital and the Global Economy"[16] and *Trust*[17] represent
a highly selective reading of Max Weber's essay, to which the
work of social scientists, including political scientists, has been
added.[18] The results illustrate the apologetic use of culture in a
manner reminiscent of the literature of the 1960s.

Economists and others have gone wrong, Fukuyama argues,
in being overly economistic in their approach, ignoring salient
noneconomic factors. In fact, Fukuyama claims, the institutions
of "property rights, contracts, and a system of commerical law"
provide inadequate answers to those who want to understand
the relative capacity of communities and societies to form productive organizations.[19] Answers may be found in the moral
realm, according to the author, which is the location of an "unwritten set of ethical rules or norms that serve as the basis of
social trust. Trust can dramatically reduce what economists call
transaction costs—costs of negotiation, enforcement, and the
like—and makes possible certain efficient forms of economic
organization that otherwise would be encumbered by extensive
rules, contracts, litigation, and bureaucracy. Moral communities,
as they are lived and experienced by their members, tend to be
the product not of rational choice in the economists' sense of the
term, but of nonrational habit."[20]

The nostalgia for corporatism is expressed in terms of the
desirability of doing away with interference in the form of protective "rules, contracts, litigation" rights that stand between "mafia
capitalism" and the individual.[21] Civil society in this context is
fated to be conformist. According to Fukuyama, the virtue of

such interpretations is that they shed light on the reasons for the comparative economic success of industrial operations in the U.S. and Japan, as distinct from France and Italy. The same arguments centering on the lack of social capital, moral community, and trust figure in assessments of "the African-American poor in contemporary American inner cities, where single-parent families predominate and larger social groups are weak."[22] As for Africa, Fukuyama points to the deficiency of "voluntary associations outside of kinship." Deficiencies in historical knowledge are apparently of little value in such arguments. So are political analyses that are replaced by references to the phenomenon of the "delinquent community," whose genesis may be traced to earlier writings on political man and the marginalization of the disaffected.[23] For Fukuyama, then, "culture, religion, tradition, and other premodern sources, will be key to the success of modern societies in a global economy."[24]

Fukuyama is by no means alone in his conviction that culture is the key to explanation and practice. "Political culture [analysis] is presently enjoying a renaissance," according to Howard Wiarda, a long time specialist on development. Wiarda cites the renewed intellectual currency of Aaron Wildavsky and Harry Eckstein, as well as earlier contributors to development studies, such as Samuel P. Huntington and Lucian Pye, among them.[25] To this list the names of others should be added, such as Lawrence E. Harrison, Robert Putnam, and Robert Inglehart, while acknowledging their differences.[26] There are others as well, including those whose work has largely been focused on regional studies who share the conviction that political culture is a critical—though by no means exclusive—explanatory variable.[27]

Like Fukuyama, Huntington has been among the exponents of this approach, as his essay "The Clash of Civilizations" and later book by the same name exemplify with their mix of politics and culture, civilization and foreign policy.[28] Huntington's thesis has critics even among politicians, business elites, and conservative scholars,but they have not stemmed the tide of its popularity.[29] The current vogue of Huntington's claims lies in their political timing, even as his message flies in the face of the global expansion of a corporate liberalism indifferent to political or geographical boundaries. In the wake of the Cold War and the burial of the communist enemy, the naming of a successor enemy is invaluable as a justification of power and politics.

This 1990s version of orientalism provides no credible examination of culture, civilization, or the politics of power. Huntington concedes that power differentials matter, but that there are more influential factors at work to explain enduring political outcomes and hostilities. These are to be found in the domain of culture—that is, "basic values and beliefs."[30] Thus, "Western ideas of individualism, liberalism, constitutionalism, human rights, equality, liberty, the rule of law, democracy, free markets, the separation of church and state, often have little resonance in Islamic, Confucian, Japanese, Hindu, Buddhist or Orthodox cultures. Western efforts to propagate such ideas produce instead a reaction against 'human rights imperialism' and a reaffirmation of indigenous values, as can be seen in the support for religious fundamentalism by the younger generation in non- Western cultures."[31]

The failure of such condemned islands to bring about democratic political institutions is attributed to their deliberate isolation from the "Western-dominated global community." Admittedly, some culture zones fare worse than others. In Huntington's repertoire, the Arab-Islamic world is consistently at the bottom of the list, matched here by Confucian civilization. Latin America, by comparison, stands the best chance, according to this hierarchy. For readers of Huntington's previous work, the current leap into the darkness represents an extension of earlier arguments in which relations of state and society were viewed as expressions of morality and culture.

The Way It Was

The conventional "classics" of academic development studies— especially those devoted to political development—have relied on similar psychosocial and cultural motifs in the rationalization of development since the 1950s. Then as now, such props have served to obscure the economic and political policies pursued and their consequences. Huntington's current arguments reflect the influence of works such as Almond and Verba's *The Civic Culture,* and that of other founding figures of the academic rationales for political development.[32] It is in this literature that the singular exploitation of culture and political culture in the analysis of the third world can be found.

In his influential 1968 work, *Political Order in Changing Societies,* Huntington acknowledged that Western-style modernization tended to destabilize Third World states, a problem that was said to be compounded by cultural factors that allegedly account for the moral and institutional weakness of government in the states concerned.[33] It would be difficult to exaggerate the influence of both points. The first relied on descriptions of Third World states fatally undermined by raging conflicts, corrupt leadership, incompetence, alienation, and the resulting near collapse of political systems. Among the critical factors allegedly responsible for such decline were a supposed moral weakness that reflected inferior institutional capacity.

These concepts have been standard fare in the work of the dominant figures who shaped academic modernization and development studies in the late 1950s and 1960s, from Daniel Lerner and his typologies of modernization, to Lucian Pye, a specialist on the military and Southeast Asia. Lerner's *The Passing of Traditional Society* took as its central theme the supposed psychosocial prerequisites of modernity.[34] Lucian Pye, a political scientist writing in 1962 about Burmese independence, and more particularly its frustrating (for American officials) propensity toward neutralism, reduced that phenomenon to the psychosocial origins of Burmese political culture. By 1965, the terminology of political culture had been integrated into the series on political development published under the aegis of the Social Science Research Council. In *Political Culture and Political Development,* edited by Pye and Sydney Verba, the authors referred to "the theory of political culture" as one "developed in response to the need to bridge a growing gap in the behavioral approach in political science between the level of microanalysis based on psychological interpretations of the individual's political behavior and the level of macroanalysis based on the variables common to political sociology."[35] The combination promised to link politics, values, personal identity and social behavior into an extravagant unified field theory of the dynamics of alien cultures. In practice, it opened the way to pseudoscientific jargon in a highly reductionist interpretation of politics.[36]

On one level, this combination represented an informal creative exchange across disciplinary lines. On another, it marked the pioneering effort of a group of social scientists in the new field of development studies, who, with support from research institutions, organized conferences and publications that defined the subdiscipline. Such studies were rooted in postwar U.S. foreign policy in the Third World, and in assumptions about its vulnerability to Soviet influence. Those who played a major role in shaping the intellectual and ideological character of development studies were the policy-oriented academics and intellectuals who shared an anticommunist and elitist outlook, which found expression in the ideology of the "end of ideology" and the "vital center." Arthur Schlesinger Jr., Daniel Bell, Edward Shils, James Burnham, William Kornhauser, Joseph Schumpeter, and Seymour Martin Lipset made crucial contributions to ambience.[37] Their speciality was not development and certainly not Third World development. Yet in practice, Shils and Burnham were involved (through their work with the Congress for Cultural Freedom) in the campaign to contain radicalism among Third World intellectuals. Others such as Gabriel Almond, who was to become a leading figure in comparative politics and political development studies, Harold Lasswell, and sociologist Daniel Lerner were well known for their work on psychological warfare, public opinion and postwar Europe before they turned their attention to the question of shaping Third World politics.[38]

Almond and Verba's *The Civic Culture* (1963) was to have an exceptional influence on the analysis of Third World politics, although its analysis of political socialization and the psychosocial prerequisites of liberal democracy focused on Great Britain, the United States, Germany, Italy, and Mexico. Their approach was elitist and conformist, and their vision of democracy closely resembled Schumpeter's. No aspect of their study was more important to the field of political development than their interpretation of the supposed threat posed by democratic participation in economic and political life and the transparent fears that inspired among elites in the U.S. and abroad. For Almond and Verba, the key to successful democracies was not merely the presence of an informed citizenry, but one sufficiently trustful of authority to desist from making undue participatory demands. "The need for elite power requires that the ordinary citizen be relatively passive, uninvolved, and deferential to elites, they wrote."[39] In their study *The Crisis of Democracy* (1975), Huntington, Crozier, and Watanuki drew out the implications of this outlook in their assessment of the excessive demands of newly mobilized constituences.[40]

Academic development studies emerged out of this intellectual and ideological environment. They have been a continuing inquiry, as David Lehmann has put it, into industrialization, class conflict, social cohesion, and the conditions for the emergence of capitalism. Such questions soon spill over into consideration of the relations between state and civil society, between theory and practice, and between the scholar and politics.[41]

Markets and politics fueled the interest in Third World states, and the policies offered in the name of development were often designed as *preventive* measures to inhibit radicalization while exploiting the common endorsement of socioeconomic and political change. From the vantage point of Washington policy makers, decolonization constituted a high risk, whether from nationalists, populists, or communists. The Third World became, in part because of this approach, the future site of U.S.-Soviet competition as well as the future arena of U.S. trade and investment. These conflicts led the U.S. government to promote development studies by encouraging dissemination of funds through major private institutions such as the Social Science Research Council and the Ford Foundation.[42] Similarly, throughout the 1950s and 1960s, Defense Department funding for social science research, including research on development, was justified in terms of "winning the Cold War." The results vastly amplified the resources, institutions, and research capacity of those engaged in government-funded projects.

In practice, the appeal of well funded development studies was virtually unlimited. It extended to a heterogeneous community of students and scholars responding to the compelling vision of Third World poverty and the prospects of socioeconomic and political change, and it included scholars from diverse disciplines.

Those who dominated academic development studies and its allied professions were a minority who generally exercised influence through noncoercive and nonformal means. Their unwritten consensus accounts for the coherence of the field. It also explains why many scholars were in effect excluded from it. To appreciate this point, one has only to consider the long list of international scholars committed to the analysis of the historic roots and evolution of capitalist development and underdevelopment whose works were often officially ignored, then selectively looted for their insights by more "acceptable" academics. Economists, sociologists, and political thinkers from Barrington Moore Jr. to Gunnar Myrdal, Raoul Prebisch, Paul Baran, and Dudley Seers, faced this, along with a myriad of intellectuals whose critical contributions to the subject challenged and altered the field from the mid-1950s through the 1970s and after.[43]

Explaining the limitations of development studies from the vantage point of the 1990s, Howard Wiarda argues that "in the 1950s when the early literature on development was published, we [that is, politically acceptable, government-funded academics—author's note] had very little actual experience with the developing nations."[44] As a result, "scholars largely fell back on the experiences they knew: the United States and Western Europe. This helps explain why, in the absence of experience or much empirical data, the models of development presented tended to be highly abstract, very theoretical, and without solid grounding in actual Third World realities."

But this greatly oversimplifies the situation. The political decision to amass information on Third World states and societies is what galvanized postwar interest in regions deemed essential to U.S. industrial development and commercial expansion as well as foreign policy. Even before the end of World War II, major foundations subsidized language training through a number of major universities, while funding the American Council of Learned Societies to facilitate its language training programs for the military.[45] Foundation grants subsidized language as well as area studies and international relations centers at major universities.The precursor of the CIA, the Office of Strategic Services (OSS), and its Research and Analysis branch relied on the services of academics and others engaged in relevant research. Three related developments in 1945 further illustrate the early concerns and cooperation that marked research efforts of government and academy. In that year, "the Social Science Research Council established a Committee on Political Behavior, the Air Force launched Project RAND, and Columbia University received $250,000 from the Rockefeller Foundation to organize the Russian Institute, as Michael Klare has reported. "In these events can be seen strands of the developing web of new approaches— foundation support, Government interest, and interdisciplinary organization of research centers—which were to exert so much influence on postwar studies in foreign affairs."[46]

During World War II the prestigious Council on Foreign Relations (CFR), a think tank of political and business elites, convened meetings and produced reports addressing issues bearing on the future of U.S. economic and defense interests in the event of Nazi as well as allied military victories.[47] Anglo-American relations figured prominently in such studies, as did the future of colonized areas. CFR reports underscored monetary, financial, tariff, and trade policies, including those relevant to international cartels, raw materials, and shipping, and the overall problem of coordinating economic and political policies. While the Eurocentrism of the State Department in the postwar years was evident, so was its concern—matched by that of defense officials—with developments outside of Europe, whether in the southern and eastern Mediterranean, or the vast land masses and sea lanes viewed as critical to U.S. military planning. The preoccupation with acquiring air force and naval bases and access to resources, and with stemming the instability of decolonized regions and containing Soviet influence, necessarily implied an extra-European vantage point. From the Truman Doctrine to the Korean War and NSC 68 of 1950, the extensive reach of Washington's policy makers was evident. The implications of such developments affected U.S. policy in Asia, Africa, the Middle East, and Latin America. Parallel to such policies was the protection accorded the expanding role of U.S. business, especially the oil and aviation industries. The State Department lost no opportunity to promote the expansion of U.S. corporate liberalism through its militant support of open doors and skies, and environments favorable to investment. The institutional structures established at Bretton Woods contributed to such objectives, as did the efforts to block competing arrangements from the periphery, whether at the United Nations or in bilateral relations with allegedly "special allies," such as Great Britain.[48]

The "preponderance" of American power in the postwar decade was undeniable.[49] It was marked by the enduring competition between Western allies, notably the United States and Great Britain, no less than by the tenacity of Western colonial control and the continued resistance to occupation throughout the colonized areas. The circumstances of competition and the commitment to maintain control became central to development strategies. Britain and France remained the preeminent colonial powers in Africa, the Middle East, and parts of Asia, while the U.S. alternately supported or undermined their roles to suit its own interests. In Latin America and the Caribbean the principles of the Monroe Doctrine held fast, as did U.S. control in the Philippines and U.S. influence over Japan's postwar political and economic course. On the heels of U.S. fear of increased Soviet trade, aid, and political and military support to these regions, came fears of the radicalization of indigeneous nationalist movements as well as many expressions of democratic civil society, such as independent trade unions.

It was in this context that a politics of preventive development (which was to be synonynous with development policies) emerged. In the Anglo-American Pentagon Talks of 1947, a major review of interests in Africa and the Middle East, U.S. and British officials agreed on the imperative of stemming widespread discontent through policies designed to improve living standards.[50] U.S. officials endorsed technical aid and assistance programs, introduced Point IV in 1949, and stressed the importance of cultivating pro-American political elites to this end. The U.S. National Security Council's (NSC) 129/1 of April 24, 1952, illustrates such objectives, underscoring the proposition that "the process of internal political change going on in these countries may lead to disorder and to a situation in which regimes subject to the influence or control of the Soviet Union could come to power."[51] Hence:

> As a means of diminishing the threat posed by nationalistic demands for the elimination of Western interests and by political instability in the area, the United States should make the fullest practicable use of psychological and political programs (including special political measures) and of economic and military aid programs and technical cooperation to influence the process of political change into channels that will effect the least compromise of Western interests and will offer the maximum promise of stable non-communist regimes. The United States should direct these programs and measures along the following lines:
>
> a. To support or develop those leadership groups in the area which offer the greatest prospect of establishing political stability oriented toward the free world.
>
> b. Place increased emphasis on measures designed to have an early and stabilizing effect upon urban groups.
>
> c. To improve or, where advisable, assist in the construction of such facilities, especially in the field of transportation and communications, as are capable of direct contribution to regional defense requirements.

    d. Continue technical cooperation programs designed to
improve the living standards and level of health and education
of the rural populations, including actions leading to solutions
of problems of land tenancy and credit.[52]

In sum, NSC 129/1 proposed systematic manipulation of
Third World political change with special attention to political
elites, since "the task is thus not so much to prevent the changes
that now impede as to guide them into channels that will offer
the least threat to Western interests and the maximum assurance
of independent regimes friendly to the West."[53] Leadership training was central. Hence, "our principal aim should be to encourage the emergence of competent leaders, relatively well-disposed
toward the West, through programs designed for this purpose,
including, where possible a conscious, though perhaps covert,
effort to cultivate and aid such potential leaders, even when they
are not in power."[54]

NSC 129/1 was issued in the spring of 1952, four years after the
Pentagon Talks between U.S. and British officials identified areas
of common interest and concern in the Middle East. Within a
year, as the Eisenhower administration took over in Washington
(1953), power relations within the Middle East changed, as challenges to Anglo-American control over petroleum resources and
transit routes multiplied. Covert attempts to subvert the Syrian
regime began even before Eisenhower came to power and were
vigorously pursued by the Dulles brothers through the 1950s,
while in Iran, Egypt, and Iraq, nationalist forces challenged Western control of—though not access to—oil. The Iranian nationalization of Anglo-Iranian oil in 1951 was followed two years later by
the covert Anglo-American coup, Operation Ajax, which toppled
the Iranian prime minister and reinstated the shah, with CIA
backing. Three years later, Egyptian President Nasser's nationalization of the Suez Canal Company was followed by the Anglo-
French invasion of Egypt and, within months, the Israeli invasion
of the Sinai. In 1958, as Britain stood stunned as the Iraqi political class was overturned in a military coup, the United States

sent over fifteen thousand troops to Lebanon in the first major post–Korean War military intervention, a highly underrated phase of its protracted intervention in Lebanese politics.[55]

Such was the background to Daniel Lerner's "classic" 1958 work on maldevelopment, *The Passing of Traditional Society,* co-sponsored by the MIT Center for International Studies (CENIS) and the Bureau of Applied Social Research of Columbia University (BASR).[56] Lerner's much-praised work, which continues to garner applause as a contribution to behavioral research, was also a major contribution to the pursuit of the Cold War in the Middle East. Its highly selective analyses and typology of the area's regimes conformed to U.S. policy, as did its emphasis on political elites and the classification of social and political forces in the region. That Turkey and Lebanon emerged as the favored states, followed by a doubtful review of Iran and negative assessment of Syria, can come as no surprise to those familiar with the publicly promoted version of U.S. policy. But Lerner's method— his integration of psychology, culture, and politics and his interpretation of modernity—won him credits from those either unfamiliar with the history and politics of the region or who uncritically accepted the unstated premises of U.S. policy implicit in Lerner's work.

A reading of declassified U.S. sources for the period offers a far more sober view of regional developments, one that is often at odds with Lerner's conclusions. There one sees that Lerner's claim that in Turkey and Lebanon the "three attributes of modernism, dynamism, stability tend to go together," was a self-serving reading of publicly announced U.S. policy in Turkey and a misinterpretation of Lebanese domestic politics. U.S. sources for the same period on Lebanon, for example, acknowledged a level of instability rooted in unresolved problems at the political level, magnified by a rapacious business class in command of politics.[57] Neither the Turkish nor the Lebanese economies had "taken off," to use Walt Rostow's terminology as employed by Lerner. Nor had political life there "reduced the cataclysmic issues of ideology to the manageable dimensions of planning," as

Lerner asserted.[58] Political life had accomplished no such thing, save to reduce the space for political differences, which was entirely compatible with U.S. policy.

To argue that violent political struggles were absent because power had been determined by elections was to further mythify the domestic politics of both states. Also misleading was Lerner's claim that both were "democratizing while Egypt and Syria tend toward bolshevizing."[59] "Bolshevizing" referred to what Lerner described as "the omnipotence of politics, a lesson impressed on the twentieth century by the Bolsheviks that has radically transformed the course of modernization in these less developed lands."[60] Lerner's work was reminiscent of the analyses of political involvement in the works of Lipset, Kornhauser, and Almond cited earlier. In the hands of Lerner, the amalgam was useful in the depiction of Syrian and Iranian politics in terms of extremism, an approach and a label that has had remarkable staying power. Nowhere, perhaps, was Lerner's misrepresentation of local developments more at odds with the now-declassified record of U.S. and British policy than in his depiction of Iran between 1951 and 1953. Mossadeq, the purported manipulator of extremists in Lerner's book, emerged in U.S. sources as a credible negotiator in the opinion of Truman's Secretary of State, Dean Acheson, though this opinion was not shared by the British directors of Anglo-Iranian Oil. In the aftermath of Mossadeq's nationalization of the Anglo-Iranian Oil Company, British as well as U.S. intelligence sources collaborated on Operation Ajax, which was facilitated by the change in U.S. administrations.[61]

Lerner's foray into the Middle East was not the only one undertaken by scholars writing within the parameters of development studies. Turkey remained a favorite topic, for reasons already cited, as did the array of pro-American regimes from Tunisia to the shah's Iran. The same selective use of data shaped the field of Middle East and North African studies.

While Lerner was designing his study on the Middle East, prolific member of the MIT CENIS team, Lucian Pye, known for his work on counterinsurgency, the military, and political development, was making his findings public. In keeping with the "culture" argument, Pye emphasized the cultural determinants of political choice. But coercion, not culture, was at the root of Pye's analyses of counterinsurgency, or, in the language of politics and the academy, "internal war." Pye's work focused on Southeast Asia—Malaya, Burma, and Indonesia—and coincided with the militarization of U.S. policy and its continued support for British pacification policies in the region. Pye's work on Malaya, *Guerrilla Communism in Malaya* (1956), was a defense of British counterinsurgency policies designed to assure continued British access to raw materials, namely, rubber and tin. In 1959, Pye participated in a conference on militarism sponsored by the RAND Corporation[62] and, two years later, authored *Military Development in the New Countries,* a report prepared for the Smithsonian and published by CENIS at MIT.

In the RAND-sponsored study support for the military was justified in terms of its potential contribution to "the growth of effective representative institutions." In the CENIS study, the explanation was more straightforward. In light of ongoing "internal wars" in southeast Asia and the inadequacy of military solutions in combating communism, "a gradually emerging American doctrine on counter-subversion," had been formed.[63] Social science research could be useful in "helping to develop a sounder and more stable United States doctrine on foreign military assistance," Pye recommended in the same source. The literature on "internal war" attests to the success of Pye's recommendation.[64]

In a work widely cited in the literature on political development, *Aspects of Political Development* (1966), Pye offered an unambiguous defense of counterinsurgency and the role of the military. Praising the dispassionate attitude of the British toward counterinsurgency—"normal police work," as opposed to what he viewed as the excesses of American moralism in politics—Pye rationalized the role of the military in Third World countries. What he omitted to disclose on this occasion was the extent to which British counterinsurgency practices affected U.S. policy in

Vietnam; and more specifically, how British policies of resettlement in Malaya were transfered to Vietnam in the U.S.backed Strategic Hamlet program.[65] In Burma and Indonesia, Pye argued, the U.S. had far better relations with the military than with civilian leaders because the former were free of insecurity and were "often the most modernized public organization in an underdeveloped country."[66] This explained their sense of self-confidence, hence their capacity "to deal frankly and cordially with representatives of the industrialized countries."

U.S. policy in Indonesia closely tracked Pye's thesis, as recent scholarship reveals. Hostile to President Sukarno's neutralist policy and convinced that Sukarno and some elements of the military in Java were communist influenced, "senior [U.S.] administration officials concluded (in the fall of 1957) that discontent in some of the islands outside Java provided an opening they could exploit to reverse this process, change the character of the Indonesian government, and move the country into an anti-Communist alignment with the United States."[67] According to the same source, the CIA acted with "substantial components of the U.S. Seventh Fleet and American planes and pilots together with supporting military personnel, facilities, and supplies from the Chinese Nationalist government on Taiwan and the government of the Philippines, with more modest but significant help from Britain and Australia."

The Eisenhower administration did not succeed in its objectives, but its successors did. Sukarno was overthrown in 1965 and the Indonesian military "engaged in mass killings to consolidate the new Suharto regime. At least 500,000 people are believed to have been killed by the army in an attempt to eradicate support for the Indonesian Communist Party (PKI). Declassified U.S. documents reveal that not only did the United States support the slaughter but it actually aided the Indonesian army in conducting it.[68]

Other members of the MIT CENIS team were in accord with the new emphasis on the military in modernization, development, and counterinsurgency. The report presented by CENIS at congressional hearings was emphatic in its endorsement of such a role, considering it a necessary complement to the incompetence of political elites, particularly since the military had the "coercive power needed to maintain stability."[69] The importance of the report and the role of members of the CENIS team in U.S. counterinsurgency policy, on the one hand, and academic studies of development, on the other, would be difficult to exaggerate. The report written under the direction of Max Milikan, the director of CENIS, on "Economic, Social, and Political Change in the Underdeveloped Countries and its Implications for United States Policy," was presented to the Senate Committee on Foreign Relations in January 1960.[70] It provided a defacto agenda for policy and development studies and was reissued with minor changes as *The Emerging Nations*.[71] Participating in the production of the original report were Rostow, Lerner, Pye, Everett Hagen, Paul Rosenstein-Rodan, de Sola Pool, and Milikan, the core group of economists, sociologists, political scientists, and communications specialists who were to shape development studies. The 1960 report, comprehensive in scope, identified the causes of social change and the economic impact of colonialism, as well as its social and political consequences. It offered a classification of the Third World in terms of traditional societies, modern oligarchies, and "potentially democratic" formations. The authors accepted the proposition that socioeconomic transformation was the condition, though not the guarantee, of political change that would increase participation and democracy. Their central concern, however, remained political stability, hence the intense interest in the role of the military, rationalized in terms of its contribution to modernization.

Walt Rostow, one of the CENIS team and the well-known author of *The Stages of Economic Growth* (1958), addressed the U.S. Army Special Warfare School at Fort Bragg in 1961, where he offered the rationale for counterinsurgency. Cuba, the Congo (Zaire), Laos, and Vietnam were the examples he used to illustrate the instability of developing countries exploited by international communism.[72] Such discussion did not include any reference to U.S. violations of the 1954 Geneva Convention and their impact on Vietnam, or to the U.S. subsidization of the Ngo Dinh Diem regime's budget, or U.S. intervention in Laos. Nor was U.S. involvement in the struggle over Zaire's resources mentioned.[73] In 1962 the Smithsonian Institution published a series of reports on "Social Science Research and National Security," in which two members of the CENIS team, de Sola Pool and Pye, recommended an interdisciplinary research effort whose objective was "the formulation of analytical models of social change and social control in underdeveloped countries."[74] In 1964 the Center for Research in Social Sciences (CRESS) channeled government funding into the study of development and the military, with the University of Chicago's Center for Social Organization Studies receiving the major subcontract for studies on the sociology of the military.[75]

"Between 1960 and 1970, the United States spent $1 billion to overcome insurgent threats to the existing order," according to the author of *War Without End*.[76] U.S. policy in Vietnam was symptomatic of the approach and its results. Huntington's, "Instability at the Non-Strategic Level of Conflict," (1961), prepared for Project Vulcan and supported by the Special Studies Group of the Institute for Defense Analyses, was a relevant primer on Third World intervention.[77] It is of interest to note that several years later, in the context of a more academically oriented work, Huntington's major opus, *Political Order in Changing Societies*, the author maintained that U.S. policy had nothing to do with the militarization of Third World regimes since military assistance was a "politically sterile"—meaning "neutral"—policy.[78]

"Winning the Cold War: The U.S. Ideological Offensive"

Huntington's claim was belied by the practice of U.S. policy and by the Defense Department's allocation of considerable funds for research on Third World development in which the collaboration of the U.S. and local military forces was repeatedly underlined. One official document that effectively conveys the objectives of such policy and the role of social scientists in providing intelligence for its implementation was the fourth report in the *Winning the Cold War: The U.S. Ideological Offensive* series of hearings by the Subcommittee on International Organizations and Movements of the Committee on Foreign Affairs of the House of Representatives. This study, part of the more comprehensive analysis on "Behavioral Sciences and the National Security,"[79] offers an unparalleled summary of the thinking of U.S. officials on the relationship between development and destabilization, and the imperative of its control.

As will be seen, information was the indispensable ingredient for the implementation of such a policy. Its accumulation and analysis frequently was in the hands of social scientists, who were also the recipients of generous funding from the Defense Department. This support, as well as that extended to universities and research institutions, had a substantial influence on the academic politics of development studies. These funds both facilitated and legitimized acceptable research, given their authoritative source and the hierarchy of social scientists dependent on them. They shaped the problems investigated, the questions pursued and equally relevant, those eliminated, subordinated or cast aside as irrelevant.

According to the introduction of Report no. 4, "during recent years, Communist support of 'wars of national liberation,' and U.S. commitments to aid the developing nations of the free world to meet this threat, propelled our Military Establishment into an expanding involvement in research relating to foreign areas and foreign populations."[80]

To facilitate the pursuit of such intelligence data, on April 24, 1964, the director of Defense Research and Engineering of the Department of Defense requested the Defense Science Board to conduct a study of Defense Department research and development programs "relating to ethnic and other motivational factors involved in the causation and conduct of small wars [deletions in text]."[81] These were viewed as promoting the accumulation of information relevant to analysis of conditons leading to local conflict, the "internal wars" that dominated development studies on the military through the early 1960s. The military was criticized for its failures in this regard, not with respect to policy but with respect to its awareness of the connection between information and practice.

As Seymour J. Deitchman, the army's special assistant for counterinsurgency explained, the U.S. military "must work with and help local military personnel at all levels plan and implement the counterinsurgency programs."[82] In pursuit of this effort, which involved collaboration with local populations, "the [Department of Defense] has called on the types of scientists— anthropologists, psychologists, sociologists, political scientists, economists—whose professional orientation to human behavior would enable them to make useful contributions in this area."[83]

The relationship among U.S. foreign policy, the role of the military, and Third World development was further underscored in congressional testimony by Dr. Theodore Vallance, director of the Special Operations Research Office (SORO), on July 8, 1965. Dr. Vallance emphasized the "Army's increasing role in military assistance and civic action [that] has focused attention on the need to better understand the processes of social and political economic development, and how the rapid changes in society which many U.S. programs are fostering in the developing countries of the world can be accomodated without a breakdown of the social order and the resultant opportunity for Communist penetration and possible takeover."[84] On the same day, the director of SORO conceded that "anticipating social breakdown and its attendant violence and destruction" was as important to the military as knowing how a regime might go about promoting change while "preventing the breakdown of social order."

It was once again Seymour Deitchman who, on July 14, reviewed postwar U.S. foreign policy, emphasizing its involvement with "the developing nations of Asia, Africa, and Latin America," and underlining the risks of communist expansion rooted in "instability and economic problems in these nations."[85] In consequence, according to Deitchman, "the State Department, the

Defense Department, and key agencies such as the CIA, AID, and USIA have increasingly had to turn their attention to meeting this purported threat. Because of its involvement in military assistance activities in these nations, and because of the all-encompassing nature of the threat—in the political, economic, social as well as military spheres, the Defense Department's missions in this area have been viewed as broader than the traditional mission of providing U.S. Armed Forces for the national defense."

SORO itself was designed to oversee social science research deemed relevant to the military role in implementing U.S. foreign policy. According to its director, this involved dealing with problems "in the orderly process of social change and national development which is of concern to the U.S. Military Establishment."[86] The establishment of the Counterinsurgency Information Analysis Center was an outgrowth of this and related SORO projects, although the agency was forced to reorganize as the Center for Research in Social Sciences under congressional pressure stemming from the Project Camelot scandal of 1964.

Estimates for Defense Department funding for behavioral and social science research in 1965 was $27.3 million, more than a third of which went to the military in deference to its role in "unconventional warfare," while the rest was subdivided between various agencies.[87] Among the beneficiaries of such largesse was the Human Resources Research Office, U.S. Army Personnel Research Office, and SORO, for "improved performance in counterinsurgency, military assistance, unconventional types of warfare and psychological operations through social and behavioral science studies of methods for predicting the reactions of indigenous troops and populations in foreign areas; and other studies as may be needed for direct support of stability operations."[88]

Short of reproducing the text of congressional hearings on the subject, it is difficult to do justice to the array of projects, the institutions and sites involved, both within and outside of the United States. Research projects identified in these hearings were classified under the headings Army, Navy, Air Force, and

Department of State, with institutional conduits through which contracts were arranged, as in the case of AID, USIA, and RAND. Thus, the Office of Naval Research's Psychological Sciences Division listed research projects under the headings of individual and group effectiveness, interaction, neural/perceptual processes; response mechanisms; human engineering; basic traits; and training and education. The Air Force defined the scope of its programs in disciplinary terms, including anthropology, economics, history, law, operations and systems analysis, political science, psychiatry, psychology, social psychology, and sociology. The relevant fields of study were classified under the overall objective of facilitating "operations with allies and foreign military organizations, and enhanc[ing] the effectiveness of airpower in cold, limited, and hot-war situations."[89] The specific projects funded ranged from those devoted to the "measurement of attitude and attitude change"[90] to "decision making in common sense situations of choice," the "influence of campus environment on student commitment to AFROTC,"[91] and "self-control under conditions of stress."[92] Policy-planning studies were offered under the aegis of the air force, with subjects including national security, nuclear proliferation, and Soviet military assistance programs, among others. The air force also funded RAND projects on defense cooperation within the NATO bloc, Chinese Communist nuclear capacity, Soviet foreign and military policy, and the "use of force in underdeveloped countries."[93]

The State Department's Agency for International Development (AID), was reported to have received some $5.7 million for twenty projects since it had gone into operation in 1962.[94] AID "participated in an informal committee on the planning of counterinsurgency research, together with representatives of the Defense Department and U.S. Information Agency."[95] Moreover, in collaboration with the State Department, AID joined with other agencies in organizing FAR, the Foreign Area Research Coordinating Group, for more effective coordination. Among the projects funded by AID were those dealing with land tenure and reform in Latin America; nation building; comparative administrative capacity; comparative social and cultural change; communication research; universities and political change in Latin America, specifically Mexico and Peru; and, more generally, political attitudes of Third World youth; social values and political responsibilities; and so on.[96]

The USIA (U.S. Information Agency) operated globally, defining its program in terms of "finding ways to reach and inform the peoples of the world, measuring their opinions and attitudes, and evaluating the U.S. Information Agency's efforts to influence them."[97] In Europe, this involved monitoring the Voice of America, Italian elections, and public opinion in France and West Germany, which included Africa and Arab students. Institutions collaborating on such projects were located in Paris, Germany, Greece, India, Iran, Kenya, Nigeria, and Brazil, among others.[98]

The above information was culled from the 1965 congressional hearings. Government support for development related projects and counterinsurgency programs did not abate.[99] They included projects under the aegis of CRESS, HumRRO, RAND, and RAC. Under CRESS, there were projects on nation building in Latin America, public opinion, on the military and modernization, and on comparative aspects of national development. Programs dealing with counterinsurgency, internal security and psychological operations focused on Afghanistan, Cambodia, China, Colombia, Congo (Zaire), Egypt, Ghana, Indonesia, Iran, Iraq, Jordan, Laos, Lebanon, Pakistan, Saudi Arabia, South Vietnam, Syria, Thailand, Turkey, Brazil, Venezuela and the Himalayan region.[100] The Human Resources Research Office (HumRRO) underwrote projects on modernization, elite studies, and the destabilizing effects of sociopolitical change from Latin America to the Middle East and North Africa. RAND continued to fund research on counterinsurgency targetted at Vietnam, Thailand and Laos.

The Research Analysis Corporation (RAC) supported counterinsurgency and strategic studies focusing on the same areas in southeast Asia, the Middle East, North Africa and Latin America, along with the USSR and eastern Europe. The Defense Department and the Institute for Defense Analyses focused on guerrilla war. Defense Department calculations of sums spent for social and behavioral science research in 1969 were in the order of $45.4 million; $48.6 million was set aside for similar projects in 1970, while some $12.7 million of this amount was designated for research relevant to foreign policy and foreign areas.[101]

The contribution of social scientists remained a critical facet of counterinsurgency in general, and in the U.S. war in Vietnam in particular. According to a former president of IDA who became vice president at MIT, Dr. Jack Ruina, U.S. counterinsurgency operations in Vietnam required the kind of information about Vietnamese society that only social scientists could provide. "When we started thinking about counterinsurgency we quickly realized that you cannot isolate these problems from people. What did we know about these people—the Viet Cong and the Vietnamese generally? We felt we needed to know a great deal more from the anthropologist, from the social scientists."[102] Similarly, Kenneth Young—a former direcctor of Southeast Asian affairs in the State Department, Ambassador to Thailand (1961–3), president of the Asia Society in 1967, and chair of the Southeast Asia Development Advisory Group (SEADAG) maintained that U.S. advisors in Vietnam were ill equipped to effectively convey "new ideas and coax new actions"[103] and lacked adequate intelligence to assure the "transfer" [of] what the Americans, either by government policy or by the technician's action, want to introduce into the mind of a Vietnamese or into a Vietnamese organization." Included among the "ideas" that were to be transferred, as Young saw it, were the U.S. administration's view of "political reform, administrative development, village and hamlet rule, drafting of constitution, and formation of political groups and leadership-using economic development, military assistance and other resources."[104] The objective was control at *any* cost.

The U.S. government was willing to pay for results. At a meeting of the Council on Vietnamese Studies in 1967, Samuel Huntington stated that "well over ninety percent of the serious social science work on Vietnam is being conducted under the auspices of the United States Government."[105] The Council itself illustrated precisely the kind of collaboration between government and social scientists that Ruina, Young and the Defense Department officials recommended. It was formed under the auspices of AID's Far East Bureau and the Asia Society at the recommendation of Young's SEADAG committee. In formal academic language the new Council indicated its intention to follow the lead of development studies, assigning "a high priority to encouraging similar studies on political development in Vietnam and to encouraging the application to Vietnam of the concepts and approaches developed in the broader reaches of comparative politics."[106] Looking back today, the nature and consequences of U.S. policy in Vietnam leaves little doubt as to the meaning of political developoment in those circumstances: it was synonymous with political pacification, a policy that ultimately failed in the face of continued resistance to U.S. technological and ideological power.

This pattern of development—plus—counterinsurgency metastasized across the Third World, with the same collaboration with local political and business elites and similar legitimization by accomodating intellectuals and academics. A comparative analysis of U.S. intervention in Latin America, the Middle East, Africa and southeast Asia, offers ample evidence of such a history, as well as the deeply rooted resistance to it in the affected countries. The public analyses produced by the approved, policy oriented, social scientists discussed in the above pages created sanitized accounts of events that were particularly effective for U.S. readers wtihout access to alternative sources.

Nevertheless, an intellectual revolt of sorts against the hegemony of development studies broke out in the late 1960s. Spurred by the evidence of Latin America and Vietnam, dissenting social scientists, students and faculty among them, took issue with the conditions and consequences of academic collaboration with government policy. In the milieu of political science, not only conventional studies of development but the mainstream approach to American politics and society itself were challenged. From inside as well as outside of the academy, questions of race, class and imperial power sometimes displaced the presumptions of liberal orthodoxy. Existing paradigms of political culture and development met the same fate, as critical studies on underdevelopment and dependency shattered the alleged consensus in the field of development studies. These distinct but overlapping constituencies joined in the contestation of politics and power, of theory and practice. Despite their very real jolt to the academic establishment, the revival of development orthodoxy and its apology in the 1990s illustrates the resiliancy of the ideology of empire. It also constitutes compelling evidence of the urgency of reconsidering our earlier experience so as to better avoid it.

Notes

1. See the essay by Laura Nader, in volume 1 of this series, *The Cold War and the University* (New York: The New Press, 1997), and that by Bruce Cummings in the present volume, for corresponding analyses in the areas of anthropology, area studies, and international studies.

2. Hearings by the Subcommittee on International Organizations and Movements of the Committee on Foreign Affairs, House of Representatives, December 6, 1965.

3. Consider the works of G. O'Donnell and P. Schmitter, *Transitions From Authoritarian Rule: Tentative Conclusions About Uncertain Democracies*, 4 vols. (Baltimore: Johns Hopkins University Press, 1986); Adam Przeworski, *Democracy and the Market*, (Cambridge University Press, 1991); S.Hag-

gard and R. Kaufman, *The Political Economy of Democratic Transitions*, (Princeton: Princeton University Press, 1995); and also Frances Hagopian, "After Regime Change: Authoritarian Legacies, Political Representation and the Democratic Future of South America," *World Politics*, 45 (April), pp. 464–500; and contesting facile pronouncements on democratic transition, E. Leeds, "Cocaine and Parallel Polities in the Brazilian Urban Periphery: Constraints on Local-Level Democratization," *Latin American Research Review* 31 (1996), no. 3, and Noam Chomsky, *Powers and Prospects*, (Boston: South End Press, 1996).

4. Benjamin DeMott, "Seduced by Civility," *The Nation*, Dec. 9, 1996, p. 11; see, in addition,

Jean L. Cohen and Andrew Arato, *Civil Society and Political Theory*, (Cambridge, Mass.: MIT Press, 1992); Ellen M.Wood, *Democracy Against Capitalism*, (Cambridge, U.K.: Cambridge University Press, 1995); Chomsky, *Powers and Prospects*, chap. 5.

5. Recent works on these issues include: M. Mamdani, *Citizen and Subject: Contemporary Africa and the Legacy of Late Colonialism*, (Princeton, N.J.: Princeton University Press, 1996), and F. Cooper, A. F. Isaacsman, F. Mallon, W. Roseberry, and S. Stern, *Confronting Historical Paradigms: Peasants, Labor, and the Capitalist World System in Africa and Latin America*, (Madison: University of Wisconsin Press, 1993).

6. Thomas L. Friedman, "Roll Over Hawks and Doves," *New York Times*, Feb. 2, 1997.

7. Larry Rohter, "Impact of Nafta Pounds Economies of the Caribbean," *New York Times*, Jan. 30, 1997.

8. William Pfaff, "Global Economy Bodes Ill for U.S.," *Sarasota Herald*, Jan. 4, 1997, p. 13A.

    Reports on the IMF's effect on Haiti in 1996 indicates that the working poor, have been abandoned not only by the nation-state but by institutions that claim to promote the economies and well-being of its people. In recent coverage of the IMF in Haiti, protesters reportedly called for the prime minister's resignation and demanded that the president break off negotiations with international lending agencies. The strike's organizers were part of the "Anti-International Monetary Fund Committee," which had the support of "more than 100 grass-roots groups" and a number of legislators. This disparate constituency came together in opposition to the regime's lack of resistance to IMF policies, which demanded the privatization of state-run enterprises and the elimination of some seven thousand out of roughly forty-three thousand government jobs. Given that an estimated 60 percent of the Haitian government's budget comes from foreign lending agencies, the options were few.

    The response of IMF visitors on such occasions has been muted. Protest may be unpleasant, but it does not appear to deflect attention from the policies to be pursued. "Protests Erupt Across Haiti as Leaders Push Austerity," *New York Times*, Jan. 17, 1997, p.3.

9. Ethan B. Kapstein, "Workers and the World Economy," *Foreign Affairs*, May–June 1996, p. 16.

10. Hillary Barnes, "Mollycoddled," in "Workers and Economists," *Foreign Affairs* 75, no. 4, p. 174.

11. Robert J. Barro, "Democracy: A Recipe for Economic Growth," *Wall Street Journal*, Dec. 1, 1994.

12. Jeff Gerth, "In Post-Cold-War Washington, Development Is a

Hot Business," *New York Times,* May 25, 1996, p. 1.

13. Ibid.

14. Ibid.

15. See for example, James Bradford de Long, "The 'Protestant Ethic' Revisited: A Twentieth Century Look," in *The Fletcher Forum of World Affairs,* special issue on culture in development, *New Perspectives,* 13, no. 2, (1989).

16. Francis Fukuyama, "Social Capital and the Global Economy," *Foreign Affairs,* Sept.–Oct. 1995.

17. Francis Fukuyama, *Trust* (New York: Free Press, 1995).

18. Max Weber, *The Protestant Ethic and the Spirit of Capitalism,* trans. Talcott Parsons (New York: Charles Scribner's Sons, 1958). see James S. Coleman, *Foundations of Social Theory* (Cambridge, Mass.: Harvard University Press, 1990).

19. Fukuyama, "Social Capital and the Global Economy," op. cit., p. 90.

20. Ibid., p. 90.

21. Michael Ignatieff, "On Civil Society," *Foreign Affairs* 74 (1994), no. 2.

22. Fukuyama, op. cit., p. 93.

23. See for example, Seymour Martin Lipset, *Political Man* (New York: Doubleday, 1960); and William Kornhauser, *The Politics of Mass Society* (Glencoe, Ill.: Free Press, 1959).

24. Fukuyama, op. cit., p. 103.

25. Howard J. Wiarda, "Political Culture and National Development," in *The Fletcher Forum of World Affairs* (For complete citation, see note 21 above), p. 199.

26. For examples of current interpretations that rely on cultural explanations of sociopolitical change, see Lawrence E. Harrison, *Underdevelopment Is a State of Mind: The Latin American Case* (Center for International Affairs, Harvard University, and the University Press of America, 1985); Robert D. Putnam, *Making Democracy Work: Civic Traditions in Modern Italy* (Princeton, N.J.: Princeton University Press, 1993); L. Diamond, ed., *Political Culture and Democracy in Developing Countries,* (Boulder, Colo.: Lynne Rienner Press, 1993); and for a critical analysis of the role of culture in development studies, see Irene L. Gendzier, *Development Against Democracy* (Hampton, Conn.: Tyrone Press, 1995), chaps. 4 and 5.

27. Wiarda, "Political Culture and National Development," p. 201.

28. Samuel Huntington, "The Clash of Civilizations," *Foreign Affairs* 72 (1993), no. 3, p. 40, and *The Clash of Civilizations,* (Cambridge, Mass.: Harvard University Press, 1996).

29. See, for example, *Foreign Affairs,* Sept.–Oct. 1993, for the rejoinders to Huntington in the journal in which he published his initial article; R. Rubinstein and J. Crocker, "Challenging Huntington," *Foreign Policy* 96 (fall 1994); R. Mottahedeh, "The Clash of Civilizations: An Islamicist's Critique," *Harvard Middle East-*

ern and Islamic Review 2 (1995), vol. 2, pp. 1–26; B. Lewis, "The West and the Middle East," *Foreign Affairs*, Jan.–Feb. 1997; and Edward W. Said, *Covering Islam* (New York: Vintage, 1997 [rev. ed.]).

30. Huntington, "The Clash of Civilizations," p. 40.

31. Ibid., p. 41.

32. Gabriel Almond, "The Development of Political Development," in *A Discipline Divided*, (Thousand Oaks, Calif.: Sage, 1990), p. 222–25; and I. L. Gendzier, *Development Against Democracy*, pp. 96, 118, 125–6, 157, 171.

33. Samuel P. Huntington, *Political Order in Changing Societies* (New Haven and London: Yale University Press, 1968), p. 28. As Huntington explained, "the moral basis of political institutions is rooted in the needs of men in complex societies." One such need is the need for community, and community presupposes trust, the cohesive and consensual force essential to the successful operation of institutions. From such expressions of the role of solidarity, Huntington concluded that "those societies dificient in stable and effective government are also deficient in mutual trust among their citizens, in national and public loyalties, and in organizational skills and capacity. Their political cultures are often said to be marked by suspicion, jealousy, and latent or actual hostility toward everyone who is not a member of the family, the village or perhaps, the tribe. These characteristics are found in many cultures, their most extensive manifestations perhaps being in the Arab would and in Latin America." The culture argument reappeared in Huntington's later works, such as *The Third Wave* and *The Clash of Civilizations*. In these later incarnations, the overall theme is not moderinization and development but democratization.

34. Daniel Lerner, *The Passing of Traditional Society* (New York: Free Press, 1958).

35. See Lucian W. Pye, in L.W. Pye and Sydney Verba, eds., *Political Culture and Political Development* (Princeton, N.J.: University Press, 1965), p. 8–9.

36. For Verba's discussion of the distinction between culture and political culture in the same volume, see ibid., pp. 521–25.

37. Daniel Bell, *The End of Ideology* (New York: The Free Press, 1962); [rev. ed.] James Burnham, *The Machiavellians: Defenders of Freedom* (New York: John Day, 1943); Seymour Martin Lipset, *Political Man*, (New York: Doubleday, 1960); Arthur Schlesinger Jr., *The Vital Center* (Boston: Houghton Mifflin, 1949); Joseph Schumpeter, *Capitalism, Socialism and Democracy*, (New York: Harper and Brothers, 1942); and Edward Shils, *Political Development in the New States* (The Hague: Mouton, 1962).

38. Gabriel Almond, *The American People and Foreign Policy* (New York: Harcourt, Brace, 1950);

The Appeals of Communism (Princeton, N.J.: Princeton University Press, 1954); "The Political Attitudes of German Business, *World Politics* 8 (Jan. 1956), vol. 2; *The Struggle for Democracy in Germany,* ed. (New York: Russell and Russell, 1965). For Harold Lasswell, consider *The Analysis of Political Behavior* (London: Routledge and Kegan Paul, 1948); *Psychopathology and Politics* (Chicago: University of Chicago Press, 1977); and "The Relation of Ideological Intelligence to Public Policy," *Ethics* 53 (Oct. 1942), vol. 1; for a selected bibliography, see, Gabriel Almond, "Harold D. Lasswell: A Biographical Memoir," in *A Discipline Divided.* For Daniel Lerner, *Sykewar* (New York: George Stewart, 1949); and *Propaganda in War and Crisis* (New York: George W. Stewart, 1951).

39. Almond and Verba, *The Civic Culture*, p. 343.

40. Samuel P. Huntington, Michael Crozier, and Joji Watanuki, *The Crisis of Democracy* (1975).

41. David Lehmann, ed., *Development Theory* (London: Frank Cass, 1979), p. 1.

42. Edward J. Berman, *The Influence of the Carnegie, Ford, and Rockefeller Foundations on American Foreign Policy* (Albany: State University of New York Press, 1983); for a recent discussion, see Joan Roelofs, "Foundations and Political Science," *New Political Science* 23 (fall 1992).

43. The contributions of these writers continue to be classified as the expression of uncritical Marxists with a concealed agenda by Almond, "The Development of Political Development," p. 225–44.

44. Howard J. Wiarda, *Introduction to Comparative Politics: Concepts and Processes* (Belmont, Calif.: Wadsworth, 1993), p. 125.

45. *The University-Military-Police Complex: A Directory and Related Documents,* compiled by Michael Klare, (North American Congress on Latin America (NACLA), 1970), p. 44.

46. Ibid., p. 45.

47. Among the relevant studies issued by the Council on Foreign Relations, see the series: "Studies of American Interests in the War and the Peace," E-B17 (1940); E-B 18 (1940); E-B (1941); E-B34 (1944).

48. See Nathan Godfried, *Bridging the Gap Between Rich and Poor* (New York: Greenwood Press, 1987), p. 79, and Joyce and Gabriel Kolko, *The Limits of Power; the World and United States Foreign Policy, 1945–1954* (New York: Harper and Row, 1972).

49. Melvin P. Leffler, *A Preponderance of Power* (Palo Alto, Calif.: Stanford University Press, 1992).

50. "The Pentagon Talks of 1947, between the United States and the United Kingdom, concerning the Middle East and the Eastern Mediterranean," *Foreign Relations of the United States,* 1947, V (1971), U.S. Government Printing Office.

51. NSC 129/1, Statement of Policy Proposed by the NSC on "United States Objectives and Policies with Respect to the Arab States and Israel," *Foreign Relations of the United States, 1952–1954,* IX (1986), pp. 4–5.

52. Ibid.

53. Ibid., p. 20.

54. Ibid., p. 22.

55. Irene L. Gendzier, *Notes from the Minefield: United States Intervention in Lebanon and the Middle East, 1945–1958* (New York: Columbia University Press, 1997); for a discussion of the events of 1958, see Pt. V, "The Minefield Explodes: U.S. Military Intervention."

56. Research began on the text in 1956 under Voice of America auspices; Lerner's 1958 text reanalyzed and recapitulated earlier studies and previously restricted data.

57. Gendzier, *Notes from the Minefield,* chaps. 4–6.

58. Lerner, *The Passing of Traditional Society,* p. 84.

59. Ibid., p. 85.

60. Ibid.

61. The literature on the subject is considerable by now, but the work of Mustafa Elm, a contemporary of the events discussed, is particularly useful in this context; see Mustafa Elm, *Oil, Power, and Principle* (Albany: State University of New York, 1994).

62. Lucian W. Pye, *Military Development in the New Countries* (Cambridge, Mass.: CENIS/MIT, 1961), p. 6.

63. Ibid.

64. See for example, Harry Eck-stein, ed., *Internal War: Problems and Approaches* (New York: Free Press, 1964).

65. Mark Curtis, *The Ambiguities of Power* (London and New Jersey: Zed Books, 1995), p. 64; and Michael Klare, *War Without End: American Planning For the Next Vietnams* (New York: Vintage, 1970), p. 105.

66. Lucien W. Pye, *Aspects of Political Development* (Boston: Little Brown and Company, 1966), p. 186.

67. Audrey R. Kahin and George McT. Kahin, *Subversion as Foreign Policy.* New York: The New Press, 1995, p. 17.

68. Mark Curtis, *The Ambiguities of Power,* (London and New Jersey: Zed Books, 1995), p. 57.

69. Max Milikan, "Economic, Social, and Political Change in the Underdeveloped Countries and Its Implications for United States Policy," prepared by the Center for International Studies, MIT, for U.S. Senate Foreign Relations Committee hearings, January 1960, p. 45.

70. For discussion of other such reports, see Gendzier, *Development Against Democracy,* bibliography, pp. 224–5.

71. Max Millikan and Donald L. M. Blackmer, eds., *The Emerging Nations* (Boston: Little, Brown, 1961).

72. See C. Maechling Jr., "Counterinsurgency, Yes—but with Controls," *Washington Post,* Feb. 12, 1981, p. 19.

73. See the work of David Gibbs, *The Political Economy of Third World Intervention* (Chicago: University of Chicago Press, 1991).

74. Cited in Klare, *War Without End,* p. 90.
75. Ibid., p. 66.
76. Ibid., p. 270.
77. Taken from I. L. Gendzier, *Development Against Democracy,* Hampton, Connecticut: Tyrone Press, 1995, p. 41.
78. Huntington, *Political Order in Changing Societies,* p. 193.
79. Behavioral Sciences and the National Security, Report no. 4, together with Part 9 of the Hearings on "Winning the Cold War: the U.S. Ideological Offensive" by the Subcommittee on International Organizations and Movements of the Committee on Foreign Affairs, House of Representatives. December 6, 1965.
80. Ibid., p. 3r.
81. Ibid., p. 3r.
82. Ibid., p. 5r.
83. Ibid.
84. Ibid., p. 11.
85. Ibid., p. 71.
86. Ibid., testimony of July 8, 1965, p. 5.
87. Ibid., p. 97.
88. Ibid., p. 27.
89. Ibid., p. 141.
90. Ibid., p. 144.
91. Ibid., p. 145.
92. Ibid., p. 146.
93. Ibid., p. 151.
94. Ibid., p. 152.
95. Ibid., p. 153.
96. Ibid., pp. 154–156.
97. Ibid., p. 157.
98. The institutions involved included: EMNID Gmbh and Co., Bielefeld, Germany, Institute for Research in Communications, Athens, Greece; Indian Institute of Public Opinion, Ltd., New Delhi; Indian Adult Education Association; National Institute of Psychology, Teheran; East African students were the object of research by Market Research Ltd., Nairobi, Kenya and Lagos, Nigeria; North African students by the Institut Francais d'Opinion Publique, Paris; student attitudes in Brazil were undertaken by the Institute for the Study of International Behavior, Sao Paulo, Brazil. The above is a partial list. Additional research sites were to be found in Latin America and Asia. Ibid., pp. 165, 167, 170.

Among the research sites for such projects were European institutions, including: EMNID Gmbh and Co., Bielefeld, Germany, prime source for surveys of political opinion among Arab and African students; Institute for Research in Communications, Athens, Greece; Indian Institute of Public Opinion, Ltd., New Delhi, India, Indian Adult Education Association; National Institute of Psychology, Teheran, Iran; East African students were the subject of research by Market Research Ltd., Nairobi, Kenya, and Lagos, Nigeria; North African students by the Institut Français d'Opinion Publique, Paris, France; student attitudes in Brazil were undertaken by the Institute for the Study of International Behavior, São Paulo, Brazil; and considerably more information on research and the institutions that conducted it appears on

99. Latin America and the Far East. The above provides an incomplete listing of subject and site of research as indicated in the pages of congressional testimony.

99. *The University-Military Police Complex*, pp. 49–62.

100. Ibid., p. 49.

101. "Winning the Cold War," p. 58. The following is a partial list of universities and research centers in the United States. American Institute for Research; Arizona State University; Berkeley Institute of Psychological Research; Bolt, Baranek and Newman, Inc., Brandeis University; Brookings Institution; Bucknell University; Center for Research on Social Behavior, University of Delaware; Educational Testing Service, Princeton; Honeywell, Inc; Cornell University; Emory University; National Academy of Sciences; Harvard Medical School; Hunter College; MIT; National New York University; Northwestern University; Purdue University; Research Center for Group Dynamics, University of Michigan; Rutgers University; Smithsonian Institution; Social Science Institute, Social Science Research Council; Research Center for Group Dynamics, University of Michigan; Science Park, Pa.; Stanford University; State University of New York, Buffalo; Texas Christian University; Teachers College, Columbia University; Tufts University; Institute for Applied Experimental Psychology; University of Akron; University of Florida, Gainesville; University of California, Los Angeles; University of Hawaii; University of Illinois, Urbana; University of North Carolina, Chapel Hill; University of Maryland; University of Massachusetts; University of Missouri; University of New Hampshire; University of North Carolina, Chapel Hill; University of Pennsylvania; University of Pittsburgh; University of Texas, Austin; University of Wisconsin; U.R.B. Singer, Inc.; Vanderbilt University; York University; Yale University: "Winning the Cold War: the ideological Offensive," pp. 131–139; 154–156.

102. Cited in Noam Chomsky, *For Reasons of State*, (New York: Pantheon Books), p. 98.

103. Kenneth T. Young, "United States Policy and Vietnamese Political Viability, 1954–1967," *Asian Survey*, 7, 8, August 1967, p. 507.

104. Ibid., p. 508.

105. Samuel P. Huntington, "Introduction: Social Science and Vietnam," *Asian Survey*, 7, 8, August 1967, p. 505.

106. Ibid., p. 505.

(Ellen Herman)

Project Camelot and the Career of Cold War Psychology

From 1945 through the Vietnam era, psychological experts shaped certain aspects of the public sphere in the United States in ways that were both decisive and unprecedented. No issue in the public conversation was more momentous than the militarism of the post–World War II era. How, in particular, could the United States prevail in the Cold War? How could we win the hearts and minds of Third World peoples?

The answers offered by psychological experts were compelling because they addressed the traumas of midcentury—the Holocaust, the ravages of world war, and a superpower rivalry that gambled the future of humanity and the planet itself—in ways that acknowledged the extent to which rationality and autonomy had been called into question. As if warning that too much faith in the sunny tenets of democratic theory could be a grave error, the events of midcentury drew urgent attention to a shadowy psychological underside, difficult to fathom and teeming with raw and unpredictable passions, as the likely controlling factor in human behavior. Persuaded that social developments and conflicts were hardly ever what they appeared to be, many observers (some eager, others reluctant) discarded habitual ways of studying and mediating social problems. Logical approaches, commonsense assumptions, and empirical commitments seemed shallow and inadequate in comparison with an alternative that promised insight into the madness lurking just beneath the thin veneer of a civilized social order. "We need to characterize American society of the mid-twentieth century in more psychological terms," the sociologist C. Wright Mills acknowledged in 1951, "for now the problems that concern us most border on the psychiatric."[1]

To their roles as Cold War military advisers and researchers, psychological experts brought evolving insights into human irrationality. A unified conception of behavior—a conviction that the relevant underlying variables were much the same whether conflicts were geopolitical or personal, whether the actors were nation-states or individual humans—was central. So, too, was the knowledge that psychology's professional and material status had reaped the benefits of war. Long after 1945, the worldview associated with the World War II generation and the early Cold War guided the history of the psychological and social sciences. Terrible arrogance and an admirable determination to make a social contribution forged enduring beliefs about the intimate links between professional responsibility and patriotic service to the state; among scientific advance, national security, and domestic tranquility; between mental health and cultural maturity; and among psychological enlightenment, social welfare, and the government of a democratic society. "Psychology is perceived," wrote John Darley, an observer of Department of Defense behavioral research in 1952, "as a vehicle that will assist in bringing about the American Creed of equality, fair play, and minimal group conflict."[2] The alliance between psychological knowledge and power may appear ideological in retrospect, but during much of the postwar era it was considered so axiomatic as to be nearly invisible.

Project Camelot illustrates these themes. Launched in 1963, Camelot was a major DOD-sponsored plan to involve behavioral experts in predicting and controlling Third World revolution and development in order to gain the upper hand in "The Minds Race."[3] A fascinating, controversial, and important episode in its own right, Camelot also documents psychology's rise to public power. Camelot had a strong psychological component, but was conceived from the start as an interdisciplinary effort on the model of World War II teamwork and in the spirit of that war's ambitious and integrated science of human behavior. It came into public view as an international scandal in July 1965, a full twenty years after the end of World War II.

Like so many other developments in postwar psychology, Project Camelot had deep roots in World War II. During that global emergency, psychological experts gained a significant and growing client base among high-level policy makers, generous financial support, and rich theoretical, methodological, and organizational experience. In return, psychologists studied the enemy mind, designed "psyops," and predicted likely responses to various policy alternatives among civilian and military populations. After 1945, experts were careful to maximize the practical military utility of their theoretical and research pursuits in areas ranging from psychological warfare to man/machine engineering and intelligence. If their functional policy orientation was less visible to the public at large than the testing or clinical work that more and more psychologists were doing during those years, it was nevertheless far more important in establishing psychology's political credentials and guaranteeing that behavioral experts would be warmly welcomed in every federal agency charged with Cold War foreign and military policy.

The boundaries between military and civilian targets, between wartime and peacetime conflicts, already beginning to blur during World War II when examined through the lens of psychological warfare, took on an eerie permanence during the Cold War. Military psychological operations experts were only stating what many Americans already felt when they pointed out that peace had lost much of its previous association with security: peace was "simply a period of less violent war."[4] Since peace and war were no longer entirely distinguishable, the services provided by experts became a permanent military asset.

The Cold War climate left few doubts about the appropriateness of fear, the dangerousness of the world, or the hope that policy enlightened by expertise might hold a key to survival in the atomic age. Psychology's Cold War trajectory was shaped by a number of broad institutional and intellectual trends—as well as by the profoundly psychological definition of Cold War itself. Between 1945 and the mid-1960s, the U.S. military was, by far, the country's major sponsor of psychological research, a living illustration of what socially-minded experts could accomplish, especially with a "not too gentle rain of gold."[5] The theoretical innovations of psychologists after 1945, especially in the areas of Third World development and revolution, also helped bring psychological perspectives to the attention of policy makers. The notion, for example, that the roots of war were to be found in the psychological particulars of national character and the universal truths of frustration and aggression found eager audiences in national security policy circles. They encouraged psychological experts to pursue questions about how to derail the development of militaristic aggressiveness, and, more ambitiously, how to construct an alterative psychology, oriented toward peaceful economic development and political stability.[6]

As a large-scale effort dedicated to translating psychological and behavioral expertise directly into the language of foreign policy and military action, Camelot shows just how far psychological experts had come since the formative years of World War II. Even an international scandal—which is what Camelot became—did not undermine their progress in the realm of public policy. Even harsh critics like Ralph Beals (an anthropologist who conducted one of the most thorough investigations of Camelot) chose to sidestep a public reassessment of the fundamental loyalty to the state that had been an axiom of the World War II worldview: "social scientists have a responsibility to government even if they do not agree with government practices."[7]

The Origins of Camelot

Project Camelot was initiated in 1963 by planners in the army's Office of Research and Development who were concerned about combating "wars of national liberation" in countries such as Cuba, Yemen, and the Belgian Congo. They were prepared to believe what the experts had been saying since 1945: behavioral expertise had a very important, perhaps the most important, contribution to make to Cold War victory over communism. Their goal—nothing less than the prediction and control of the social and psychological preconditions of Third World revolution—reflected the most lavish ambitions of psychological experts. In the words of its architects, "Project Camelot is a study whose objective is to determine the feasibility of developing a general social systems model which would make it possible to predict and influence politically significant aspects of social change in the developing nations of the world."[8] In spite of the code name (chosen to "connote the right sorts of things . . . the development of a stable society with domestic tranquility and peace and justice for all") and the ill-fated effort to disguise its military sponsorship in Chile (the lie that led to the project's exposure), Camelot was not officially classified.[9]

Camelot's mandate to "predict and influence" the process of Third World development marked it as a product of the World War II worldview. Additionally, it embodied the trend toward counterinsurgency and special operations that was so firmly identified with the Kennedy administration and its pledge to undermine the Soviet Union's support for liberation movements around the world, which Khrushchev had announced in his famous 1960 speech "For New Victories of the World Communist Movement."

The project was funded through the Special Operations Research Organization (SORO), one of the many campus-based contract research organizations that appeared after 1945 to service the Defense Department's scientific research effort. A nonprofit organization founded in 1956, SORO existed for the purpose of conducting "nonmaterial research in support of the Department of the Army's missions in such fields as counterinsurgency, unconventional warfare, psychological operations, and military assistance."[10] SORO was so loosely affiliated with the American University that some critics retrospectively dismissed its campus setting as clever camouflage. Its director, Theodore Vallance, had been a psychological researcher during World War II, when he was an army lieutenant in charge of a field laboratory that studied B-29 gunsights and gunners at Laredo Army Air Field, in Texas.[11]

By the early 1960s, Vallance was predicting a big role for "paramilitary" psychology in the "cultural engineering" of emerging Third World states, a logical outgrowth of the military's "trend away from emphasis on human components for hardware systems toward emphasis on human components of social systems."[12] Vallance was a staunch partisan of a politically neutral military psychology, very much like Charles Bray's "technology of human behavior." He was careful to describe Camelot as "an objective, nonnormative study concerned with *what is or might be* and *not* with what *ought to be*."[13] In addition to Camelot, SORO's work included providing the army with dozens of country-specific handbooks on psychological operations, case studies of Southeast Asia focusing on the exploitation of psychological vulnerabilities, and a comprehensive data bank called the Counter-Insurgency Information Analysis Center.

Camelot's projected research plan bore all the telltale traces of the World War II–era conception of an ambitious and integrated behavioral science. Psychology, cultural anthropology, and sociology were all slated to make important contributions to the final goal of the project: a model of a social system experiencing internal war accurate enough to be predictive, and therefore useful, to military planners. To reach that goal, Camelot's designers anticipated moving ahead in several phases. Phase I consisted of reviewing the existing data on internal war, a largely theoretical challenge already engaging the talents of many mainstream behavioral scientists. Phase II would produce twenty-one case studies of post–World War II insurgencies and five contemporary field studies with the explicit goal of developing predictive indicators. Phase III would bring the work of the first two phases to bear on a single in-depth analysis of an undetermined country. Phase IV would validate the findings of Phase III, and the project as a whole, by applying the model to yet another national case.[14]

The project's focus was Latin America, and Rex Hopper, a Brooklyn College sociologist and Latin America expert, was chosen as Camelot's director. Countries in Asia and Africa, however, were also found on Camelot's list of foreign areas in need of study. Vietnam, for example, was a clear target for research, and the project exploded into public view at precisely the moment when U.S. involvement in Vietnam escalated: mid-1965.[15] It was also a bare two months after marines had landed in the Dominican Republic, intervening to prevent a purported communist takeover.

Had it come to fruition, Camelot would have been the largest, and certainly the most generously funded, behavioral research project in U.S. history. With a $4–6 million contract over a period of three years, it was considered a veritable Manhattan Project for the behavioral sciences, at least by many of the intellectuals who saw opportunities there.[16] Prominent behavioral scientists, including the sociologists Jessie Bernard, Lewis Coser, and Neil Smelser, were among the project's consultants, and the National Academy of Sciences agreed to provide Camelot with an advisory committee.

Camelot Exposed

But the project backfired. The University of Pittsburgh anthropologist and Camelot consultant Hugo Nutini tried to promote the plan among Chilean scholars by lying to them about its fiscal sponsors; he told them it was funded by the National Science Foundation (NSF). But a concerned Norwegian sociologist, Johan Galtung, had already leaked preliminary versions of Camelot's research design, and the crucial fact of its military sponsorship, to Chilean colleagues. When they heard about it, outraged left-wing journalists in Chile decried the plan as an ominous indication that U.S. policy was shifting its sights from bananas to behavior, and predicted that social science research would replace dollars as the leading edge of U.S. diplomacy.

Even though Chile had not been among those countries mentioned by Camelot's planners, the project was publicly denounced in a special session of the Chilean Senate, where politicians called it "a plan of Yankee espionage" masquerading as science.[17] Protests were lodged in Washington by the incensed U.S. ambassador to Chile, Ralph Dungan, who had never been informed about Camelot's existence. Finally, the whole project was canceled by Secretary of Defense Robert McNamara on July 8, 1965, because of the unfavorable publicity. A subsequent memo from President Johnson, dated August 2, 1965, ordered that all future foreign area research be cleared by a new review agency, the Foreign Affairs Research Council, located in the Department of State's Bureau of Intelligence and Research. (This adjustment in the bureaucratic location of final decisions apparently had little short- or long-term effect on the nature or funding of overseas research for government agencies, but was intended to calm fears that civilian authorities had lost their grip on the direction of the U.S. military.[18])

On the very day Camelot was canceled, the Subcommittee on International Organizations and Movements of the House Committee on Foreign Affairs convened hearings intended to get to the bottom of the scandal.[19] The testimony of army and SORO bureaucrats made it clear that they saw Camelot as a logical continuation of behavioral experts' role in World War II, Korea, and in a wide spectrum of intelligence agencies, such as the OSS and the CIA. They reiterated that, as far as they were concerned, "the U.S. Army has an important mission in the positive and constructive aspect of nation building as well as a responsibility to assist friendly governments in dealing with active insurgency problems."[20] Obviously, they had absorbed the mainstream social scientific view that militaries were the leading edge of the modernization process.

Military planners pinned the blame for Camelot's cancellation on either communist distortions or bureaucratic rivalries between the Departments of Defense (DOD) and State (DOS). While they realized that Camelot-like projects would have to be handled more discreetly in the future, they were also somewhat surprised by all the fuss. In the end, Camelot could hardly have been as consequential to its military funders, who had very deep pockets, as it was to the behavioral scientists who saw it as either the crowning achievement, or failure, of their careers. Camelot's fiscal sponsors had plenty of money and behavioral science was a relative bargain. Even a multimillion dollar project, such as Camelot, was described by its military sponsors as a "feasibility study."[21] The scandal, in any case, did not put even a tiny dent into levels of DOD funding.[22]

Dante Fascell (D–Fla.), chair of the investigating subcommittee, was typical of Camelot's congressional critics. For him, the episode proved that the DOS was being bypassed on key foreign policy decisions and the DOD was all too willing to jeopardize foreign alliances in sensitive areas of the world. Fascell accused the DOD of inappropriately involving itself in nonmilitary business and concluded that behavioral science had not been at fault. Support for foreign area behavioral research was repeatedly expressed during the hearings; it was called "one of the vital tools in the arsenal of the free societies."[23]

The committee ended by chastising the DOS for not spending enough money on behavioral science (the DOS accounted for less than one percent of the federal government's total for foreign area research, according to Secretary of State Dean Rusk.)[24] Fascell's committee recommended that civilian foreign policy bureaucrats invest in a much bigger behavioral research program and that the executive branch establish an Office of the Behavioral Science Adviser to the President. In June 1966, Dante Fascell filed House bills designed to further these goals and correct civilian policy makers' relative neglect of behavioral science.

Intellectuals Debate Professional Ethics

Camelot's demise was also followed by considerable debate among intellectuals, who saw the project's significance rather differently than did its military sponsors or its congressional critics.[25] Some observed that Camelot's consequences for experts were rather surprising. The credibility of behavioral science, they suggested, survived the ordeal of the Congressional probe not only unscathed, but strengthened. As Robert Nisbet put it, "Let it be trumpeted far and wide: The federal government, starting with the subcommittee whose job it was to look into Camelot's coffin, and going all the way across town to Secretaries Rusk and McNamara, love the behavioral sciences; love them not despite but, apparently, because of their sins. . . . With the kind of luck that . . . God grants to children, fools, drunkards, and citizens of the United States of America, the behavioral sciences emerged from this potentially devastating hearing with their luster untarnished, their prestige, if anything, higher."[26] What began as a Pandora's box may have ended as a lucky break in the coming-of-age story of behavioral experts, but intellectuals themselves were divided on Camelot's lessons. Some insisted that Camelot had been an excellent opportunity to shape policy, unforgivably squandered by incompetent operators. Others wondered about the acceptability of contracts from military agencies and compared what behavioral scientists were doing for the Defense Department to the huge amounts of work being conducted under the auspices of the Department of Health, Education, and Welfare (HEW) and other domestically oriented bureaucracies by the mid-1960s. A very few, worried that researchers were being turned into the unwitting servants of power, ventured so far as to ask whether any form of federal support could be ethical.

In the end, they reached no consensus. Few participants were naive enough to defend Camelot for its basic scientific value, but many maintained their remarkable optimism about the potential of behavioral science in government. They regarded Camelot as an example of socially engaged research, even as a rare opportunity for science "to sublimate" the military's unfortunate tendency toward violence.[27] David Riesman, not a participant in Camelot himself, was not alone when he suggested that the episode proved "the top management of the Defense Department often seems to have a wider perspective on the world than its counterpart in State."[28] The next year, Gabriel Almond was still scolding DOS policy makers for their backward intellectual tastes. "They believe in making policy through some kind of intuitive and antenna-like process," Almond noted testily, "which enables them to estimate what the prospects of this and that are in this or the other country."[29]

Ithiel de Sola Pool, a political scientist who had worked with Harold Lasswell at the Library of Congress during World War II, was a key figure at the MIT Center for International Studies, which had been created to "bring to bear academic research on issues of public policy."[30] De Sola Pool was probably the most enthusiastic proponent of a purportedly "humanizing" alliance between social science and government, writing that "They [the social sciences] have the same relationship to the training of mandarins of the twentieth century that the humanities have always had to the training of mandarins in the past. . . . The only hope for humane government in the future is through the extensive use of the social sciences by government."[31] Far from considering Camelot's participants to be spies, de Sola Pool went so far as to accuse its critics of "a kind of neo-McCarthyism."[32]

Neither Camelot's supporters nor its detractors were politically homogeneous, and the project cannot, therefore, be easily dismissed as a perverse brainchild of rabid cold warriors. Many, perhaps even a majority, of participants were liberal anticommunists; some were critics of U.S. involvement in Vietnam. For them, deploying the theories and techniques of behavioral science to prosecute the Cold War efficiently and nonviolently was evidence of the democratic values embedded in U.S. policy. Indeed, Camelot's critics and defenders all tended to venerate the vital and progressive role that behavioral expertise could and should play in government. The sociologist Irving Horowitz, who endorsed this position and called it the "Enlightenment Syndrome," was the most influential academic observer of the project's "life and death," "rise and fall."[33] In his articles on the subject and in the book he edited, *The Rise and Fall of Project CAMELOT* (1967) (which gathered primary documents as well as critiques), Horowitz expressed the anxieties of many intellectuals when he interpreted Camelot's cancellation as a serious attack on behavioral scientists' intellectual freedom and public contribution: "The degree to which the development of the social sciences is permitted within a nation operates as a twentieth-century index of freedom. . . . I do not think anyone can participate in social research and fail to see a high correlation of good social science and a good society."[34]

Unlike Horowitz's belief in the freedom-reflecting quality of behavioral expertise, Charles Bray and the Smithsonian's Research Group in Psychology and the Social Sciences (an immediate predecessor of Camelot), had argued that psychothechnologies were capable of application to repressive as well as benevolent ends. Awareness of the negative potentials of behavioral science was never, of course, entirely absent during the period after World War II. Bray's group followed the lead of important World War II–era figures such as the social psychologist Kurt Lewin and the sociologist and NSF administrator Harry Alpert, who, while deeply committed to a vision of behavioral scientists bringing order and enlightenment to public policy, were nevertheless alert to the danger that their wisdom could still be used for manipulative purposes. "Science gives more freedom and power to both the doctor and the murderer, to democracy and Fascism," wrote Lewin in a 1946 essay.[35] Alpert restated the message more than a decade later: "Whether the atom is used for peace or destruction, whether bacteria are mobilized for purposes of health or disease, whether knowledge of human motivations is used to provide happiness or to sell soap, are alternatives which the scientist as seeker of knowledge and truth cannot determine."[36] Such warnings seemed to lose their force under the pressure of Cold War conflicts and opportunities, at least until the antiwar movement gained the loyalty of many intellectuals in the late 1960s. During the 1950s and early 1960s, few doubts surfaced that U.S. policy makers would use behavioral expertise exclusively in the interests of freedom or justice, just as there was correspondingly little skepticism about the repressive reach of the Soviet psychological and psychiatric professions.[37]

Horowitz was among the most thoughtful commentators on Camelot and its implications at the time. His own political views were decidedly left-wing; he was, for example, a great admirer of the radical sociologist C. Wright Mills well before the New Left turned Mills into a hero. Yet Horowitz embodied many of the assumptions of the World War II worldview: for example, that intellectuals' social responsibilities included special obligations to government, even when they opposed government policies.

In the case of Camelot, Horowitz criticized Camelot contractors for their unscientific reluctance to look a gift horse in the mouth. Swallowing military objectives without question was a serious mistake for which intellectuals should, Horowitz felt, be held responsible. But he was also convinced that congressional contempt for social and behavioral science—rather than defective method or botched research design—was the real motive behind Camelot's termination. He regarded the whole affair—particularly Johnson's memo requiring new clearance procedures for foreign area research—to be "a gross violation of the autonomous nature of science."[38] For Horowitz, Camelot's unhappy end threatened the fragile hold that behavioral expertise had on public policy. He chose to emphasize the virtues of socially engaged intellectuals over their ideological sins. They were, after all, at least trying to survive as the voice of reason in an unreasonable political system.

Some intellectuals on the left, such as the social psychologist Herbert Kelman, were more willing than Horowitz to concede that behavioral research could serve repressive ends, that "even under the most favorable conditions manipulation of the behavior of others is an ethically ambiguous act."[39] Yet Kelman, too, maintained that psychological expertise was a prerequisite for democratic policy and that it could and should be a profoundly "constructive and liberating force" in U.S. public life.[40] Overcoming all the negatives required insuring that psychological research would proceed uncontaminated by mundane political considerations and that experts would be able to do their work autonomously and in the spirit of international scientific cooperation.

Horowitz and Kelman were only two of the canceled project's public critics in the social sciences and psychology. The questions they raised about the ethical values and social responsibilities of behavioral scientists, and the relationship of research to government policy, were both timely and sincere. It does not detract from the validity of their critique to point out that they were also self-interested. Few voices were heard, one notes, calling for a halt to government-funded research. Dismay about Camelot did not alter the conviction, widespread among behavioral scientists across the political spectrum, that such research should be continued, and preferably expanded.

The belief that science required complete political independence in order to generate positive results was entirely compatible with insistence that whatever controls over socially useful research were needed should be retained by the professionals themselves. Keeping the material and status benefits of government research contracts while expanding the authority of experts over the conditions and applications of their work was part of the ongoing, successful bargaining process that marked the public history of psychological expertise in the decades after World War II. Because experts whose political views led them to disagree about everything else (the Vietnam War, for example) could still agree about this, practically no ground was lost in the fight for government research support. Considering the international proportions of the Camelot scandal, this was a remarkable feat.

For historical and practical reasons, the few criticisms of Camelot that questioned the very foundations of the behavioral science–government bond tended to be voiced by cultural anthropologists. Their discipline, inextricably bound to the establishment of global empires by European states, had been shaken by espionage charges earlier in the century. In 1919, Columbia University's Franz Boas accused four anthropologists of "prostitut[ing] science by using it as a cover for their activities as spies" during World War I.[41] Even though his campaign to bring sanctions against them was outvoted in the American Anthropological Association (AAA), the discipline carried the burden of its imperial heritage uncomfortably; anthropological work sensitized scholars to the impact of Western rule on the underdeveloped world. Moreover, anthropology depended more heavily than any of the other disciplines on foreign field opportunities, and these could readily evaporate if foreign authorities doubted the sincerity of researchers' scientific intentions.

After Camelot, the AAA appointed a Committee on Research Problems and Ethics, sponsored a wide-ranging inquiry into the responsibilities of social scientists, and strongly urged other behavioral science organizations to do the same. The AAA adopted a series of resolutions such as the following: "Constraint, deception, and secrecy have no place in science. . . . Academic institutions and individual members of the academic community, including students, should scrupulously avoid both involvement in clandestine intelligence activities and the use of the name of anthropology, or the title of anthropologist, as a cover for intelligence activities."[42] The anthropologists were not, however, entirely certain about how either "science" or "intelligence" should be defined. Ralph Beals, one of those most concerned with the negative consequences of Project Camelot for the profession, was also aware that the CIA extracted most of its information from civilian research. He was forced to conclude that "today there is practically no information that may not, under some circumstances, have military significance."[43]

That this dilemma represented something more than a definitional problem was well illustrated when the alarm over Camelot in 1964 escalated into a tidal wave of shock over revelations of CIA involvement in academic life in the years that followed.[44] Advocates of an "engaged anthropology" gained momentum from news about colleagues' secret activities, as they did from the gathering strength of the antiwar movement, and young leftists formed professional groups like Anthropologists for Radical Political Action.[45] The anthropological establishment reacted publicly, too, stepping up its campaign to erect impermeable barriers between legitimate intellectual work and cloak-and-dagger intelligence gathering. The difference between the two, however, was far less obvious than caricatured images of scientists and spies would suggest, as they well knew.

As if to underscore the enduring confusion between research and espionage, antiwar activists brought evidence of counterinsurgency activities by social scientists to members of the AAA's Committee on Research Problems and Ethics in 1970, five years after Camelot had been put to rest. The Student Mobilization Committee to End the War in Vietnam documented numerous instances of cooperation between anthropologists and the U.S. military, including a counterinsurgency project in Thailand run by the American Institutes for Research (an organizational descendent of SORO) and the Center for Research in Social Systems, (CRESS), which had superseded SORO at the American University in 1966. In spite of the AAA's formal position that an unbridgeable gulf ought to exist between covert activities and anthropological field work, the two committee members who went public with this information (Eric Wolf and Joseph Jorgensen) were reprimanded by the AAA for acting outside the bounds of their authority. They finally resigned in protest.[46]

Aftermath: Direct Consequences

After Camelot, Hugo Nutini, the consultant whose lie had led to Camelot's initial exposure, was banned from returning to Chile. The scandal's impact, however, extended well beyond his case. Many foreign governments devised restrictions to prevent U.S. meddling and, in a few cases, even slammed the door shut entirely on U.S. researchers.[47] U.S. academics worried that "the natives will all say you're working for the CIA," regardless of what the facts of research sponsorship and design actually were.[48]

Still, remarkably little about behavioral science funding or design changed after Camelot was canceled. A similar project was uncovered in Brazil less than two weeks after the Chilean scandal broke, and others were soon launched in Colombia (Project Simpatico) and Peru (Operation Task). Each was sponsored by SORO and funded by the DOD, exactly as Camelot had been.[49] Project Agile, a study of Vietnamese National Liberation Front (NLF) members' motivation, the attitudes of villagers, and communication patterns among South Vietnamese troops, was carried out in the years after Camelot's demise, as were studies of the "Potential for Internal Conflict in Latin America."[50] Whatever objections existed to such activities were clearly ineffective and did not interfere with the completion of the research. A confidential DOD memo written five weeks after Camelot's cancellation simply stated that counterinsurgency research involving foreign areas was "highly sensitive" and "must be treated in such a way that offense to foreign governments and propaganda advantage to the communist apparatus are avoided."[51] Four years later, the DOD admitted that not a single one of its social or behavioral science projects, or for that matter anything at all involving foreign area work, had been terminated in the years after Camelot's exposure.[52]

Two years after Camelot was canceled, the officers of most major behavioral science organizations gave their blessings to defense research in a congressional hearing on that topic. Arthur Brayfield, the director of the American Psychological Association (APA), had this to say: "I think the military should be free to use all reasonable, ethical, and competent tools at its command to help carry out its mission, and I would say strongly that the use of behavioral science and behavioral scientists is one of those useful tools."[53] Such endorsements were qualified by warnings that it would be wise to pay closer attention to appearances in the future since it was inevitable that someone, somewhere, would always label behavioral research sensitive and accuse behavioral experts of being surreptitious manipulators.

Some visionary advocates tried to turn Camelot's negative

public relations impact into a plus by arguing that the behavioral sciences deserved a federal foundation of their own and should no longer have to rely on the largesse of the military because of their secondary status in the NSF. "Senator for Science" Fred Harris (D–Okla.) led a movement in Congress in 1967 to establish a National Social Science Foundation. He agreed with Dante Fascell that foreign area research, in particular, needed to be "civilianized." Harris pointed to Camelot as a turning point in his own thinking on the matter, but he often employed the shining example of World War II behavioral experts to make his case for the importance of social research in government.

Although Harris's battle for a separate foundation was ultimately lost, it appears that the social sciences won their funding war with the federal government during the 1960s.[54] In 1968, President Johnson signed a bill amending the NSF's founding legislation and granting social science the formal status it initially lacked as part of the NSF mandate. Throughout the 1960s, the NSF steadily increased the proportion of its budget devoted to social science and tilted its priorities toward the applied research with which social science was commonly associated.[55]

Barely affected by Camelot's immediate fallout, the DOD nevertheless took a number of steps to shine up its tarnished image in the academic world after Camelot, and by the end of the decade such efforts were calculated as much to counteract storms of student antiwar protest as to dispel the doubts of hesitant faculty members. For example, in 1967 the DOD launched Project Themis, a program designed to encourage increasingly skeptical universities to consider the advantages of putting social and behavioral scientists to work for the DOD, and improving the caliber of those who did. In its first year alone, Themis doled out $20 million worth of support; the budget for its third year was projected at almost twice that.[56]

The Defense Science Board, the DOD's highest ranking advisory group, also convened in the wake of Camelot to mend the tattered relationship between Defense and academic experts. Its members, eager to bury for good the uncomfortable questions that Camelot had raised, issued a report that took as axiomatic the view that intellectuals' obligation to serve their society and work for federal government agencies were one and the same.[57] The report did not even consider the consequences, ethical or otherwise, of the specific military requirements and purposes of DOD behavioral science research. Instead, it concluded that, "The DoD mission now embraces problems and responsibilities which have not previously been assigned to a military establishment. It has been properly stated that the DoD must now wage not only warfare but "peacefare," as well. Pacification assistance and the battle of ideas are major segments of the DoD responsibility. The social and behavioral sciences constitute the unique resource for support of these new requirements and must be vigorously pursued if our operations are to be effective."[58]

Over the next decade, the Vietnam War put great pressure on the military to wage "peacefare." Behavioral research and its operational, "psychological warfare" counterpart remained in high demand partly because that war illustrated so dramatically the failure of great military might in the absence of basic cultural and political comprehension. Vietnam "sykewarriors" simply replicated, on a grander scale, many of the techniques used during World War II. In a typical month in 1969, 713 million leaflets were dropped from the air and two thousand hours of propaganda were broadcast—all to encourage NLF defections.[59]

Other Vietnam-era studies reflected the evolution of psychological expertise since 1945. General Westmoreland demanded repeated studies of NLF psychology. He got them, pronounced them invaluable, and made them required reading for his staff.[60] The most renowned of the Vietnam motivation and morale studies, and surely among the most elaborate field studies on revolutionaries and the revolutionary process, were those conducted by the RAND Corporation between 1964 and 1969.[61] Apparently not at all affected by the Camelot scandal, the Viet-Cong Motivation and Morale Project (VC M&M) outlasted its original conception as a six-month pilot study in 1964, and became more secure and ambitious as the 1960s wore on. A classified project that studied prisoners, defectors, and refugees, sixty-two thousand pages of interviews were finally made public in 1972.

VC M&M was a classic example, during the Vietnam era, of the axiom about bureaucratic survival and expertise that policy makers had learned during World War II: the government uses social science the way a drunk uses a lamp post, for support rather than for light.[62] Its authors' conclusions—that the enemy was near the breaking point and that heavy bombing would quickly end the conflict—told the policy makers exactly what they wanted to hear in 1965, the precise moment of military escalation. And there is quite a bit of evidence that policy makers were paying close attention to the findings of VC M&M, rewarding the project's researchers for their good efforts with a 100 percent increase in funding in 1966.[63]

The light-at-the-end-of-the-tunnel mentality would, of course, come to seem tragically misguided later on. One of the project's own staff members would go so far as to call it "a whitewash of genocide."[64] The RAND studies nevertheless illustrated how politically useful psychological intelligence was to the policy making process, even when it was entirely wrong.

The Progress of Cold War Psychology

In retrospect, it seems clear that policy oriented behavioral expertise was neither fragile at the time of Camelot nor seriously jeopardized by the outcome of the scandal. In 1966, SORO, Camelot's sponsoring organization, reconstituted itself as the Center for Research in Social Systems (CRESS) and continued, under its new name, to provide the army with detailed information about the Third World. The name change was virtually the only change. Camelot's spirit lived on. Its outlines continued to inform the work of CRESS and other research organizations long after 1965. A number of subsequent studies bore more than a passing resemblance to the shelved project.

A three-volume CRESS study, *Challenge and Response in Internal Conflict* (1968), provides some clues about what Camelot might have looked like had it been completed. Like Camelot, it was launched in 1963 under the watchful eyes of SORO's director, Theodore Vallance. Its purpose was to provide the army with an "institutional memory bank" that could guide counterinsurgency planning. Although its authors declined to evaluate the specific military purposes to which their research might be put because "counterinsurgency might be undertaken by either 'good' or 'bad' governments in an assortment of 'good' and 'bad' ways," they were quite certain that U.S. counterinsurgency efforts always assisted morally virtuous and popular regimes.[65] The finished product encompassed the work of forty-five experts from fourteen universities, detailed fifty-seven cases of twentieth-century insurgencies (twenty-nine since World War II), and literally covered the globe.

CRESS also produced a number of Camelot-like behavioral studies spotlighting the Vietnamese insurgency.[66] One, *Human Factor Considerations of Undergrounds in Insurgencies,* surveyed twenty-four postwar cases, but an analysis of National Liberation Front psychology was its centerpiece. In their effort to understand why normally law-abiding individuals were drawn into the orbit of revolutionary movements, the psychologists Andrew Molnar, Jerry Tinker, and John LeNoir emphasized all the basic social psychological factors that had been identified as key variables as early as World War II: group membership and cohesiveness, patterns of leadership, the advantage of emotional over rational appeals.[67] Like their predecessors in World War II–era psychology, they placed the individual firmly at the center of inquiries into social and political phenomena.

The study also featured a developmental stage model of the revolutionary process, based on the claims of crowd psychology, very much like the one Rex Hopper had outlined in 1950.[68] It concluded with the familiar theme that the best counterinsurgency strategy was preventive treatment. But when nipping upheavals in the bud was impossible, as was the case in Vietnam, soldiers should be trained as "agents of pacification." They should be made into admirable models of civic action, engaged in the necessary work of building roads and bridges and, at the same time, capable of coercively channeling popular frustrations into the "catharsis" provided by loyalty to the existing government.[69]

Many CRESS studies considered the frustration of personal needs an adequate and convincing explanation for revolutionary upheaval—a theory that was in many respects an extension of yet another strand of World War II–era psychological warfare. One sophisticated 1969 survey, subcontracted by CRESS to the Princeton Center for International Studies, began by noting that: "It seems obvious that most riots and revolutions are made by angry men, not dispassionate ones, and that the more intense their anger, the more destructive their actions are likely to be. . . . [M]ost human aggression occurs as a response to frustration."[70]

Ironically, Camelot's spirit was destined to have its most lethal reincarnation in Chile, the country where it had been exposed, but which had never been one of its intended targets of research. In 1973, almost a decade after Camelot was canceled, its mark could be seen in the secret, CIA- sponsored coup against the socialist-leaning government of Salvador Allende.

The connection came through Abt Associates, a research organization located in Cambridge, Massachusetts, whose president, Clark Abt, had been one of Camelot's consultants. In 1965, the DOD's Advanced Research Projects Agency (ARPA) contracted with Abt to design a computer simulation game to be used for monitoring internal war in Latin America. Except for the addition of sophisticated computer technology, Camelot's goal remained intact. Dubbed "Politica," the game was first loaded with data about hundreds of social psychological variables in a given country: degree of group cohesiveness, levels of self-esteem, attitudes toward authority, and so on. Then it would "highlight those variables decisive for the description, indication, prediction, and control of internal revolutionary conflict."[71]

In the case of Chile, according to Daniel Del Solar, one of Politica's inventors, the game's results eventually gave the green light to policy makers who favored murdering the elected president, Salvador Allende, and toppling Chile's leftist government.[72] Politica had predicted that Chile would remain "stable" even after a military takeover and the president's death. The character of this stability was in time demonstrated by the post-coup regime in the form of mass arrests, thousands of political murders and disappearances, and a series of economic "adjustments" targeting the poorer two-thirds of Chile's population. Politica proved to be as useful to the planners of military and covert action as had been the RAND study of VC M&M, and more accurate.

Precisely because it was a fiasco, Camelot's story illustrates the stamina of the World War II and early Cold War worldview in the face of a significant challenge. It helps to explain the political distance that behavioral science—and psychology in particular— had traveled in the twenty years between 1945 and 1965, and the intimate links that had been forged among psychology's diverse public uses. By 1965, a majority of elected officials and top policy makers thought they understood why "we have psychiatrists and psychologists running out of our ears in this Government of ours today."[73] With regular prodding from the experts, they proclaimed that behavioral scholarship was indispensable to foreign and military policy. In Camelot's case, the aggressive political deployment of psychological expertise was effectively obscured through psychology's old scientific and new theraputic reputation.

Ironically, the government's decision to cancel Camelot (while continuing analogous projects in Brazil, Peru, and other countries) can be traced in part to psychologists' claims that their knowledge about human societies should be considered to be neutral technology or basic research, even when they were working under contract to military or intelligence agencies with clear political missions.[74] As of 1965, the legacy of George Lundberg's classic formulation of social scientists' expertise and objectivity— the ability "to predict with high probability the social weather, just as meteorologists predict sunshine and storm,"[75] as he put it—still remained relatively secure. Its rhetoric had up till then provided considerable social and scientific legitimacy to the behavioral sciences. Camelot's antiseptic language often emphasized the allegedly apolitical character of behavioral science, by referring, for example, to creating an "insurgency prophylaxis" rather than a counter-revolution.[76]

But the public's growing experience with Cold War politics and clandestine operations was taking a toll on those myths, notwithstanding the many layers of mediation that tended to protect them. Once the spotlight of public attention focused on Camelot, its supporters found themselves in the awkward position such that defending Camelot's *military utility* tended to undermine the profession's claims of *objectivity and social responsibility,* and vice versa. In the end, both polls of thought found it easier to kill the project and procede secretly rather than defend a position that had beome untenable.

One of Camelot's lessons was that even a significant international scandal, which in an earlier period might have elicited much debate about the proper relationship between knowledge and power, did not noticeably interrupt psychology's political progress. The heated debate among intellectuals that followed the project's cancellation revealed more about the insecurities felt by a group of intellectuals new to power than it did about any serious threat to their public status. Many of the official architects of the Vietnam War, after all—policy makers such as McGeorge Bundy, Robert McNamara, and Walt Rostow—were the very models of the new "mandarins" de Sola Pool had so hopefully proclaimed to be the vanguard of a humanistic future.[77]

They, along with the researchers put to work on Cold War projects like Camelot, generally had politically liberal, behaviorally-oriented educational backgrounds. They had dutifully absorbed the lessons of recent wars, hot and cold: that political passions, ideas such as freedom, and military conflicts were contaminated by toxic emotions in need of immediate treatment and firm containment. They studied the chaotic compound known as "national character," subsequently renamed "political culture," in hopes of producing effective management techniques. For the Cold War generation, "population control," the calculated shaping of behavior at home and abroad, was both a realistic and responsible goal. (This use of the term "population control" should not be confused with the global family planning programs it has frequently denoted since the 1960s.) Prediction and control via behavioral management was the enduring refrain of World War II–era experts, and it was constantly reiterated during the years that followed 1945. According to the morale specialist Rensis Likert, "The important problems of our times concern human behaviour. . . . Problems of human behaviour underlie each of the many kinds of organized group effort on which nations are becoming increasingly dependent. . . . The larger social problems of nations and of the world also involve human behaviour."[78] Cold War managers were, after all, charged with nothing less than overseeing the awful dangers of superpower conflict. Because they saw themselves as strategists involved in a global "Minds Race," the very future of the planet seemed to depend on how well they could stabilize the emotional and behavioral disorder caused by aggression, fear, self-interest, primitive loyalties, and the ever-present human quest for security, which took so many irrational forms. Is it any wonder, in the face of such imposing emotional obstacles during the postwar decades, that one of the most famous psychologists in the United States—B. F. Skinner—would reject individual autonomy and suggest that psychology's biggest challenge was to move "beyond freedom and dignity?" Skinner defined his profession's toughest problem as follows: "to induce people not to be good but to behave well."[79]

As the years wore on, the booming postwar economy would slow and the quagmire of U.S. policy in Vietnam would become more obvious and elicit more protest. Cold War psychology, one product of the World War II worldview, would later come to be more seriously challenged than it was as the moment of Camelot's exposure.[80] By the end of the decade, even Harold Lasswell, the very embodiment of World War II—era faith in psychological expertise, was expressing grave doubts about the enlightening potential of scientific expertise. "If the earlier promise [of science] was that knowledge would make men free, the contemporary reality seems to be that more men are manipulated without their consent for more purposes by more techniques by fewer men than at any time in history."[81] By the time Lasswell spoke these discouraging words at the 1969 APA meetings, psychological experts had long since found secure new homes and enthusiastic new sponsors in federal bureaucracies devoted to cleaning up U.S. domestic social problems.[82] Total federal expenditures on the "psychological sciences" steadily increased throughout most of the 1960s, from $38.2 million in fiscal year 1960 to a high of $158 million in fiscal year 1967.[83] While the source of most of the funds did shift decisively from the DOD to HEW early in the decade, defense-related research spending never dipped. Camelot had little impact on the financial resources the military made available to psychological experts.

Similarly, in 1965, intellectuals of the sort involved in Camelot had not yet been redefined in the eyes of some of their colleagues and students as a repressive "secular priesthood," as Noam Chomsky put it, whose job it was "to ensure that the people's voice speaks the right words."[84] Eventually, the antiwar movement would convert many Americans to views directly opposed to the World War II worldview. With a civilian population sharply divided on the merits of U.S. involvement in Vietnam, it became possible to think that psychology (and other varieties of expertise) helped the state maintain ideological control over a potentially unruly population, shielded a murderous foreign policy from public view, and "manufactured consent" by insisting that U.S. motives were pure and its power legitimate.

The notion that mercenary experts were reinforcing U.S. dominance around the world in hopes of gaining status for themselves was a far cry from the World War II image of exemplary citizen-intellectuals putting their social responsibility on display by going to work for the government. In 1972, Margaret Mead, compelled by the idea of a "generation gap" and exceptionally receptive to the ideas of young people, admitted as much when she reflected on what her own wartime activities had taught her: "that psychological warfare rebounded on those who perpetrated it, destroyed trust and simply prepared for later trouble — discoveries which the young radicals were to make over again in the 1960s but about which we had no doubt in the late 1940s."[85]

When Camelot unfolded, however, most of the antiwar movement's history (including the partial takeover of the 1969 APA conference by antiwar activists) still lay in the future.[86] The teach-in movement, which did so much to expose the military-industrial-*academic* complex, was just getting off the ground with novel, all-night gatherings on the campus of the University of Michigan in Ann Arbor. The ideological beliefs of the World War II and early Cold War generation were still, for the most part, quite solid. Momentous conflicts seemed to exist between good and evil. A U.S.-style republic seemed infinitely superior to any political alternative. And government could be trusted to use the power of science responsibly.

For a brief moment in the early 1960s, the dreams inspired by World War II psychological operations seemed to have come true. Psychological experts were no longer required to prove the benefits they brought to the military and foreign policy elites — a task they had been forced to perform in earlier years. The political benefits of psychology had become, for the moment at least, seemingly self-evident, while its ideology remained largely invisible. Society had become the patient. Psychology had become the cure.

Notes

1. C. Wright Mills, *White Collar: The American Middle Classes* (New York: Oxford University Press, 1951), p. xx.

2. John G. Darley, "Contract Sup-port of Research in Psychology," *American Psychologist* 7 (December 1952), p. 719.

3. This phrase was used by Theodore Vallance, the director

of Project Camelot's sponsoring organization, the Special Operations Research Office (SORO) at the American University. See Theodore R. Vallance, "Psychological Aspects of Social Change Mediated Through the Interaction of Military Systems of Two Cultures," in U.S. Army Behavioral Science Research Laboratory, *Technical Report S-1, Psychological Research in National Defense Today* (June 1967), p. 314. Vallance presented this material (which was not published until 1967) as a talk at the September 1964 meetings of the American Psychological Association, before Camelot was canceled.

4. Department of the Army, *Psychological Operations,* Department of the Army Field Manual, FM 33-5 (Washington, D.C.: Dept. of the Army, January 1962), p. I.

5. Darley, "Contract Support of Research in Psychology," p. 720. On the institutionalization and scope of psychological research for the military in the immediate postwar period, see Lyle H. Lanier, "The Psychological and Social Sciences in the National Military Establishment," *American Psychologist* 4 (May 1949), pp. 127–47.

The critical postwar role of DOD funding has been more widely acknowledged by historians of the physical sciences than is the case in the history of psychology, probably because the sums involved and absence of other public sources of support were even more dramatic. See Paul Forman, "Behind

Quantum Electronics: National Security as Basis for Physical Research in the United States, 1940–1960," *Historical Studies in the Physical and Biological Sciences* 18 (1987), pp. 149–229.

6. For a fuller account of psychology's Cold War career, see Ellen Herman, *The Romance of American Psychology: Political Culture in the Age of Experts* (Berkeley: University of California Press, 1995), chap. 5.

7. Ralph Beals, *Politics of Social Research: An Inquiry into the Ethics and Responsibilities of Social Scientists* (Chicago: Aldine, 1969), p. 18.

8. Irving Louis Horowitz, ed., *The Rise and Fall of Project Camelot: Studies in the Relationship Between Social Science and Practical Politics* (Cambridge, Mass.: MIT Press, 1967), p. 47.

9. Excerpt from Theodore Vallance's congressional testimony, reprinted in "Testimony Before House Subcommittee on International Organizations and Movements of the Committee on Foreign Affairs, July 8, 1965," *American Psychologist* 21 (May 1966), p. 469. (Subcommittee on International Organizations and Movements of the House Committee on Foreign Affairs, *Behavioral Sciences and the National Security,* Report No. 4, Together With Part IX of the "hearings on Winning the Cold War: The U.S. Ideological Offensive," 89th Cong., 2nd sess., H.R. Report 1224, testimony of Theodore Vallance, director of SORO, p. 20.)

10. Subcommittee on International Organizations and Movements of the House Committee on Foreign Affairs, *Behavioral Sciences and the National Security,* testimony of Lt. Gen. W. W. Dick Jr., chief of research and development, Department of the Army, p. 28.

11. Charles William Bray, *Psychology and Military Proficiency: A History of the Applied Psychology Panel of the National Defense Research Committee* (Princeton, N.J.: Princeton University Press, 1948), p. 171.

12. Charles Windle and Theodore R. Vallance, "The Future of Military Psychology: Paramilitary Psychology," *American Psychologist* 19 (February 1964), p. 128. See also Theodore R. Vallance and Charles D. Windle, "Cultural Engineering," *Military Review* 42 (December 1962), pp. 60–64.

13. Theodore R. Vallance, "Project Camelot: An Interim Postlude," *American Psychologist* 21 (May 1966), p. 441, emphasis in original.

14. For a detailed chronology of Camelot's projected research, see Subcommittee on International Organizations and Movements of the House Committee on Foreign Affairs, *Behavioral Sciences and the National Security,* testimony of Lt. Gen. W. W. Dick Jr., pp. 30–32.

15. Ibid., p. 32.

16. Irving Louis Horowitz, "The Life and Death of Project Camelot," *American Psychologist* 21 (May 1966), p. 452; Horowitz, *The Rise and Fall of Project Camelot,* p. 27.

17. Aniceto Rodriguez, "A Socialist Commentary on Camelot," in Horowitz, *The Rise and Fall of Project Camelot,* p. 229.

18. See the review of federally sponsored research in the year immediately after Camelot's exposure in Subcommittee on Government Research of the Senate Committee on Government Operations, "Hearings on Federal Support of International Social Science and Behavioral Research," June–July 1966, 89th Cong., 2nd sess. In these hearings, Thomas L. Hughes, director of intelligence and research, Department of State, noted that many projects similar to Camelot had in fact been classified and these, obviously, never came to public attention. For a list of classified projects in military psychology during this period, see Peter Watson, *War on the Mind: The Military Uses and Abuses of Psychology* (New York: Penguin, 1980), p. 30.

    Later, Hughes declared that the futility of structural reform, such as that mandated by Johnson's memo, was an inevitable product of the confusing relationship between objective expertise and policy making, unequal experts and policy makers, and the unpredictability of human personality in general: "[I]t is the human variables that defy the jurisdictional reforms, mock the machinery of government and frustrate the organizational tinkering. These are the phenomena that help assure that no rejuggling of administrative charts can finally surmount the uneven qualities of the men who inhabit the institutions. The human material, much as the institutional framework, will in the end determine whether intelligence and policy, either or both, have feet of clay" (Thomas L. Hughes, "The Fate of Facts in a World of Men: Foreign Policy and Intelligence-Making," *Headline Series*, no. 233 [New York: Foreign Policy Association, December 1976], p. 60).

19. Howard Margolis, "McNamara Ax Dooms Camelot," *Washington Post*, July 9, 1965, p. B6.

20. December 4, 1964, description sent by SORO to scholars in Camelot, quoted in Horowitz, *The Rise and Fall of Project Camelot*, p. 48.

21. The term "feasibility" was used in Camelot's own documents, and the project was described as a "feasibility study" by SORO's director, Theodore Vallance, in his "Project Camelot," p. 442.

22. The total DOD budget for behavioral and social science research was $27.3 million in 1965, when Camelot was exposed. In 1966, the figure had reached $34 million and it was almost $50 million in 1970. See Subcommittee on International Organizations and Movements of the House Committee on Foreign Affairs, *Behavioral Sciences and the National Security*, p. 97, and Michael T. Klare, *War Without End: American Planning for the Next Vietnams* (New York: Knopf, 1972), p. 373, app. C.

23. Subcommittee on International Organizations and Movements of the House Committee on Foreign Affairs, *Behavioral Sciences and the National Security*, p. 5R.

24. Subcommittee on International Organizations and Movements of the House Committee on Foreign Affairs, *Behavioral Sciences and the National Security*, p. 6R and testimony of Dean Rusk, secretary of state, p. 108.

25. The most useful single source on the response to Camelot among social and behavioral scientists is Horowitz, *The Rise and Fall of Project Camelot*. See also his "The Life and Death of Project Camelot," pp. 445–54, reprinted from *Trans-action* (1965), pp. 3–7 and 44–47.

26. Robert A. Nisbet, "Project Camelot and the Science of Man," in Horowitz, *The Rise and Fall of Project Camelot*, pp. 316 and 323. See also Nisbet's "Project Camelot: An Autopsy," in *On Intellectuals: Theoretical Studies/Case Studies*, ed. Philip Rieff (New York: Anchor, 1970), pp. 307–39.

27. Horowitz, "The Life and Death of Project Camelot," p. 448. See also Robert Boguslaw, "Ethics and the Social Scientist," in Horowitz, *The Rise and Fall of Project Camelot*, pp. 107–27. Of all the experts involved in Camelot, Boguslaw defended most strongly the noble motive—"to find nonmilitary and nonviolent solutions to international problems."

28. "Feedback from Our Readers," *Trans-action* 3 (January–February 1966), p. 2. For another statement of the view that

the U.S. military's patronage of behavioral science demonstrated more enlightenment than was evident in civilian government agencies, see George E. Lowe, "The Camelot Affair," *Bulletin of the Atomic Scientists* 22 (May 1966), p. 48.

29. Gabriel Almond, testimony before the 1966 congressional hearings on "Federal Support of International Social Science and Behavioral Research," quoted in *Social Scientists and International Affairs: A Case for a Sociology of Social Science*, eds. Elisabeth T. Crawford and Albert D. Biderman (New York: John Wiley and Sons, 1969), p. 243.

30. Walt Rostow, quoted in Allan A. Needell, "'Truth Is Our Weapon': Project TROY, Political Warfare, and Government-Academic Relations in the National Security State," *Diplomatic History* 17 (summer 1993), p. 417. For more on the center's CIA ties, and for the role of the new intelligence community in supporting research on mass communication, see Christopher Simpson, *Science of Coercion* (New York: Oxford University Press, 1994), pp. 53–54, 81–84, 89–90.

31. Ithiel de Sola Pool, "The Necessity for Social Scientists Doing Research for Governments," in Horowitz, *The Rise and Fall of Project Camelot*, pp. 267–68.

32. De Sola Pool, "The Necessity for Social Scientists Doing Research for Governments," p. 277.

33. Horowitz, *The Rise and Fall of Project Camelot*, p. 7.

34. Irving Louis Horowitz, "Social Science and Public Policy: Implications of Modern Research," in *The Rise and Fall of Project Camelot*, p. 341.

35. Kurt Lewin, "Action Research and Minority Group Problems," in *Resolving Social Conflicts: Selected Papers on Group Dynamics* (New York: Harper and Brothers, 1948), p. 213.

36. Harry Alpert, "Congressmen, Social Scientists, and Attitudes Toward Federal Support of Social Science Research," *American Sociological Review* 23 (December 1958), p. 685.

37. For a concise statement of this position, see Daniel Lerner, "Social Science: Whence and Whither?" in *The Human Meaning of the Social Sciences*, ed. Daniel Lerner (New York: Meridian, 1959), pp. 13–39.

38. Horowitz, "The Life and Death of Project Camelot," p. 454; Irving Louis Horowitz, "The Rise and Fall of Project Camelot," in *The Rise and Fall of Project Camelot*, p. 40.

39. Herbert C. Kelman, "Manipulation of Human Behavior: An Ethical Dilemma," in *A Time to Speak: On Human Values and Social Research* (San Fransisco: Jossey-Bass, 1968), p. 16.

40. Herbert C. Kelman, "The Social Consequences of Social Research," in *A Time to Speak: On Human Values and Social Research*, p. 33.

41. Franz Boas, "Scientists as Spies" (1919 letter to *The Nation*), reprinted in this volume. See also the reference to this episode in Beals, *Politics of Social Research*, p. 51.

42. "Statement on Problems of Anthropological Research and Ethics," in Beals, *Politics of Social Research*, pp. 193 and 195–96. Beals' *Politics of Social Research* was based on the report he did under AAA auspices in the aftermath of Camelot. For the original text of the report, see "Background Information on Problems of Anthropological Research and Ethics," *American Anthropological Association Newsletter* 8 (January 1967). See also Stephen T. Boggs's and Ralph L. Beals's testimony in Subcommittee on Government Research of the Senate Committee on Government Operations, "Hearings on Federal Support of International Social Science and Behavioral Research," pp. 72–93; Bryce Nelson, "Anthropologists' Debate: Concern Over Future of Foreign Research," *Science* 154 (Dec. 23, 1966), pp. 1525–27.

43. Beals, *Politics of Social Research*, p. 78.

44. See, for example, the testimony of Stephen T. Boggs, AAA executive secretary, in Subcommittee on Government Research of the Senate Committee on Government Operations, "Hearings on Federal Support of International Social Science and Behavioral Research," pp. 72–77. He discusses, among other things, anthropologists' deep concerns over the revelations of a CIA-funded project on Vietnam at Michigan State University. For more on the CIA-MSU connection, see Max Frankl, "University Project Cloaked C.I.A. Role in Saigon, 1955–59," *New York Times*, April 14, 1966, pp. 1–2, and Warren Hinkle, "The University on the Make," *Ramparts* 4 (April 1966), pp. 11–22.

45. Personal communication, Martin Diskin, Oct. 26, 1990.

46. Eric R. Wolf and Joseph G. Jorgensen, "Anthropology on the Warpath in Thailand," *New York Review of Books* 15 (Nov. 19, 1970), pp. 26–35. For more on the debate within anthropology, see "Social Responsibilities Forum," *Current Anthropology* 9 (December 1968).

47. There were, predictably, far more restrictions erected in Latin America than in Asia or Africa, but repercussions were felt by researchers working in Burma, Nepal, Afghanistan, Iran, Pakistan, Iraq, Yemen, Saudi Arabia, Sudan, Egypt, and South Africa, among other countries. See Beals, *Politics of Social Research*, pp. 20–25. Accounts of research directly and negatively effected by Project Camelot can be found in: *American Anthropological Association Fellow Newsletter* 6 (December 1965), pp. 2–3; Elinor Langer, "Foreign Research: CIA Plus Camelot Equals Troubles for U.S. Scholars," *Science* 156 (June 23, 1967), pp. 1583–84; letter to the editor by Dale L. Johnson, *American Anthropologist* 68 (August 1966), pp. 1016–17; Kalman H. Silvert, "American Academic Ethics and Social Research Abroad: The Lesson of Project Camelot," in Horowitz, *The Rise and*

Fall of Project Camelot, pp. 81–82.

48. Gabriel Almond, at an American Political Science Association forum on Project Camelot in September 1965, quoted in Lowe, "The Camelot Affair," p. 47.

49. Horowitz, *The Rise and Fall of Project Camelot*, p. 20; Subcommittee on Government Research of the Senate Committee on Government Operations, "Hearings on Federal Support of International Social Science and Behavioral Research," p. 20; Jean Hardisty Dose, "A Social and Political Explanation of Social Science Trends: The Case of Political Development Research" (Ph.D. diss., Northwestern University, 1976), p. 197. For a senior SORO researcher's defense of Project Task as "a most uncynical and unsinister project" and complaint that the debate surrounding Camelot's demise had been dishonest and shrill, see Milton Jacobs, "L'Affaire Camelot," letter to the editor, *American Anthropologist* 69 (June–August 1967), pp. 364–66.

50. On Project Agile, see Gene M. Lyons, *The Uneasy Partnership: Social Science and the Federal Government in the Twentieth Century* (New York: Russell Sage Foundation, 1969), p. 197; Watson, *War on the Mind*, p. 319. On post-Camelot research aimed at preventing revolution in Latin America, see Senate Committee on Foreign Relations, "Hearings on Defense Department Sponsored Foreign

Affairs Research," May 1968, pts. 1–2, 90th Cong., 2nd sess., pp. 64–65.

51. Memo from Director of Defense Research and Engineering to Assistant Secretaries for Research and Development of the Army, Navy, Air Force, and the Director, Advanced Research Projects Agency, August 18, 1965, NRC Committee on Government Programs in Behavioral Sciences, Central Policy Files, National Academy of Sciences, Washington, D.C. I am indebted to Mark Solovey for sharing this document with me.

52. Senate Committee on Foreign Relations, "Hearings on Defense Department Sponsored Foreign Affairs Research," testimony of John S. Foster Jr., director of defense research and engineering, p. 93.

53. Subcommittee on Government Research of the Senate Committee on Government Operations, "Hearings on Federal Support of International Social Science and Behavioral Research," testimony of Arthur Brayfield, executive officer, American Psychological Association, p. 66.

54. Mark Solovey, "Social Science and the State during the 1960s: Senator Fred Harris's Effort to Create a National Social Science Foundation" (paper presented at "Toward a History of the 1960s," Madison, Wisconsin, April 30, 1993).

55. Subcommittee on Government Research of the Senate Committee on Government Operations, "Hearings on National Foundation for Social Sci-

ences," February, June, July
1967, 90th Cong., 1st sess., pts.
1–3. For a general discussion of
the effort to establish a separate social science foundation
and changes within the NSF
during the 1960s, see Otto N.
Larsen, *Milestones and Mill-
stones: Social Science at the National Science Foundation, 1945–
1991* (New Brunswick, N.J.:
Transaction, 1992), chap. 4.

56. Senate Committee on Foreign
Relations, "Hearings on Defense Department Sponsored
Foreign Affairs Research," pt. 1,
pp. 52–55.

57. A clear statement of this equation was offered by Milton Jacobs, a senior researcher at
SORO during the Camelot era,
who noted several years later
from a perch in academia that
"Working for the United States
Government should not suddenly become sinful. . . . I am
sure that most university professors and intellectuals, in and
out of government, feel responsibility to their society as well as
to their chosen field of endeavor. I doubt that these responsibilities need be
contradictory. If they are, our
nation is in deep trouble"
(quoted in Jacobs, "L'Affaire
Camelot," p. 366).

58. Quoted in Senate Committee
on Foreign Relations, "Hear-
ings on Defense Department
Sponsored Foreign Affairs Re-
search," p. 16; and in Klare, *War
Without End,* p. 98. For a critical
analysis of the Defense Science
Board's *Report of the Panel on
Defense Social and Behavioral
Sciences,* which treats it as evi-

dence of "the ominous conver-
sion of social science into a
service industry of the Pentagon," see Irving Louis Horowitz, "Social Science Yogis &
Military Commissars," *Trans-
action* 5 (May 1968), pp. 29–38.

59. Watson, *War on the Mind,* p.
307.

60. Senate Committee on Foreign
Relations, "Hearings on Defense Department Sponsored
Foreign Affairs Research," pt. 1,
testimony of John S. Foster Jr.,
pp. 10 and 18. See also Subcommittee on International
Organizations and Movements
of the House Committee on
Foreign Affairs, *Behavioral Sciences and the National Security,*
testimony of Maj. Gen. John W.
Vogt, director, policy planning
staff, Office of the Assistant
Secretary of Defense for International Security Affairs, pp.
81–82.

61. For a general discussion of the
evolution of these morale studies and their relationship to the
conduct of the Vietnam War,
see Watson, *War on the Mind,*
pp. 27–28, 263–67, 299–300,
326, and "The RAND Papers,"
Ramparts 11 (November 1972),
pp. 25–42 and 52–62.

62. The source of this oft-repeated
phrase appears to be Alexander
Leighton, who wrote: "The administrator uses social science
the way a drunk uses a lamp-
post, for support rather than
illumination." (See Alexander
H. Leighton, *Human Relations
in a Changing World: Observa-
tions on the Use of the Social
Sciences* [New York: E. P. Dut-
ton, 1949], p. 128.) That this

phrase had become conventional wisdom among experts and bureaucrats is illustrated by the fact that Thomas L. Hughes, director of intelligence and research, Department of State, from 1963–69, used it, without attribution, almost thirty years later in his "The Fate of Facts in a World of Men," p. 24. Leighton was a psychiatrist who worked in the Postan, Arizona, Japanese-American relocation center and then headed the Office of War Information's Foreign Morale Analysis Division, set up by the Military Intelligence Service of the War Department in 1944. Leighton and his group of behavioral scientists studied Japanese-Americans, and then Japanese citizens, by taking a "psychiatric approach in problems of community management."

63. Project head Leon Goure, for example, regularly briefed most of the war's top policy makers—Bundy, McNamara, Rostow, and Westmoreland—and the VC M&M office in Saigon was a central gathering place for high-level bureaucrats passing through South Vietnam. Carl Rowan, former head of the U.S. Information Service, also wrote in 1966 that the VC M&M "lies at the heart of President Johnson's strategy." (See "The RAND Papers," pp. 60–61.)

64. Anthony Russo, "Looking Backward: RAND and Vietnam in Retrospect," *Ramparts* 11 (November 1972), p. 56.

65. D. M. Condit, Bert H. Cooper Jr., et al., *Challenge and Response in Internal Conflict*, 3 vols. (Washington, D.C.: American University, Center for Research in Social Systems, 1968), pp. xxi and xxiii.

66. See *Annotated Bibliography of SORO Publications* (Washington, D.C.: American University, Special Operations Research Office, February 1966); *Annotated Bibliography of CRESS Publications* (Washington, D.C.: American University, Special Operations Research Office, August 1966); *Annotated Bibliography of CRESS Publications* (Washington, D.C.: American University, Special Operations Research Office, April 1969).

67. The study refers repeatedly to World War II attitude investigations, such as Samuel Stouffer's *The American Soldier.* For an example, see Andrew R. Molnar with Jerry M. Tinker and John D. LeNoir, *Human Factors Considerations of Undergrounds in Insurgencies* (Washington, D.C.: American University, Center for Research in Social Systems, 1966), p. 80.

68. Rex D. Hopper, "The Revolutionary Process: A Frame of Reference for the Study of Revolutionary Movements," *Social Forces* 28 (March 1950), pp. 270–79.

69. Molnar with Tinker and LeNoir, *Human Factors Considerations of Undergrounds in Insurgencies*, pp. 270 and 274–75.

70. Ted Gurr with Charles Ruttenberg, *Cross-National Studies in Civil Violence* (Washington, D.C.: American University, Cen-

ter for Research in Social Systems, May 1969), pp. 11–12.

71. M. Gordon et al., "COCON—counterinsurgency (POLITICA): The Development of a Simulation Model of Internal Conflict under Revolutionary Conflict Conditions," quoted in Carol Cina, "Social Science for Whom? A Structural History of Social Psychology" (Ph.D. diss., State University of New York, Stony Brook, 1981), p. 326.

72. Cina, "Social Science for Whom?, p. 331.

73. This comment was made by Iowa congressional representative H. R. Gross during the Camelot hearings. See Subcommittee on International Organizations and Movements of the House Committee on Foreign Affairs, *Behavioral Sciences and the National Security*, p. 94.

74. For an example of an ambitious, apolitical vision for psychotechnological aid to defense organizations and policy making, see Charles W. Bray, "Toward a Technology of Human Behavior for Defense Use," *American Psychologist* 17 (August 1962), pp. 527–41.

75. George A. Lundberg, *Can Science Save Us?* (New York: Longmans, Green, 1947), p. 30.

76. Horowitz, *The Rise and Fall of Project Camelot*, p. 48. For some interesting comments on the language of Camelot documents, see Marshall Sahlins, "The Established Order: Do Not Fold, Spindle, or Mutilate," in *The Rise and Fall of Project Camelot*, pp. 77–78.

77. For a portrait of these and other individuals whose commitments to a military policy informed by behavioral expertise decisively shaped the Vietnam War, see David Halberstam, *The Best and the Brightest* (New York: Penguin, 1969).

78. Rensis Likert, "Behavioural Research: A Guide for Effective Action," in *Some Applications of Behavioural Research*, eds. Rensis Likert and Samuel P. Hayes (Paris: UNESCO, 1957), p. 11.

79. Skinner's *Beyond Freedom and Dignity* analyzed the political function of psychology and made explicit recommendations for the public roles of psychological experts. B. F. Skinner, *Beyond Freedom and Dignity* (New York: Knopf, 1971), p. 67. See also B. F. Skinner, "Freedom and the Control of Men," *American Scholar* 25 (winter 1955–56), pp. 47–65.

80. For the argument that, in spite of such challenges, "the military uses of psychology have been pursued with ever more energy and increasing imagination" since the early 1960s, see Watson, *War on the Mind*.

81. Harold D. Lasswell, "Must Science Serve Political Power?" *American Psychologist* 25 (February 1970), p. 119.

82. For comparative data on levels of funding by the DOD and HEW (and other domestically oriented agencies), see National Science Foundation, *Federal Funds for Science*, 1950–62 (Washington, D.C.), followed by *Federal Funds for Research, Development, and Other Scientific Activities*, 1962–70 (Washington, D.C.).

83. National Science Foundation,

Federal Funds for Science, 1960, 1961, 1962, p. 100, table 15; *Federal Funds for Research, Development, and Other Scientific Activities: Fiscal Years 1965, 1966, and 1967,* vol. 15, p. 102, table C-13.

84. Noam Chomsky, "Intellectuals and the State," in *Towards a New Cold War: Essays on the Current Crisis and How We Got There* (New York: Pantheon, 1982), p. 65.

85. 1972 draft of *Blackberry Winter,* quoted in Virginia Yans-McLaughlin, "Science, Democracy, and Ethics: Mobilizing Culture and Personality for World War II," *History of Anthropology* 4 (1986), p. 214.

86. For a description of the conference action, see "Psychology and Campus Issues," in Frances F. Korten, Stuart W. Cook, and John I. Lacey, eds., *Psychology and the Problems of Society* (Washington, D.C.: American Psychological Association, 1970), pp. 366–76. In this instance, protest was leveled not against the foreign area research activities of psychologists, but against a research project being conducted on the student New Left itself by Alexander W. Astin and the American Council on Education.

(**Kevin Gaines**)

The Cold War and the African American Expatriate Community in Nkrumah's Ghana

In 1968, Harold Cruse's classic study, *The Crisis of the Negro Intellectual* became an immediate best-seller, capitalizing on the popular mood of militancy, Black Power, and angry disenchantment with the gradualism and limitations of the reforms achieved by the 1960s-era social contract between corporate liberalism and the civil rights establishment. Cruse's text presented itself as bolder and more radical than other approaches to African American liberation popular in black intellectual discourse of the day.

In retrospect, however, it would appear that the book's reception actually benefited at least as much from Cold War liberalism as it did from the popular mood of militancy.[1]

Cruse singled out the previous generation of black left intellectuals—Paul Robeson, W. E. B. Du Bois, Richard Wright, Lorraine Hansberry, and others—to support his contention that black militants had hitherto failed to make an independent social and historical analysis of African-American oppression within the United States. Cruse's indictment of the black left remained strikingly silent about the Cold War and the forces that shaped the African-American experience of that conflict. Instead, his book is a sustained black nationalist polemic against many of the most prominent black left intellectuals of the postwar era, whose international political outlook and support for national liberation struggles abroad, Cruse said, had led them into debilitating compromises with the white left and a new form of failed integrationism.

But as Penny Von Eschen has recently argued, the besmirched reputation of these intellectuals, and the demise of the radical anticolonial politics they espoused after World War II, were to a large degree the result of a campaign against them led by the U.S. government and Cold War liberals.[2] Julian Mayfield, the Harlem-based novelist, actor, and one of the radical internationalist intellectuals named in Cruse's indictment, castigated Cruse for pursuing personal vendettas through his "spiteful" assault on black left intellectuals. Mayfield's review of Cruse's book for *Negro Digest* provoked an acrimonious response from Cruse, unenlightening on political and ideological questions and saturated with innuendo regarding Mayfield's activities while in exile in Ghana as an adviser to its head of state, Kwame Nkrumah.[3]

This heated exchange between Mayfield and Cruse, so far removed from the catastrophic assassinations, mass protests, and challenges to the legitimacy of U.S. and Western society in 1968, has long been overshadowed by the influence Cruse's text has exerted on numerous black intellectuals. Cruse articulated a tendency, now commonplace within much of the academy, that privileged the local over the cosmopolitan. In other words, despite a growing body of critical scholarship in African American studies, the continuing insular, neonationalist preoccupations with identity and "authentic" blackness have often prevailed over a more internationalist, inclusive, and, most importantly, historical notion of black consciousness.[4] However valid Cruse's critique of the paternalism of the white-dominated left, his conflation of the *black* left internationalism of Du Bois, Robeson, and others with the suspect category of integrationism effectively consigned much of the independent black radical activist tradition to the dustbin of history, at least on American campuses. By consolidating the Cold War's marginalization of the black left in the minds of many of his readers, Cruse might well be understood as an unwitting soldier in the Cold War. Cruse's avowed commitment to historical analysis and recuperation ultimately took a back seat to his evident preoccupation with identity, which found expression in his assertion of a more authentically grounded black nationalist intellectual praxis.

Cruse's identity-driven theorizing diminished many of those artists, activists, and intellectuals whose political commitments throughout the Cold War era have contributed to their ambiguous legacies: Wright, Robeson, Hansberry, James Baldwin, Mayfield, and others (Mayfield criticizes Cruse for having little to say about W. E. B. Du Bois, and wonders why Cruse devoted considerably more space to his attack on Lorraine Hansberry than to any discussion of Du Bois). These radical intellectuals and their internationalist views, articulated in such journals as *Freedomways* and the *Liberator*, were, by Cruse's reckoning, out of touch with the needs of black communties in Harlem and the U.S. According to Cruse, "This generation [of intellectuals was] deeply impressed by the emergence of the African states, the Cuban revolution, Malcolm X and Robert Williams himself. They were witnessing a revolutionary age of the liberation of oppressed peoples. Thus they were led to connect their American situation with those foreign revolutionary situations. They did not know of course, that to attempt to apply foreign ideologies to the United States was more easily imagined than accomplished."[5]

For Cruse, then, the exile from the United States taken after World War II by Wright, Baldwin, Chester Himes, and other black writers seeking an intellectual and personal freedom unavailable in the United States under Jim Crow had been a failure. Mayfield's own flight into exile to Ghana, to escape prosecution for his involvement with Robert Williams's armed self-defense movement, was attacked by Cruse as proof of the critical cul de sac of the internationalism of both of these militants and of their purported disengagement with the struggles of African Americans for economic self-sufficiency and control of their communities.[6]

For better or worse, Cruse's book marked a turning point in black politics. With the War on Poverty then perishing in the flames of Watts and Vietnam, the assassination of Malcolm X, the implosion of the Student Nonviolent Coordinating Committee after its failed challenge to the Democratic Party's pact with Mississippi segregationists, and the overthrow of Kwame Nkrumah in February of 1966, Cruse's text signaled a decisive shift away from the internationalism that shaped the sensibilities of many black intellectuals of the 1940s and 1950s, and which once had culminated in widespread support for the expatriates' vision of a liberated Ghana.[7] Ironically, given the popularity of Cruse's call for an independent black intellectual project (and his scathing critique of white left paternalism), Cruse's assertion of the radicalism of black nationalism, with its scorn for "foreign" ideologies, was at the time widely hailed by white liberals and leftists, a reading emblematic of the American exceptionalism fashionable among liberal critics of New Left internationalism. Indeed Cruse, distortions and all, continues to be invoked by liberals as authenticating their dismissals of black left internationalism.[8]

Cruse's disparagement of internationalism as irresponsible integrationism echoed the constraints and outright dismissals imposed by the Cold War on black radical thought and politics. However valid his advocacy of black community control of economic and cultural institutions, Cruse's nationalism precluded serious consideration of independent black freedom struggles on a global scale, such as those represented by Nkrumah's Pan-Africanism, or manifested in the outrage among African American militants over the assassination of Patrice Lumumba, prime minister of the independent Congo.[9] True, Mayfield's personal stake in rebutting Cruse, through the review and in subsequent writings, was animated in part by his direct involvement in Nkrumah's Ghana from 1961 to 1965. But more fundamentally, much more was at stake in Ghana's first republic than the success or failure of a handful of radical African American intellectuals. Ghana poses historical questions about the legacy of independent black social movements and political projects, and the relationship between their domestic and global dimensions, that are unaddressed by Cruse and are still, with few exceptions, largely unexplored.[10]

Though overlooked in many Black studies programs today, Ghana and its Pan-African politics were by no means peripheral to the concerns and interests of African Americans throughout the 1950s and early 1960s. Indeed, Ghana embodied for many the very independent black left political ideals and objectives sought by Cruse himself. It would be a fallacy to brand the internationalism represented by black Americans' interest and involvement in Ghana as an integrationist retreat from black interests and communities, as Cruse did. Instead, it is crucial to recognize the centrality of race to the Cold War itself in order to appreciate the singular challenge Mayfield and the Ghana expatriates faced in defining black opposition to American racism. Mayfield and African American radicals in Ghana and in the United States contended with the U.S. government's Cold War ideology, its subordination of black struggles to East-West conflicts, and its frequently successful attempt to impose the limits of Cold War liberalism on the political discourse and tactics of many black activists and movements.[11]

On a symbolic level, at least, Nkrumah's Ghana's embodiment of black power and its proudly independent role in Cold War geopolitics briefly made this small country seem to be as immediate a threat to U.S. domestic and foreign policy as the Americans' nuclear-armed superpower rivals. The radical promise of Ghana's first republic, and its potential influence on the nature of black opposition in the United States itself, led to concerted diplomatic, economic and political U.S. government strategies for "containment" of Ghana's influence in world affairs.[12] In addition, fears of an economically independent Africa prompted the United States to attempt to prevent Nkrumah's Pan-African socialist politics from gaining adherents across the continent and spurred an intense propaganda campaign by U.S. embassies throughout Africa to counter the adverse worldwide coverage of racial oppression in the United States.

The first sub-Saharan African nation to gain its independence from colonial rule, Ghana during the 1950's and early 1960's was a magnet for radical African Americans supporting Nkrumah's politics of nonalignment, socialism, African continental unity, and revolutionary transformation. Their enthusiasm for Ghana's progress was reinforced by their frustration at the racial inequities, unredressed bloodshed, and Cold War constraints of U.S. society. Mayfield joined hundreds of African Americans, including many key intellectuals, technicians, teachers, artists, and trade unionists who left the United States for Ghana. To name only one example, Malcolm X's 1964 visit among the black expatriates in Ghana and his meeting with Nkrumah—both described at length in his posthumous autobiography—appear to have been far more significant for refining his political and social analysis of the plight of black peoples in the U.S. and Africa during the weeks that remained to him than his celebrated religious pilgrimage to Mecca.[13]

Nkrumah's overthrow in a military coup, in 1966, marked not only the demise of Ghana's leadership of struggles for economic and political independence for African peoples. It also occasioned the dispersal of many of the American expatriates, whose close political ties to Nkrumah made them suspect in the eyes of the new military regime.

Understanding Mayfield and other African American expatriates in Ghana is critical for an assessment of the impact of the Cold War on black politics and social movements. In the late 1950s and into the next decade, Mayfield joined efforts by African American intellectuals, at home and abroad, to forge an independent black radical politics. Mayfield and other activists among the Ghana expatriates worked to transform African American political identities by fostering communication between participants in domestic and international freedom struggles.

Today, the relative obscurity of Mayfield and other Ghana expatriates is a consequence of the enduring legacy of the Cold War's constraints on black thought and politics. From U.S. government controls on the freedom and mobility of African American intellectuals of the postwar period (the most notable examples being W. E. B. Du Bois, Richard Wright, and Paul Robeson) and the prosecution of anticolonial political activists, to the state-sanctioned repression against the Black Panthers, to the amnesia with regard to the internationalist arguments of Malcolm X and Martin Luther King, the persistence of that Cold War legacy is affirmed by the silence that continues to shroud it today. Mayfield and the Ghana expatriates are instructive precisely because they insisted on the inherent value of all struggles for racial and social justice, as distinct from many liberals' tendency to subordinate the domestic issue of civil rights to Cold War foreign policy imperatives. Moreover, Mayfield and his allies resisted anticommunist propaganda that portrayed domestic struggles against segregation and African nation-building projects as spearheaded by Soviet "outside agitators."[4]

Mayfield's journalistic writings from Ghana were prolific and widely circulated throughout anglophone West Africa and the United States. Nevertheless, Mayfield was unsuccessful, on his return to the States, in publishing three separate manuscripts of his analysis of Ghana under Nkrumah.[5] Although Mayfield's legacy was certainly not helped by his death in 1984, in Washington, D.C., at the age of 56, his failure to publish in the U.S. also suggests, in part, the persistence of Cold War limitations on black oppositional thought and politics.

While acknowledging the plight of those harrassed out of the country, such as Mayfield and the political philosopher Preston King,[16] exile was in many respects an enabling condition for Ghana's expatriates, yielding a critical and largely overlooked perspective on the origins and legacy of black popular movements of the 1950s and 1960s. Mayfield's unpublished accounts of his work in Ghana, read against his surviving correspondence from that period with other expatriates and colleagues back in the States, attest to the rich complexity of the expatriate experience.

The many ambiguities of their location in Ghana—being of African descent, yet socially and culturally foreign; remote from the racial controversies of the U.S. scene, yet situated at the center of international anticolonial projects; sympathetic to the politics of African liberation, yet marginal, as junior partners of Pan- Africanism, so to speak, within Nkrumah's Ghana—all provided expatriate intellectuals a unique perspective from which to reflect on events both near and distant, an outlook that was simultaneously expansive and liberating, yet constrained by their outsider status within Ghanaian political culture.

Mayfield's account of "our crowd" in Ghana offered an account of the genealogy and formation of his cohort of black intellectuals. For Mayfield, the true crisis of the Negro intellectual was defined by the pressures of U.S. racism, segregation, and Cold War hysteria:

> As Afro-Americans [in Ghana] we were testing the parameters of the Western world. Our heroes, inevitably, were . . . Paul Robeson, Malcolm X, and most of all, W.E.B. DuBois, who was still alive, and who lived just around the corner. . . . All of these men had been international in their thinking. They had recognized long ago something that we had to work out for ourselves in Ghana: That being a member of a persecuted minority in a racist nation like the United States almost automatically stunted one's psychological and intellectual growth. Minority thinking limited your vision and scaled down the demands you made on yourself, and on the nation. You asked for one school instead of the whole school system, for a town instead of a country. . . .[17]

Mayfield praised Robeson and Du Bois, who had been victims of Cold War repression for their advocacy of anticolonial struggles. For Mayfield, their radical legacy resisted the political and ideological constraints imposed on black intellectuals within the United States. Ghana, to Mayfield, heralded a revitalized global black identity, rising from the ashes of political persecution and historical erasure.

In Ghana, Mayfield defined black American identities within a dialectic of domestic and international politics. The expatriates' experiences went to the heart of the deeply politicized matter of black identity in these years. The Ghana expatriates, and their allies back in the United States, had a considerable stake in debates in the U.S. on the extent to which African Americans identified with Africa and, in addition, with socialism or the interests of working people generally. While this was an old debate, it took new forms in the Cold War context of the 1950s. Following the McCarthyite purges, explicit claims of solidarity with anticolonial struggles on the African continent and working-class movements globally were perceived as dangerously militant criticisms of the U.S. government and its policies at home and abroad. The anticolonial activist and scholar W. Alphaeus Hunton, for example, was imprisoned in 1951, cited for contempt of court for failing to cooperate with a federal court investigation of communist activities. He spent six months in a segregated federal prison in Virginia. Hunton subsequently could not find a teaching job in the United States. Thus exiled, he later joined Du Bois in Ghana to work on the *Encyclopedia Africana*. In 1970, Hunton died in Lusaka, Zambia, where he and his wife Dorothy had relocated after the Ghana coup.[18]

For the expatriates, "home" was where they identified the vanguard of black struggle, and from the late 1950s onward, this was increasingly understood to be Ghana. The expatriates reveled in the expanded horizons of black statehood in Ghana and, concomitantly, of black identity as well. The advent of a new era of defacto black power (not to be confused with the post–civil rights slogan "Black Power") elicited a range of responses among the expatriates, from romantic longings to pragmatic assessments of the obstacles, both internal and external, to nation building in Ghana and by extension, throughout Africa.

Ghana's potential impact on black American identities and, by extension, on U.S. domestic politics, made it a target for U.S. government efforts to contain, or redefine, its significance. The Eisenhower's administration's presence at Ghana's independence festivities was to some degree a concession to anger in the

U.S. black press at the administration's inaction against a spate of racist bombings throughout the South, which it contrasted to the administration's intense concern about the Soviet invasion of Hungary. Black American opposition seized on the evident double standard of a U.S. government more forthright in opposing Soviet aggression abroad than moving against segregationist terror in the "free world" itself. The U.S. government's preoccupation with its image abroad at the height of the Cold War, its propaganda stressing purported U.S. racial harmony and progress, and its duplicitous tendency to discipline civil rights activists and protests, instead of segregationist mobs and demagogues, combined to make Ghana an unpredictable challenge for a government seeking to minimize any catalyst for criticism of U.S. policy.

The Eisenhower administration's post-*Brown* policy of appeasement of massive southern resistance to desegregation was followed by well-publicized and embarrassing encounters of diplomats from the new African states with Jim Crow laws in the United States. Such incidents undermined U.S. attempts to shape emergent African and Asian states and their economic policies, not to mention efforts to manage domestic racial unrest.[19] When the press reported that Ghana's minister of finance, Komla Gbedemah, accompanied by his assistant, the African American pacifist Bill Sutherland, were insulted and refused breakfast at a Howard Johnson's restaurant in Dover, Delaware, Eisenhower had "a first-class international incident" on his hands, as E. Frederic Morrow, the lone black on the White House staff, characterized the event. Morrow's diary of his tenure as a presidential aide during this crisis-ridden period records his frustration: "On top of the Little Rock situation, this is the kind of thing that makes our country look bad abroad and gives the world the idea that we are first-class hypocrites when we prate about our wonderful democracy." (Morrow's discomfort, in the wake of the recent Little Rock school desegregation standoff between Arkansas governor Orval Faubus and Eisenhower, was eased somewhat by Eisenhower's invitation of Gbedemah and Sutherland to the White House for breakfast.)[20]

Just as the sight of African diplomats elicited racist responses from benighted whites, Ghana's image of black statehood on the world stage at the United Nations, and Nkrumah's nonaligned foreign policy at the height of the Cold War, challenged the political outlook of Americans of a variety of political persuasions. Despite Ghana's initially cordial relations with the United States, its very existence as a socialist state was a challenge to official Cold War policy and pronouncements. For African Americans, Ghana and the prospect of new African states gave the lie to segregationist assertions that peoples of African descent had no history and no prospects. Indeed, Ghana was understood by some as a catalyst for southern black college students to make history themselves through the sit-in movement, energizing civil rights struggles in the United States. After observing activists at Florida A & M college in 1960, for example, James Baldwin explained that the students were born as Africa was breaking free of European colonialism. "I remember . . . the invasion of Ethiopia and Haile Selassie's vain appeal to the League of Nations, but they remember the Bandung conference and the establishment of the Republic of Ghana."[21]

Like Mayfield, many of the Ghana expatriates had activist backgrounds in antiracist and social democratic struggles. Sutherland had been imprisoned for refusing to serve in World War II and had campaigned against segregation in the armed forces with A. Philip Randolph and Bayard Rustin in the late 1940s. Disenchanted with racism in the United States, Sutherland reached Ghana in 1953 and later married the Ghanaian playwright, Efua Sutherland. Although only a few—such as Du Bois, and Dr. Robert Lee, originally from Charleston, South Carolina—went so far as to renounce their U.S. citizenship, the expatriates' embrace of Ghana was reinforced, generally, by their abhorrence of racism in America's domestic politics and their conviction that Jim Crow and right-wing anticommunism combined to shape the nation's foreign policy toward non-Western African and Asian states as well.[22]

Accordingly, the expatriates shared Nkrumah's Pan-African conviction that domestic struggles for black freedom were inseparable from African liberation movements. For example, in 1963 they staged a demonstration at the U.S. embassy in Accra in conjunction with the famous March on Washington, enacting their view of solidarity between the struggles of black Americans and African peoples. Their protest, vehemently condemning President Kennedy's broken promises on racial justice and his interventionist foreign policy in Cuba and Vietnam, was far more militant and critical of the U.S. government than the officially vetted speeches delivered at the Lincoln Memorial. Alice Windom, a Ghana expatriate, provided a description of the demonstration (which coincided with the death of W. E. B. Du Bois) which was circulated among black activists in the United States. Even before this, however, through their links with activists in the United States, expatriates and their allies brought their vision of Ghana and internationalism to discussions of black American politics and society, manifested in the Harlem-based Liberation Committee for Africa and the armed self-defense movement led by Robert Williams in the late 1950s and into the next decade.[23] "Tales of the Lido," Mayfield's final unpublished account of the period written between the early 1970s and 1984, situates the Ghana expatriates within a radical tradition that, as early as the 1950s, challenged both right-wing Cold War anticommunism *and* the Cold War liberalism espoused by the civil rights establishment. Mayfield actively dissented from Martin Luther King's philosophy and strategy of nonviolence during the 1950s. With African Americans and organizers in the Deep South terrorized by segregationists, Mayfield, (who was born in 1928 in Greer, South Carolina) hastened to point out that non-violence enjoyed less than universal popularity.

Mayfield, a journalist, soon became involved with the armed self-defense movement led by Robert Williams, an NAACP leader in Monroe, North Carolina. Williams had rescued a local NAACP chapter that had been decimated by racist intimidation after the *Brown* decision. He organized a black paramilitary force to thwart resurgent Klan attempts to harass black professionals suspected of supporting the NAACP. That, however, led to Williams' dismissal from the NAACP. In *Commentary*, Mayfield argued Williams' case, contending that his example posed a stark challenge to establishmentarian black leaders incapable of responding effectively to the boycotts, sit-ins, and other forms of black mass protest from below. Mayfield applauded Williams's efforts to turn the Cold War (and the second amendment of the Bill of Rights) to his advantage, putting pressure on the federal government by giving antiblack violence world exposure. Holding black working-class insurgency as the unknown variable in civil rights struggles, Mayfield argued that the legalistic and passive resistance strategies of the black leadership class failed to address the needs of the black masses. Grass-roots leaders such as Williams, "who have concluded that the only way to win a revolution is to be a revolutionary," would then rise to the fore, Mayfield wrote.[24]

Pressured by the FBI to provide information about Williams, Mayfield quit the country, reaching Ghana in 1961. In Ghana, Mayfield became a speechwriter and publicist for Nkrumah. He maintained later that he had only a limited influence on the Ghanaian president. From Ghana, Mayfield learned of Harold Cruse's critique of Williams's Monroe movement, which faulted Williams for using militant, armed self-defense tactics for what were ultimately, in Cruse's estimation, moderate goals of racial integration. Not surprisingly, Mayfield vehemently objected to Cruse's dismissal of Williams, suggesting the longstanding nature of their dispute.[25]

Mayfield's activities paralleled the deterioration of relations between Ghana and the United States, as Nkrumah, along with leaders of other radical new states, such as Sekou Toure in Guinea, pursued a foreign policy of nonalignment. By seeking trade-and-aid agreements with Soviet bloc countries—in effect playing the Cold War antagonists against each other—Nkrumah confirmed the worst fears of anticommunists. As Basil Davidson has written, "that sort of non-alignment has become an everyday affair: when Nkrumah embarked upon it, [Westerners] saw it as a hostile challenge or a dastardly betrayal."[26] Mayfield meanwhile edited a volume for Nkrumah's information bureau on nuclear disarmament, *The World Without the Bomb*, culled from presentations from the international left at a conference held in Accra. Mayfield also worked as the West African correspondent for the Middle East News, a press agency with bureaus in New York, Cairo, London, and throughout Europe, and as a frequent contributor to the Ghanaian *Evening News*. His articles also discussed Nkrumah's program of African unity and nonalignment.[27]

Mayfield worked to expose the hypocrisy of the official U.S. endorsement of a limited domestic civil rights agenda, which he contended was primarily a means of keeping new African states within the West's sphere of influence. Mayfield frequently published in Ghanaian newspapers accounts of U.S. racism and violence, often with graphic illustrations of lynching victims.[28] Mayfield's exposés of U.S. racial atrocities were deployed against the American embassy's propaganda portraying the United States as committed to resolving the so-called dilemma of racial segregation. Tattered copies of U.S. embassy memoranda located in the Mayfield papers border on hysteria in denouncing Mayfield as the author of several "racist" pieces designed to undermine claims of racial progress and American policies seeking to secure Ghana's membership in the "free world."

Ghana's challenge to U.S. foreign policy is further glimpsed in Mayfield's correspondence and writings on African Americans and others he deemed unfriendly to the cause of independent Ghana and an emancipated Africa. This, too, was an abiding legacy of the Cold War, during which government informants were paid to provide names of real or imagined subversives to U.S. authorities.[29] Among the more immediate causes for Mayfield's and the expatriates' suspicion was the crisis in the former Belgian Congo, where the resource-rich Katanga province attempted to secede with the help of Belgian economic and military interests. This culminated in the brutal assassination of the independent Congo's prime minister, Patrice Lumumba.[30] The murder of Lumumba sparked outrage among African American intellectuals, including, most notably, James Baldwin and Lorraine Hansberry. In a letter to the *New York Times,* Hansberry excoriated U.N. Undersecretary Ralph Bunche for his comments at the U.N. on this issue and his role in the U.N. mission in the Congo. Baldwin warned Cold War liberals that they were dangerously mistaken in perceiving black Americans' protest at the United Nations (whose peacekeeping mission in the Congo was widely believed to be implicated in Lumumba's removal) to be communist-inspired. Indeed, this accusation of communist influence, to Baldwin, was deeply insulting in its suggestion that blacks would otherwise be complacent in the face of dreadful conditions, north and south, and at home and abroad. From Ghana, Mayfield defended Baldwin (in *Freedomways*) against attacks by black American militants for whom Baldwin's success and his candid writing about homosexuality all but proved his suspect racial credentials. Asserting the priority of global politics over their parochial notions of blackness, Mayfield reminded critics that Baldwin, like Hansberry, had taken the unpopular stand in aligning themselves with the pro-Lumumba demonstrators.[31]

The expatriates, along with Baldwin and Hansberry, symbolized a broader tendency among black radicals to view the political status and identity of African Americans through the lens of African liberation struggles. Correspondence shows that Mayfield and his cohorts called themselves "Afros," tellingly omitting their American identity, but always with a ironic awareness that blackness in itself was no guarantee of loyalty to Ghana or Nkrumah. Mayfield became increasingly preoccupied with those black Americans flocking to Ghana under the auspices of the U.S. government. He disclosed that he personally intervened to cancel the invitations of several "old colored Uncle Toms" to the Accra assembly on disarmament. In an essay laced with caustic wit, Mayfield took the measure of "Uncle Tom in Africa," typically retiring on race and social questions at home but a militant advo-

cate of socialism on African soil, maintaining against all contradictory appearances that his subsistence on the U.S. payroll
scarcely compromised his solidarity with the African revolution.[32]

Despite, perhaps because of, Ghana's post-Bandung challenge of nonalignment, the nation remained beset by Cold War
pressures, internally and externally. This state of affairs certainly
shaped Mayfield's highly specific notion of the Uncle Tom as the
African American enemy of the African revolution. As editor in
chief of the *African Review,* a magazine published from Nkrumah's ministry of information in his executive offices at Flagstaff
House, Mayfield found himself by 1964 floundering in the turbu-
lent domestic politics surrounding Nkrumah, who by this time
had weathered several assassination attempts. Mayfield had obtained an article for the magazine by C. L. R. James, already
sharply critical of Nkrumah's leadership, on Lenin's analysis of
the unfinished business of the Bolshevik revolution. To Mayfield's dismay, James's article, intended as a lesson for the Ghanaian situation, was spiked by either Nkrumah or his overzealous
aides.[33] Domestic opposition from conservatives and intellectuals primarily from the cocoa-producing Ashanti region had long
been strident and had elicited such repressive policies as Nkrumah's Preventive Detention Act of 1958.[34]

Such internal tensions were reinforced by the external pressure of Cold War constraints on Ghana and the black power it
represented. Opposition leaders were keen to exploit anticommunist hysteria at nonalignment. From exile, Dr. Kofi Busia testi-
fied before Congress in 1962 that Ghana was the springboard for
communist subversion on the African continent, and thus not a
good candidate for further financial aid. Opposition spokesmen
such as Busia were effective in characterizing Nkrumah's support for nationalist parties still struggling against colonial rule as
communist-inspired.[35]

The February 1966 coup found Mayfield, like Nkrumah, away
from Ghana. Nkrumah learned of the coup in China, en route to
North Vietnam on an ill-fated peace mission. Mayfield was on the
island of Ibiza, staying in a government-owned villa. He re-

mained there writing his first unpublished manuscript on Nkrumah, Ghana, and the coup. Almost a year after the coup, Mayfield had concluded that while Nkrumah's flaws certainly contributed to his undoing, the determination of Africa's enemies, as he put it, to obstruct African liberation movements and prevent unity was decisive in Ghana's crisis. For Mayfield, the Ghana coup, along with the deaths of Malcolm X, Lumumba, and others, affirmed that "this power struggle is a murderous game. . . . The enemy plays for keeps."[36]

Although widely understood at the time as an advancement in the struggle, late 1960s declarations of black power in the United States ultimately reflected the fragmentation of African American politics. Before this fragmentation, the latter careers of Martin Luther King and especially Malcolm X had been transformed in the internationalist image epitomized by Ghana. They had attempted to broaden the civil rights agenda to one of human rights, linking antiracism with struggles for economic democracy. They had argued that inequality at home was inseparable from—and epitomized by—the escalation of the war in Vietnam. Black Power rhetoric notwithstanding, the deaths of these martyred leaders tended to enforce civil rights liberalism as the normative black political discourse, further marginalizing strategies linking race and class struggles within an internationalist politics.

From the mid-1960s onward, radical black politics in the United States was effectively neutralized by a combination of state repression and increasingly unaccountable, undisciplined leadership.[37] What remained was in large part a highly rhetorical popular conception of black power, or the new black aesthetic. Some internationalist black intellectuals and activists forged ahead with organizational initiatives inspired by ongoing anti-colonial struggles and such Pan- African revolutionaries as Amilcar Cabral, Sekou Toure, Walter Rodney, and the exiled Nkrumah.[38] Nevertheless, new articulations of Black Power in the United States were often depoliticized, anti-intellectual, fratricidal and ineffectual, despite their frequently proclaimed revolutionary potential. Although from exile Nkrumah managed to publish critiques of neocolonialism in Africa, Black Power rhetoric in the United States tended toward the sort of bourgeois nationalism that Frantz Fanon had identified as the Achilles' heel of independent African states. Undeniably, black solidarities were fragmented from above. In addition to the repressive force of U.S. counterintelligence, President Nixon demonstrated anew the U.S. political establishment's vested interest in imposing its own vision of freedom on black Americans. For Nixon, Black Power was best expressed through promoting petty capitalist enterprises in inner cities.[39]

Cruse's slighting of Nkrumah's Ghana and Mayfield cannot be wholly explained by their personal animosities. The destruction of Nkrumah's leadership, combined with concerted U.S. efforts to neutralize independent black politics both at home and abroad doubtless bred a sense of betrayal and disillusionment among many African Americans. Mayfield's writings strongly suggest that the role and influence of African American expatriates within independent Ghana was severely restricted by the complex political realities established by Nkrumah's policies. Inhibited in thought as well as action by their marginality, the Ghana expatriates were indeed vulnerable to charges of naïveté in failing to perceive the manifold contradictions of "African socialism" as practiced by Nkrumah.[40]

Yet it can also be said that the largely ad hominem style of Cruse's writing and his evident need to construct and topple straw men precluded any serious reflection on Ghana and the independent black left activism that had flourished there. The downfall of Nkrumah and Ghana's project cannot be explained by Cruse's thesis of the black left's subservience to the Communist Party. Expatriate sympathizers of Nkrumah and other writers remain convinced that his military overthrow was not, in fact, a purely internal matter, but was in fact orchestrated in large part by Western powers, including the United States.[41] Whatever one's analysis of the Pan-Africanism represented by Mayfield and the African American expatriates in Ghana, it appears that

Cruse's influence often has been the opposite of what he claims to have intended in penning *The Crisis of the Negro Intellectual*. By misleadingly characterizing internationalist black militants of the 1950s as integrationist, the work's legacy for future generations has been one of discontinuity and confusion rather than that of advancing his avowed project of critical inquiry into the history of independent black politics.

Long after Nkrumah's fall, the appearance of Cruse's obfuscatory text, and Mayfield's passing, Ghana still retains its significance, albeit as the locus of profoundly unresolved histories. Today, Ghana often is advertised as an economic success story, the showcase for the International Monetary Fund's structural adjustment programs—despite its declining exports and the erosion of real incomes and living standards for most Ghanaians.[42] But in the late 1950s, Ghana and all it stood for potentially debunked for African Americans the racial myths, both imposed and internalized, that trapped them in what Mayfield called "minority thinking;" myths that prevented them from defining and pursuing an independent vision of human freedom. With the destruction of Nkrumah's vision of an independent, unified African continent, Ghana has come to symbolize unresolved silences and continuing aspirations that are the legacy of the Cold War and the postcolonial condition.

Notes

1. Harold Cruse, *The Crisis of the Negro Intellectual* (New York: Quill, 1984).
2. Penny Von Eschen, *Race Against Empire: Black Americans and Anticolonialism, 1937–1957* (Ithaca, N.Y.: Cornell University Press, 1997).
3. Julian Mayfield, "A Challenge to a Bestseller: Crisis or Crusade?" *Negro Digest* (June 1968), pp. 10–24. Amid his defense against Mayfield's charges that

personal animosity informed Cruse's assessments of Paul Robeson and Lorraine Hansberry, Cruse calls for Mayfield to be more forthcoming about his romantic pursuits in Harlem, Puerto Rico, and Ghana: "But, damn, Mayfield, here you are sittin' on all that fantastical experience about black writers in love (and also exile) with your poor readers thirsting for knowledge, literary exaltation, and a bit of honest, healthy titillation. . . . Give us the livin' lowdown on what went down in Ghana." For Cruse, exile was reduced to sexual adventurism. This particular response to Mayfield seems more revealing about Cruse's personal preoccupations than anything else. See Harold Cruse, "Replay on a Black Crisis: Harold Cruse Looks Back on Black Art and Politics in Harlem," *Negro Digest* (November 1968), p. 25.

4. For a recent example, see Wahneema Lubiano, ed., *The House that Race Built* (New York: Pantheon, 1997).

5. Cruse, *The Crisis of the Negro Intellectual,* p. 354. For a listing of several organizations reflecting African American linkages to African independence movements, see Martin Kilson and Rupert Emerson, "The American Dilemma in a Changing World: The Rise of Africa and the Negro American," *Daedalus* (fall 1965), pp. 1055–84.

6. Michel Fabre, *From Harlem to Paris: Black American Writers in France, 1840–1980* (Urbana: University of Illinois Press, 1991); Fabre, *The Unfinished Quest of Richard Wright* (New York: William Morrow, 1973); Ernest Dunbar, *The Black Expatriates* (New York: Pocket Books, 1970); the fictional treatment by John A. Williams, *The Man Who Cried I Am* (New York: Signet, 1968); and Tyler Stovall, *Paris Noir: African Americans in the City of Light* (Boston: Houghton Mifflin, 1996) are among the few works which address the black expatriate experience after World War II, in either Europe or new African states such as Ghana. For a groundbreaking discussion of African American expatriates in Ghana, see Ronald Walters, *Pan Africanism in the African Diaspora* (Detroit: Wayne State University Press, 1993), pp. 89–125.

7. Cruse's attack on black left internationalism is at its most mean-spirited in his discussion of the late Lorraine Hansberry. Taking his cues from the anti-integrationist moment, Cruse dismisses her play *Raisin in the Sun* as an exercise in bourgeois integrationism, and denounces its author as not only cliquish and middle-class in her interpersonal relations, but also as the owner of slum property. See Cruse, *The Crisis of the Negro Intellectual,* pp. 267–84. In an analysis of the assassination of Hansberry's reputation by both white liberals and black nationalists, Hansberry's widower and literary executor calls Cruse's accusation that she owned slum property "an outright lie." See Robert Nemiroff to Julian Mayfield, August 24, 1979, in the folder, "Correspondence re: Lorraine Hansberry" in the Julian Mayfield Collection, Schomburg Center for Research in Black Culture, New York Public Library.

8. Cruse was favorably reviewed by Christopher Lasch on this basis. The review is reprinted in Lasch, *The Agony of the American Left* (New York: Vintage, 1970). On the belief that the

New Left was compromised by foreign ideologies, see John P. Diggins, *The American Left in the Twentieth Century* (New York: Harcourt Brace Jovanovich, 1973). Sadly, Cruse remains the only introduction for many readers to Robeson, Hansberry, and other African American radical intellectuals.

9. See, for example, the virtually forgotten essay by James Baldwin, "A Negro Assays the Negro Mood," *New York Times Sunday Magazine* (March 12, 1961), pp. 25 and 103–4, penned in the aftermath of the protest by African American activists at the United Nations after Lumumba's death.

10. Notable exceptions to this silence include Cedric Robinson, *Black Marxism* (London: Zed, 1983); Manning Marable, *From Kwame Nkrumah to Maurice Bishop* (London: Verso, 1987); Jan Carew, *Ghosts in Our Blood: Malcolm X in England, Africa and the Caribbean* (Chicago: Lawrence Hill, 1994); and Von Eschen, *Race Against Empire*.

11. Although it generally does not address the experiences of African American expatriates, much of the literature on the civil rights movement addresses the conflict between black activism and Cold War perceptions and policy. See Clayborne Carson, *In Struggle: SNCC and the Black Awakening of the 1960s* (Cambridge, Mass.: Harvard University Press, 1981); Taylor Branch, *Parting the Waters: America in the King Years, 1954–1963* (New York: Simon and Schuster, 1988); Manning

Marable, *Race, Reform and Rebellion: The Second Reconstruction in Black America, 1945–1982* (Jackson: University Press of Mississippi, 1988); and Godfrey Hodgson, *America in Our Time: From World War II to Nixon* (New York: Vintage, 1976). On federal surveillance of black intellectuals and activists, see Kenneth O'Reilly, *Racial Matters: The FBI's Secret File on Black America* (New York: Free Press, 1989).

12. Richard Mahoney, *JFK: Ordeal in Africa* (New York: Oxford University Press, 1983).

13. For accounts of Malcolm's visit to Ghana, see Malcolm X, *The Autobiography of Malcolm X* (reprint, New York: Ballantine, 1984), pp. 352–60, which contains a detailed description of the African American expatriate community's welcome for him; Maya Angelou, *All God's Children Need Traveling Shoes* (New York: Vintage, 1984); Leslie Alexander Lacy, *The Rise and Fall of a Proper Negro* (New York: 1970); and Julian Mayfield, *Tales of the Lido* (unpublished manuscript).

14. On federal surveillance of black intellectuals and activists, see O'Reilly, *Racial Matters: The FBI's Secret File on Black America*; Ward Churchill and Jim Vander Wall, *The Cointelpro Papers: Documents from the FBI's Secret Wars Against Dissent in the United States* (Boston: South End Press, 1990).

15. These unpublished manuscripts are preserved in box 14, "Ghana manuscripts," in the Mayfield collection at the

Schomburg Center. The first, "The Lonely Warrior," written immediately after the coup, is divided between a political biography of Nkrumah and an analysis of the coup. Journalistic and anecdotal, it presents a balanced assessment of Nkrumah's flaws and failed policies within a critique of the continued dominance of foreign economic interests in post-independence Ghana. The second, "When Ghana Was Ghana," is a revised version of the first manuscript, maintaining the validity of Nkrumah's project of African unity while seeking to strengthen this analysis with more documentation and research. The final manuscript, "Tales of the Lido," was evidently written between the late 1970s and Mayfield's death in 1984. In its surviving fragments, this memoir of Mayfield and the Ghana expatriates abandons the scholarly tone of the previous works, interspersing historical and political analysis with a more informal, gossipy, and sexualized remembrance of Ghana. This manuscript suggests that Mayfield eventually heeded, to some extent, Cruse's mocking criticism of his activities in Ghana.

16. Preston King, the brother of the civil rights attorney and activist Slater King, refused to serve in the U.S. Army on grounds of discriminatory treatment, challenging his draft board in Albany, Georgia, in the late 1950s. Fleeing federal and local prosecution, King exiled himself to England. When the U.S. government attempted to extradite King to face charges of draft evasion, the British government deported King, claiming that he had an invalid passport. Ghana granted King political asylum, and he taught political science at the University of Ghana at Legon. King believes his was not an isolated case of forced exile by the U.S. government. Letter, Preston King to author, January 28, 1997.

17. Mayfield, "Tales of the Lido," (unpublished manuscript), p. 32, and Julian Mayfield Collection, Schomburg Center, New York Public Library.

18. See Von Eschen, *Race Against Empire*, pp. 137 and 183–84.

19. Thomas Borstelmann, *Apartheid's Reluctant Uncle: The United States and Southern Africa in the Early Cold War* (New York: Oxford University Press, 1993); Von Eschen, *Race Against Empire*.

20. E. Frederic Morrow, *Black Man in the White House*, (New York: Coward-McCann, 1963), pp. 126–27.

21. James Baldwin, "They Can't Turn Back," reprinted in Baldwin, *The Price of the Ticket: Collected Nonfiction, 1948–1985* (New York: St. Martin's/Marek, 1985), p. 228.

22. The backgrounds of Sutherland and Lee are provided in Dunbar, *The Black Expatriates*.

23. For a thorough report of the expatriates' demonstration and petition, see Department of State Airgram A-125, September 1, 1963, State Department Records, National Archives. For an expatriate's version of the

protest, see Alice Windom's untitled account, September 11, 1963, in box 6, folder "Alice Windom," in the Julian Mayfield papers, Schomburg Center, New York Public Library. Ronald Walters mentions the Ghana expatriates' demonstration in *Pan Africanism and the African Diaspora*, pp. 119–20. For a description of the Kennedy administration's management of the March on Washington and its support by liberal foundations, see Hodgson, *America in Our Time*. For an American-based version of the expatriates' internationalist left project, see the pamphlet *Nationalism, Colonialism and the United States* (New York: Liberation Committee for Africa, 1961); and on Williams, see Robert Williams, *Negroes With Guns* (New York: Marzani and Munsell, 1962).

24. Julian Mayfield, "Challenge to Negro Leadership: The Case of Robert Williams," *Commentary* (April 1961), pp. 297–305. The Xerox copy in the Mayfield papers at the Schomburg Center carries a 1971 note with instructions to have copies of the piece made for Mayfield's students, indicating Mayfield's commitment to acquainting younger generations with prior, forgotten struggles.

25. Harold Cruse, "Revolutionary Nationalism and the Afro-American," *Studies on the Left*, 2 (1962), no. 3, reprinted in Cruse, *Rebellion or Revolution* (New York: William Morrow, 1968), pp. 74–96. Cruse reported that Mayfield's violent

objection to Cruse's article on revolutionary nationalism had been communicated to him by John Henrik Clarke. See "Harold Cruse Looks Back," *Negro Digest* (November 1968), pp. 20–21.

26. Basil Davidson, *Black Star: A View of the Life and Times of Kwame Nkrumah* (London: Allen Lane, 1973), p. 172.

27. For examples, see Julian Mayfield, "What Nkrumah Means by a United Africa," *Egyptian Gazette*, July 22, 1964; Mayfield, "Ghanaian Sketches," in Roger Klien, ed., *Young Americans Abroad* (New York: Harper and Row, 1962), pp. 176–204.

28. Mayfield, "Why They Want to Kill Mae Mallory," Ghanaian *Evening News,* March 30, 1962.

29. On the pervasiveness of informants, surveillance, and "no-holds-barred warfare on 'subversives,'" see Addison Gayle, *Richard Wright: Ordeal of a Native Son* (Gloucester, Mass.: Peter Smith, 1983) p. 235.

30. Madeline G. Kalb, *The Congo Cables: The Cold War in Africa—from Eisenhower to Kennedy* (New York: Macmillan, 1984).

31. Baldwin, "A Negro Assays the Negro Mood"; Lorraine Hansberry, "Congolese Patriot, *New York Times Sunday Magazine* (March 26, 1961), p. 4; Mayfield, "And Then Came Baldwin," *Freedomways* (1963), pp. 143–55.

32. Julian Mayfield to John Henrik Clarke [1962], Julian Mayfield folder, John Henrik Clarke papers, Schomburg Center for Research in Black Culture, New

York Public Library. Mayfield, "Uncle Tom Abroad," *Negro Digest* (June 1963), pp. 37–39.

33. Mayfield's account is from an unpublished fragment of his manuscript "Tales of the Lido," box 14, Julian Mayfield collection, Schomburg Center. James's essay "Lenin and the Problem" eventually appeared in *Nkrumah and the Ghana Revolution* (London: Allison & Busby, 1982).

34. For a detailed analysis of the political and economic strategies which contributed to Nkrumah's downfall, see Bob Fitch and Mary Oppenheimer, *Ghana: End of an Illusion* (New York: Monthly Review Press, 1968).

35. Davidson, *Black Star,* p. 174.

36. Mayfield to John Henrik Clarke, February 1, 1967, in Mayfield correspondence folder, John Henrik Clarke papers, Schomburg Center.

37. Clayborne Carson, "African American Leadership and Mass Mobilization," *Black Scholar* 24, no. 4 (Fall 1994).

38. Walters, *Pan Africanism and the African Diaspora*, catalogs these organizational efforts.

39. On Nixon's co-optation of Black Power, see Daniel Schechter, Michael Ansara, and David Kolodney, "The CIA as an Equal Opportunity Employer," in Ellen Ray et al., eds., *Dirty Work 2: The CIA in Africa* (Seacaucus, N.J.: Lyle Stuart, 1980), pp. 50–69.

40. These contradictions are detailed in Fitch and Oppenheimer, *Ghana: End of an Illusion*.

41. On the role of the CIA station in Accra in the coup, see John Stockton, *In Search of Enemies* (New York: Norton, 1978); for a general discussion of CIA interventions in Africa, see Ray et al., eds., *Dirty Work 2*.

42. Lareef Zubair, "Ghana I.M.F. Program Drains the Country," letter to *New York Times,* November 2, 1994, p. A22.

(**Bruce Cumings**)

Boundary Displacement:

Area Studies and International Studies During and After the Cold War

The channel is more important than that a lot of water should be running through it
— McGeorge Bundy

In this essay I propose to examine the displacement and reordering of the boundaries of scholarly investigation of "foreign areas" in the postwar period, through three phases: the first, determining burst of academic work that accompanied the early years of the Soviet-American confrontation and often led to astonishing levels of collaboration between the universities, the foundations, and the intelligence arms of the American state; the 1970s turn toward the "Pacific Rim" as geopolitical tensions eased in East and Southeast Asia; and the contemporary revaluation of American studies of the rest of the world occasioned by the end of the Cold War and the collapse of the USSR. My position is that the ultimate force shaping scholarly studies of what used to be called "the non-Western world" is economic and political power, but the most interesting effects of such power were often the least observed, at those local points where (in Foucault's phrase) power becomes "capillary"—as in universities and academic departments.[1] In this process of power going capillary but in newly rearranged rivulets, we can discern both the original flaws of the "area" boundaries, the disordering occasioned by watershed changes in world politics, and new relationships between power and knowledge.

159

For a generation after World War II, the bipolar conflict between Moscow and Washington and the hegemonic position of the United States in the world economy drew academic boundaries that had the virtue of clarity: "area studies" and "international studies" had clear reference to places or to issues and processes that became important to study, backed with enormous public and private resources. The places were usually countries, but not just any countries: Japan got favored placement as a success story of development; China got obsessive attention as a pathological example of abortive development. The focus of these studies were processes such as modernization, or what was for many years called "political development" toward the explicit or implicit goal of liberal democracy. Before 1945 little attention had been paid to, nor was there much funding for, these things.

Countries inside the containment system, such as Japan and South Korea, and those outside it, such as China and North Korea, were clearly placed as friend or enemy, ally or adversary. In both direct and indirect ways the American government and the major foundations traced these boundaries by directing scholarly attention to distinct places and to distinct ways of understanding them (for example, communist studies for North Korea and China and modernization studies for Japan and South Korea). To be in "Korean studies" or "Chinese studies" was daily to experience the tensions that afflicted Korea and China during the long period of the Cold War.

Over time this revaluation by power gave us two tropes, yielding an entire inventory of East and Southeast Asia. The first trope was "Red China" and the second (accomplished by a Nixonian transition in the 1970s in response to defeat in Vietnam) was "Pacific Rim." Each trope valued and revalued East and Southeast Asia, as Westerners (mostly Americans) recognized and defined it, in ways that highlighted some parts and excluded (or occluded) others. When East Asia was "painted Red," it held an apparent outward-moving dynamic whose core was Beijing: "400 million Chinese armed with nuclear weapons," in Dean Rusk's

1960s scenario, threatened nations along China's rim with oblivion: South Korea, South Vietnam, Taiwan, Indonesia, Thailand, and, most importantly, Japan. "Pacific Rim" was the post-1975 artistry, an era of forward movement and backward occlusion, as Americans sought to "put Vietnam behind us."

"Pacific Rim" heralded a forgetting, a hoped-for amnesia in which the decades-long but ultimately failed American effort to obliterate the Vietnamese revolution would enter the realm of Korea, "the forgotten war." But more importantly, it looked forward: suddenly the rim became the locus of a new dynamism, bringing pressure on the mainland of Asia. The "success stories" of Rimspeak were any countries that sought export-led capitalist development; the "basket cases" were any countries still foolish enough to remain committed to self-reliant or socialist development, from Burma to North Korea. This new discourse was also solicitous of these same benighted and laggard socialist economies and therefore proclaimed a formal end to ideology: "Pacific Rim" invoked a new-born community that anyone, socialist or not, could join . . . as long as they were going capitalist. Rimspeak continued to look with curiosity if not disdain on anyone who did not privilege the market. The many working-class and antisystemic movements of the region in the past decades remained poxes, irrationalities that illustrated immature "political development" in the Rim.

The people of the Pacific Rim did not know they inhabited a bustling new sector of the world system until they were told, just as our "Indians" did not know they were in America (or "West India") until Columbus told them so. If "Pacific" is a Euro-American name in itself, measuring, delineating and recognizing living space for the people who live there, "Rim" is an American construct, an invention just like the steam engine, incorporating the region's peoples "into a new inventory of the world."[2] (That these are Western social constructions, of course, does not mean that the natives think them unimportant or have self-confident definitions themselves.) Organized into the new inventory were "miracle" economies in Japan, South Korea, Taiwan, Hong Kong,

Malaysia, and Singapore, with honorable mention for Thailand, the Philippines, Indonesia, and post-Mao (but pre-Tiananmen) China. The centerpiece in the region was Japan, a newly risen sun among advanced industrial countries—indeed, "Number One" in Ezra Vogel's perfectly timed book, published in 1979.[3] The miracles were also "NICs" (Newly Industrializing Countries), and books about Asian industrialization proliferated.

Reflective of these tendencies was the nearly instantaneous revaluation of China in the late 1970s. The very real slaughters of Mao's failed Cultural Revolution—many directed against the intellectual class—became for American intellectuals the signifier to rename and parenthesize the entire history of the Chinese revolution, not to mention occasioning a vast rewriting throughout the scholarly apparatus of the China field. But the same thing happened throughout the Rim: postwar history was revalued and rewritten across the region.

When the Cold War ended and Western communism collapsed in 1989–91, a third revaluation unfolded. One set of rationales for studying "areas" (or areas in particular kinds of ways, namely communist studies) collapsed, while another— "development," whether economic or political—deepened. In effect the previous boundaries disappeared as the framework of inquiry distended to approximate the reach of the world market; the dawning "world without borders" collapsed area studies into international studies. Even "Pacific Rim" gave way to a new globalism, as Japan's economic bubble burst and the U.S. emerged finally as the mature hegemonic power of the century. We were now living in a world economy, something that radicals had written about for decades but that now materialized as the essential domain of American activity and academic endeavor. This globalized domain is not our past, however, but our present—one that will be with us for a long time. Accordingly, in this essay I will revisit the origins of area and international studies in the early Cold War period, examine how both changed with the end of the Cold War, and suggest how we might rethink boundaries (of area and discipline) and reengage our minds with the task of understanding the world outside American boundaries.

Area Studies in the Early Cold War

It is a curious fact of academic history that the first great center of area studies . . . [was] in the Office of Strategic Services. . . . It is still true today, and I hope it always will be, that there is a high measure of interpenetration between universities with area programs and the information-gathering agencies of the government.
—McGeorge Bundy, 1964[4]

The Association for Asian Studies was the first "area" organization in the United States, founded in 1943 as the Far Eastern Association and reorganized as the AAS in 1956.[5] In that period the area programs instantly confronted the existing boundaries of the social sciences and humanities; this often made for interesting intellectual confrontation. William Nelson Fenton was present at the creation of area studies, and in 1947 he wrote that area programs "faced fierce resistance from the 'imperialism of departments' since they challenged the fragmentation of the human sciences by disciplinary departments, each endowed with a particular methodology and a specific intellectual subject matter."[6] But those were not the power lines that counted. The state was less interested in the feudal domains of academe than in filling the vacuum of knowledge about a vast hegemonic and counter-hegemonic global space, however, and it was the capillary lines of state power that shaped area programs. This was effected in the first instance by the relocation of the OSS' Soviet division to Columbia University, as the basis for its Russian Institute which opened in September 1946, and in the second instance by a Carnegie Corporation grant of $740,000 to Harvard to establish the Russian Research Center in 1947.[7] Soon the Ford Foundation put in much more money, a total of $270 million to 34 universities for area and language studies from 1953 to 1966.[8]

This munificent funding created important area programs throughout the country and provided numerous fellowships that allowed scholars to spend years in the field acquiring languages and other forms of area knowledge. McGeorge Bundy, however, was much closer to the truth in linking the underpinnings of area studies to the intelligence agencies—the OSS and, subsequently, the CIA. William ("Wild Bill") Donovan, director of the wartime OSS, was also in many ways the founder of the CIA. In his papers, combed through by the CIA and then deposited at the Army War College, there is a brief account of the original development of "foreign area studies," in which Donovan, George F. Kennan, and John Paton Davies played the major roles. Davies had a plan to transform area studies and bring enormous amounts of government and foundation funding into American universities, through what was originally to be an institute of Slavic studies, but which subsequently became a model for the organization of studies of the communist world and threatened Third World areas.

Donovan, who was then with the Wall Street firm Donovan, Leisure, was at the center of this effort, working with Davies in 1948 and helping him to get foundation funding. The organizers specified that the government was not to be involved publicly in developing area studies, thus to allay suspicions that such programs were little more than "an intelligence agency." Their work should be "impartial and objective," clear of conflicts of interest, and so on. (Indeed, the files on this project are full of concern with academic independence and proper procedure.) However, in a letter to Donovan, Clinton Barnard of the Rockefeller Foundation—which, with the Carnegie Corporation, funded this effort at the beginning—wrote, "the most compelling aspect of this proposal is the intelligence function which the Institute could perform for government."[10]

Sigmund Diamond greatly expanded our understanding of the establishment of area studies centers during the early years of the Cold War in his book, *Compromised Campus*. Diamond paid particular attention to the Russian Research Center at Harvard, which, following Davies's Slavic studies institute, became a model for other area programs on Eastern Europe and China. It was also a model of cooperation with the CIA and the FBI.

Although Diamond's government documents on Harvard in this period have been greatly expurgated—and Harvard's own papers remain closed to scholars under a fifty-year rule—he was able to document that the Harvard Russian Research Center was based on the wartime OSS model; that the center was deeply involved with the CIA, the FBI, and other intelligence and military agencies; that several foundations (Carnegie, Rockefeller, Ford) worked with the state and the center to fund projects and, in some cases, to launder CIA funding; that the same scholars who undertook this activity often were subjects of FBI investigations themselves; that some of these scholars, in turn, were responsible for denouncing other scholars to the FBI; and, finally, that these academics were major figures in the postwar development of Russian area studies in the nation as a whole—not to mention the major figures in other fields who populate Diamond's account, such as Talcott Parsons in sociology and Clyde Kluckhohn in anthropology.[11]

By 1949 Harvard and the Russian Research Center had established a mutually satisfactory relationship with the local FBI office: indeed, results of the center's work were "made available to the Bureau officially through contact with President James B. Conant of Harvard University, who has on occasion indicated his respect for the Bureau's work and his understanding for its many and varied interests in connection with internal security matters." At roughly the same time, Conant also negotiated basic arrangements between Harvard and the CIA.[12] It is only a bit of an exaggeration to say that for those scholars studying potential enemy countries, either they consulted with the government or they risked being investigated by the FBI; working for the CIA thus legitimized scholars and fended off J. Edgar Hoover (particularly for the many scholars born in foreign countries).[13]

Diamond's papers contain large files of FOIA material on FBI investigations of academics in the early 1950s, throughout the country. I frequently chide myself for running afoul of what I might call the fallacy of insufficient cynicism. I had not, for example, imagined the lengths to which the FBI would go to investigate even the most trifling aspects of life in academe in the early Cold War period. Although most of the files are thoroughly blacked out by "declassification" censors (in truth there has been hardly any declassification on this issue), the papers still contain enough information to indicate that any hearsay, any wild charge, any left-of-center organization joined, any name entered on a petition for whatever cause unacceptable to the FBI (such as peace or racial integration), any subscription to a magazine the FBI did not like (for example, *The Nation* or *The New Republic*), was enough to get an entry in the file. The FBI routinely checked the credit records of academics, monitored their lectures, questioned their colleagues and students, tailed them around, and sought out reliable campus informants (William F. Buckley Jr. distinguished himself at Yale by becoming an important source for the FBI, as did Henry Kissinger at Harvard).[14]

One FBI memorandum on Harvard has a detailed account of its courses on the USSR, complete with syllabi, teachers, and the content of the courses. It goes on for forty-two detailed pages.[15] Another has extensive reports on the content of lectures at Harvard sponsored by the John Reed Club, which future Japan scholar Robert Bellah chaired and which had among its members future China scholars Albert Feuerwerker and Franz Schurmann.[16] Academics working on East Asia, of course, were particularly vulnerable to FBI harassment; those working on the USSR were as well, but for reasons deeply involved with the history of those fields (for example, the USSR never inspired much sympathy among academics in the postwar period, but China, pre- and post-1949, did), more Asianists seemed to have come to the FBI's attentions. The Korean War, for example, had an immediate impact on Harvard's policies toward the John Reed Club. In August 1950 Harvard banned the club from using Harvard facilities, unless it went through a lot of formalistic procedures (membership lists, sources of funds, and so on) not required of other groups. In the same month, Harvard security people blocked

China hand Israel Epstein from speaking at a club gathering. An FBI informant in the John Reed Club reported that the war in Korea was the cause of this new policy, and that some club members did not want to register with Harvard for fear that their names would be turned over to the government.[17]

Mosely at Columbia

If Harvard's Russian Research Center had been the only place where such intelligence ties and government interference went on, it could be dismissed as an aberration. Unfortunately, it was the central model for area programs around the country. Philip Mosely ran Columbia University's Russian Research Institute for many years and was one of the most important figures in Russian studies and American foreign policy in the 1950s. In addition to directing Columbia's center, he was head of the Council on Foreign Relations from 1952 to 1956, a member of various boards and committees at the Ford Foundation, and a prominent leader of the American Political Science Association in the early 1950s. His papers raise the same question Sigmund Diamond did in his book: Why did so many of the major figures in academe and the foundations, particularly the leaders of area centers, have CIA ties and background? More broadly, his papers show that the Ford Foundation, in close consultation with the CIA and with the help of its munificent resources, helped to shape the entire field of modernization studies and comparative politics that were later mediated through well-known Social Science Research Council projects.[18]

Although Mosely's papers contain little formerly classified material, his nearly constant involvement with secret government agencies is clear from the late 1940s through his retirement from Columbia in the early 1970s.[19] The sketchy and incomplete nature of his papers makes it impossible to know exactly what he did for the CIA and other agencies, and whether he had such clearances at all times. But his continuing relationship with intelligence groupings is clear. One example would be the letter he received from Walt W. Rostow in 1952 about which portions of

Rostow's "classified project" on the "dynamics of Soviet society" should be released for publication, a project for which Mosely was an advisor.[20] Another would be Frederick Barghoorn's letter to Mosely in the same year, asking for Mosely's help in getting government work for the summer: "In addition to some sort of official interview project or intelligence operation, it has occurred to me that perhaps I might obtain some connection with the State Department's educational exchange project.[21] In 1955 John T. Whitman of the CIA wrote to Mosely, asking that Mosely schedule recruitment interviews for him with students at Columbia's Russian Institute, "as you so kindly did for Messrs. Bloom, Bradley and Ferguson last year." Mosely was happy to oblige.[22] Meanwhile Mosely was an active partisan in the politics of the McCarthy era, testifying before the Subversive Activities Control Board in 1953, for example, that an unnamed "respondent's" views and policies "do not deviate from those of the Soviet Union." This testimony was part of the Justice Department's attempt to get the Communist Party USA to register under the McCarran Act, whereupon its members could be jailed.[23]

Mosely was a central figure at the Ford Foundation throughout the formative years of American area studies centers. On May 5, 1953, Ford's Board on Overseas Training and Research approved an agenda for implementing a program of "Coordinated Country Studies." Shortly thereafter Paul Langer wrote to Mosely, stating that the first item in regard to implementation would be consultation with the CIA's Director, Allen Dulles. After suggesting that a person high in the foundation should consult with Dulles, the other items to be discussed were listed as follows:

(b) In what terms are the projects to be presented to the CIA?
(c) To what extent will the Foundation assume responsibility toward the government in regard to the political reliability of the team members?
(d) Should mention be made of the names of persons tentatively selected?
(e) Should the directors of the proposed study projects be informed of the fact that the CIA has been notified?[24]

Another memorandum from the Ford Foundation concerning "implementation of the proposed country studies,"[25] said in the second paragraph that "Carl Spaeth [of Ford] offered to call Allen Dulles to explain in general terms the nature of the proposed studies," to be followed up by a more detailed presentation of the projects in a meeting between Cleon Swayze, also of Ford, and Allen Dulles. (Here, however, the purpose of these contacts with the CIA was said to be "merely to keep interested government agencies informed.")

Other memoranda in Mosely's files show that plans for these "country studies" spawned some of the most important works later published in the field of comparative politics; for example, Langer recommended Lucian Pye for work on guerrillas in Malaya, and suggested "a broadly conceived" study of Burmese government and politics" (which Pye also did somewhat later, although he was not recommended for it in this memorandum). Langer also wanted a study of Turkey as "a special case in the Near East" of "smooth development toward democracy" and immunity "to the appeals of communism." Among other scholars, he thought Dankwart Rustow would be good for the task; Rustow, together with Robert Ward, later published a central work on how Japan and Turkey modernized successfully.[26] (There is no evidence in these memoranda that Pye or Rustow knew that they were under consideration for such tasks.)

Later in 1953 the Ford Foundation sponsored a conference on Soviet and Slavic area studies, to discuss a program of fellowships in that field. Major academic figures in Soviet studies, such as Mosely, Merle Fainsod, Cyril Black, and Frederick Barghoorn, attended; also attending was the China specialist George Taylor. Government figures present included George Kennan, Paul Nitze, Allen Dulles, and several CIA officials. Pendleton Herring of the SSRC also attended.[27] Among other things, the conferees fretted about "loyalty" checks on grantees, and therefore suggested denying fellowships to "partisans of special Soviet movements and recognized supporters of political parties inimical to the best interests of the United States." Although this stricture was directed primarily at the Communist Party USA, the language was broad enough to include, say, supporters of Henry Wallace's Progressive Party; the Carnegie Corporation also extended such concerns to a variety of liberal academics.[28]

One apparent result of this program was a CIA-sponsored study entitled "Moslems of the Soviet Central Asia" done by Richard Pipes, a well-known Harvard historian of Russia who eventually became responsible for Soviet affairs on Reagan's first and most ideologically committed National Security Council.[29] Langer, Mosely and others also sought in 1953 and 1954 to develop Chinese studies along the lines of their previous work in Russian studies.[30]

According to Christopher Simpson's study of declassified materials, this interweaving of foundations, universities, and state intelligence agencies extended to the social sciences as a whole: "For years, government money . . . not always publicly acknowledged as such—made up more than 75 per cent of the annual budgets of institutions such as Paul Lazarsfeld's Bureau of Applied Social Research at Columbia University, Hadley Cantril's Institute for International Social Programs at Princeton, Ithiel de Sola Pool's CENIS program at MIT, and others." Official studies in 1952 reported that "fully 96 per cent of all reported [government] funding for social sciences at that time was drawn from the U.S. military."[31]

That Mosely provided a working linkage among Ford, the CIA, and the ACLS/SSRC into the 1960s is suggested by Abbot Smith's 1961 letter to him, referring to lists of possible new CIA area studies consultants whom he wished to clear with Mosely, William Langer, and Joseph Strayer. (Smith was described as the director of the CIA's "consultants' group.")[32] In Mosely's response, he recommends among other people the China scholar John M. Lindbeck of Columbia, A. Doak Barnett (a China watcher then with the Ford Foundation but soon to join the Columbia faculty), and Lucian Pye of MIT ("my first choice").[33] The Ford Foundation's decision in the late 1950s to pump at least $30 million into the field of China studies (to resuscitate it after the

McCarthyite onslaught, but also to create new China watchers) drew on the same rationale as the Russian programs examined above: "The investment strategy was based on the model designed just after World War II by cooperation on the part of the Carnegie Corporation of New York and the Rockefeller Foundation in supporting Soviet studies, initially and principally through grants to Columbia and Harvard Universities."[34]

International Studies during the Cold War

"International studies" has been a more muddled field than area studies. One can count on most members of area programs to have competence on those areas, but international studies is such a grab bag that almost any subject or discipline that crosses international boundaries can qualify for inclusion. The annual meetings of the International Studies Association have an extraordinary range of panels, with political scientists predominating but with a profusion of disciplines and subfields typically represented on the program. It is anything and everything, perhaps with a bias toward international relations and policy-relevant research. International studies is an umbrella under which just about everything gathers, from fine work and fine scholars to hack work and charlatans.

Among the earliest and the most important of international studies centers was MIT's Center for International Studies, or CENIS. In its early years in the 1950s, the CIA underwrote this center almost as a subsidiary enterprise. This is evident in the transcript of a visiting committee meeting at MIT in 1959, attended by MIT faculty such as W.W. Rostow, Pool, Max Millikan, and James Killian (president of MIT for several years); the visitors included Robert Lovett, McGeorge Bundy, and several unidentified participants.[35] Queried as to whether the center served just the CIA or a larger group of government departments, for example, Millikan remarked that over the five years of the center's relationship with the CIA, "there has been some continuing ambiguity as to whether we were creatures of CIA or whether CIA was acting as an administrative office for other agencies." He also admitted that the Center had "taken on projects under pressure" to have work done that the CIA wanted done (these were among "the least successful projects" from MIT's standpoint, he thought). At one point in the transcript Millikan also says that "[Allan] Dulles allowed us to hire three senior people," suggesting that the CIA director had a hand in CENIS's hiring policies. The center provided an important go-between for the CIA, since "top notch social scientists" and "area experts" had no patience for extended periods of residence at CIA headquarters: "A center like ours provides a way of getting men in academic work to give them [sic] a close relationship with concrete problems faced by people in government."

This transcript illustrates that the two big objects of such work were the Soviet Union and China, with various researchers associated with the center doing internal, classified reports that subsequently became published books —for example, Rostow's *Dynamics of Soviet Society*. The primary impetus for this, of course, was the professorial desire to "get a book out of it." But Millikan also noted another motivation: "In an academic institution it is corrosive to have people who are supposed to be pursuing knowledge and teaching people under limitations as to whom they can talk to and what they can talk about." One way to remedy that problem was to take on no project "whose material we can't produce in some unclassified results [sic]." McGeorge Bundy, however, thought that the value of classified work was not in its "magnitude," but in the connection itself: "the channel is more important than that a lot of water should be running through it."

Lovett acknowledged that there could be "very damaging publicity" if it were known that the CIA was funding and using CENIS, since the CIA was "a good whipping board"; he thought they could set up a "fire wall" by making the NSC "our controlling agent with CIA the administrative agent." Killian responded that "I have a strange animal instinct that this is a good time to get ourselves tidied up. We shouldn't take the risk on this." Another participant named McCormack said he had always thought "that others would front [for] the CIA"; a participant named Jackson said that the NSC could be "a wonderful cover." In the midst of this discussion (which resonates with Hollywood versions of Mafia palaver), Lovett then gave them the bottom line: "If this thing can be solved you will find it easier to get more money from the foundations."[36]

The Present Moment in Area and International Studies

Perhaps there is enough detail above to convince independent observers that the major American centers of area and international studies research came precisely from the state/intelligence/foundation nexus that critics said they did in the late 1960s (always to a hailstorm of denial). If we now fast-forward to the 1990s, we find that proponents of the state's need for area training and expertise decided to put the intelligence function front and center, with a requirement that recipients of fellowships consult with the national security agencies of the government as a quid pro quo for their funding. I refer, of course, to the National Security Education Act (NSEA, also known as the Boren Bill, after Senator David Boren). At least three area associations (for the Middle East, Latin America, and Africa) have refused participation in this program.

In a discussion of the issues that scholars raised about the NSEA,[37] the administrator in charge of the program (at that time, Martin Hurwitz) suggested that "the buffer approach is 'traditional clandestine tradecraft'" and that "aboveboard is the way to go" for this program. (Hurwitz would know, since his background is in the Defense Intelligence Agency). Others commented that some academics worry that students in the program "may appear to be spies-in-training," while Anne Betteridge, the author of the summary, noted that "academic representatives do not wish to obscure the source of funding, but do wish to assure the integrity of academic processes." The NSE's public board apparently was to be supplemented by a "shadow board," and some administrators wanted to find non-Pentagon housing for the NSEA and call the new office "The David L. Boren Center for International Studies"—with no substantive changes otherwise. On February 14, 1992, three area associations (not including the Association for Asian Studies [AAS]) wrote to Senator Boren, expressing worries about "even indirect links to U.S. national security agencies." Each of those three organizations had extant resolutions on their books urging members not to participate in defense-related research programs.

The secretary-treasurer of the AAS, L. A. Peter Gosling, introduced the issue to the membership as follows: "The goal of our continued discussions about and with the NSEA [*sic*—he refers to discussions with Martin Hurwitz] has been to make it as useful and acceptable to the scholarly community *as possible,* which in turn involves insulating it *as much as possible* from the Department of Defense where it is funded and located [my emphasis]."[38] Gosling went on to fret that "there are no [*sic*] other sources now, nor in the immediate future" for funding international studies, and that, although the NSEA only supplemented Title VI funding, "there are those who fear that the traditional Defense Department/intelligence community whose support has so often saved Title VI funding from extinction may [now] be less motivated to do so." Defense Department control, Gosling thought, might be mitigated by "using re-grant agencies," such as the Fulbright program; he argued that the program will benefit Asian studies at both the undergraduate and graduate levels and that all Asian languages are included in the NSEA's list of priority languages (and isn't that wonderful). Even though the NSE board "sets the priorities for the program," this can be mitigated again by "the use of re-grant organizations" in administering parts of the program. Gosling closed by saying that the AAS has "made clear the desirability of distancing this program from Department of Defense design and control."

A fair reading of these two statements, it seems to me, suggests that Betteridge and the area associations from Latin America, Africa, and the Middle East raised important objections to the NSEA, whereas the secretary-treasurer of the Association for Asian Studies seemed concerned primarily with (1) getting the money, (2) showing how important NSEA would be for Asian studies, and (3) showing no concern whatever for the "traditional clandestine tradecraft" that makes "re-granting agencies" mere window dressing—perhaps because of a different "tradition": that of intelligence-agency support for Title VI that I, for one, have never seen in print before.

Important changes have also come to the Social Science Research Council (SSRC) and the American Council of Learned Societies (ACLS) in the 1990s. These organizations have been the national, joint administrative nexus of American academic research since the 1930s. The SSRC has not been a center of social science research as most social scientists would define it (the Institute for Social Research/Survey Research Center at Michigan, for example, would come much closer), but a point at which the existing disciplines find meeting ground with "area studies." As such, of course, it is a more important organization than any of the area associations. Therefore we can hearken to how the SSRC vice president, Stanley J. Heginbotham, appraised the NSEA.[39]

First, he welcomed it by saying that "new forms of federal support for higher education "have been extremely difficult to mobilize" in the recent period of spending cuts, budget deficits, and the like. Boren, he explained, wanted the NSEA to facilitate area studies education at the graduate and undergraduate levels, and had hoped the program would be part of an independent governmental foundation. However the Office of Management and Budget blocked this and ruled that for defense funds to be disbursed for the NSEA (under the 1992 Intelligence Authorization Act), it would have to be located in the Department of Defense. Heginbotham then adds in a footnote that Boren decided further to strengthen "the credibility of the program in academic circles" by putting the administration of the program under the Defense Intelligence College. Although Heginbotham writes that "few observers were reassured by this provision," the Defense Intelligence College retained a "nominal" role in the program—whatever that means.

Heginbotham expressed particular concern with "merit review" provisions in the NSEA: "the academic and scholarly communities need firm assurance that selection processes will be free from political or bureaucratic interference beyond assuring compliance with terms of reference. . . . It would not seem *acceptable* [my emphasis], for example, to have candidates screened on the basis of their political views . . . [or] their ability to obtain security clearances." Heginbotham went on to recommend that grants to individuals be made by "independent panels of scholars," that the academics on the "oversight board" be selected by a means "transparently independent" of the agencies making up the board. "Most worrisome," Heginbotham wrote, were the service requirements of the NSEP. He described the postgrant requirements for individuals as follows:

> Finally, the legislation includes important but ambiguous 'service' requirements for individuals who receive funds. . . . Undergraduates receiving scholarships covering periods in excess of one year, as well as all individuals receiving graduate training awards, are required either to serve in the field of education or in government service for a period between one and three times the length of the award. The legislation also prohibits any department, agency, or entity of the U.S. government that engages in intelligence activities from using any recipient of funds from the program to undertake any activity on its behalf while the individual is being supported by the program.[40]

Heginbotham suggested that the post-grant term be limited to a year, and limited not just to positions in "government and education," but enabling any employment that used the training to benefit the nation's international needs.[41]

Heginbotham's analysis is similar to Gosling's in three respects: one, the analysis and recommendations are almost entirely procedural; nowhere does either Heginbotham or Gosling defend independent academic inquiry as essential in itself, or international and area studies as important apart from what the state (let alone the "intelligence community") may want. Second, both assume that any funds of such size are ipso facto worth having, regardless of provenance, assuming merely that the procedures can be "as good as possible," in Heginbotham's words; third, the guarantees that they ask for have not only been routinely bypassed by the state and area studies academics that we examined earlier, but even powerful senators complain that the very "oversight" committees responsible for monitoring the CIA have been ignored and subverted—especially in the most recent period (I refer mainly to the revelations of "Iran-Contra" and the murders of Americans by CIA-associated militarists in Central America). The SSRC's Heginbotham, however, seems both more responsible and more concerned than the AAS's Gosling about "re-granting agencies" being little more than laundries for DOD funding. Finally, of course, Heginbotham's calls for merit review, independence, recognition of the difference between scholarship and government "service," and so on, were the same ones harped on by the early leaders of area education, and they did little to hold back the proliferation of CIA-service faculty and students.

The *Bulletin of Concerned Asian Scholars* (BCAS), a publication that has its roots in the antiwar movement of the late 1960s, provided periodic coverage of the NSEA.[42] Mark Selden argued correctly that the NESA "poses anew the issue of scholarship and power that lay behind the origin" of the Committee of Concerned Asian Scholars (mother organization to the BCAS, but now defunct), and noted that unlike earlier such activities, this one "saw no reason to conceal the military and intelligence priorities and powers shaping the field." The *BCAS* drew particular attention to article three of the "purposes" section of the NSEA, calling for it "To produce an increased pool of applicants for work in the departments and agencies of the U.S. Government with national security responsibilities."

In 1994 the cunning of history gave us the "Gingrich Revolution," and a hacksaw approach to cutting budgets: thus the NSEA got what it deserved, namely, a quick and polite burial. No doubt Newt Gingrich thought the NSEA was just another boondoggle for academia (and maybe he was right). At first Congress cut all its funds, but then restored some of them—or so it seems, since NSEP scholarships were again available to students in early 1996. Still, it is limping along into the post-Gingrich era.

If government funding for area studies seems to be drying up, so is funding from the foundations. One result is the contemporary restructuring of the Social Science Research Council. For forty years SSRC committees have been defined mostly by area: the Joint Committee on . . . China, or Latin America, or Western Europe, and so on; there were eleven such committees as of early 1996. That is all changing now, under a major restructuring plan.[43] Instead of eleven committees, there will apparently be three, under the following general rubrics: area studies and regional analysis; area studies and comparative analysis; area studies and global analysis. There may also be a fourth committee designed to support and replenish the existing scholarly infrastructure in the United States, and to develop similar structures in various other parts of the world.

Although this effort is still unfolding, making it unwise to hazard generalizations about how it will end, the SSRC has justified its restructuring by reference to the global changes and challenges of the post-Cold War era, the very "boundary displacements" that I began with this essay with. In the mid-1990s major funding organizations like the Mellon Foundation and the Ford Foundation have also made clear their declining support for area studies and their desire for cross-regional scholarship, so in that subtly coercive context a new beginning for the SSRC becomes obligatory (apparently the SSRC has been teetering on the edge of bankrupcy for several years).

As this restructuring project got off the ground, the SSRC sought to justify it by reference to the unfortunate Cold War shaping of area studies in the early postwar period and the need for "rethinking international scholarship" now that the Cold War is over.[44] This odd return of repressed knowledge stimulated a sharp response: several scholars associated with Soviet and Slavic studies weighed in to deny that political pressures deriving from the Cold War agenda of U.S. foreign policy had much affect on their field, which often produced scholarship "strikingly independent of assumptions driving U.S. political preferences"; various area institutes may have been formed "partially in response to the Cold War," but nonetheless were able to conduct scholarship "without compromising their academic integrity." The authors also argued that the new SSRC framework "will tear international scholarship from the rich, textured empirical base that has been assiduously developed through decades of research, moving it instead to a nebulous 'global' framework for research."[45] This is a very nice statement of the likely outcome of the current SSRC/ACLS restructuring, but, as we have seen, Heginbotham is clearly right about the state's role in shaping the study of "foreign areas"; honest and independent scholarship was possible in the early area institutes, but the academic integrity of the institutes themselves was compromised by a secret and extensive network of ties to the CIA and the FBI. It is a bit much, of course, for the SSRC only to acknowledge this now by way of justifying its new course, when it spent all too much time in the 1960s and 1970s denying that the state had any influence on its research programs.[46] More important, however, is the contemporary denial of the same thing, and here the SSRC's critics had a point.

Perhaps the most disappointing aspect of the SSRC's restructuring and the new directions announced by the major foundations is the absence of any reference to the basic motivation for so many of the new tendencies in the 1990s world that it hopes to adapt itself to, namely, the transnational corporation. This is the motive force and modal organization for "globalization" and the technologies that speed it. Bill Gates's Microsoft is as dominant in this new sphere as John D. Rockefeller's Standard Oil was a century ago; and no doubt our grandchildren will vote for various governors and senators, if not presidents, named Gates— and the ones who become academics will go to the "Gates Foundation" for their research grants. Another symbolic American corporation, Coca-Cola, has become the first U.S. multinational to place overall corporate management in the hands of its world office rather than its historic national center in Atlanta. In that sense, SSRC is merely following Coca-Cola's lead by making the United States of America just another subsidiary, just another "area committee." The globally competitive American corporations are all-out for multiculturalism, multiethnic staffs, a world without borders, and the latest high technology, no matter what its impact on human beings, something evident in their media advertising: "Oil for the Lamps of China" may have been Standard Oil's slogan for selling kerosene worldwide, but now Michael Jordan as the high-flying, globe-trotting logo for Nike might as well be the logo for America, Inc. (Jordan and his Chicago Bulls are particularly popular in "Communist China"—just as they are in my household, I hasten to add.)

If the current American administration has one "doctrine," it is a Clinton Doctrine of promoting American-based global corporations and American exports through the most activist foreign economic policy of any president in history. Clinton's achievements in this respect—NAFTA, APEC, the new World Trade Organiation and many other alphabet-soup organizations, and the routine, daily use of the state apparatus to further the export goals of U.S. multinationals—are all justified by buzzwords that crop up in the new directions of the foundations and the SSRC: a world without borders, increasing globalization, the wonders of the Internet and the World Wide Web, the growth of multiculturalism, the resulting intensification of subnational loyalties and identities (and isn't that a problem that needs to disappear), and so on.

This is not a matter of SSRC raising a challenge to the global corporation, which is hardly to be expected, but it is a matter of not abandoning hard-won scholarly knowledge and resources that we already have. Because of the ferment of the 1960s, social science scholarship of the 1970s met a high standard of quality and relevance. In political science, sociology, and even to some extent economics, political economy became a rubric under which scholars produced a large body of work on the multinational corporation, the global monetary system, the world pool of labor, peripheral dependency, and American hegemony itself. A high point of this effort was Immanuel Wallerstein's multivolume *The Modern World-System,* but there were many others.

It was amazing to witness the alacrity with which social scientists abandoned this political economy program, however, especially since the abandonment seemed roughly coterminous with the arrival of the Reagan and Thatcher administrations. Often, the very social scientists who produced serious scholarship in political economy in the 1970s became the leaders of a march into the abstractions of rational choice and formal theory in the 1980s. Be that as it may, there remains a fine body of work in American political economy that could be the basis for a revival of scholarship on the global corporation and the political economy of the world that it creates before our eyes.

Conclusion

The Clinton administration has stamped the 1990s with its predominant emphasis on foreign economic policy, just as the foundations, in the wake of the collapse of Western communism, moved quickly to attenuate their support for area studies, emphasizing instead interregional themes (such as "development and democracy"). The source of power had shifted in the 1990s, from the state's concern with the maintenance of Cold War boundary security to transnational corporations that, as the organized expression of the market, saw no geographic limit on their interests. The state (in the form of the Clinton administration) and the foundations were the quickest to sense this displacement and to redirect practical and scholarly efforts. Sponsors' expectations of area experts likewise changed quickly: a Kremlinological opinion abut "China after Mao or Deng" was suddenly less interesting than an informed judgment on "China's economic reforms: whither the old state sector,"? and the like. The entire field of communist studies found itself alone with the intelligence agencies and the Pentagon, searching for a function after the object of their desire had rolled itself back to nothing.

As postwar history unfolded, in other words, scholars caught up in one historical system and one discourse that defined discipline, department, area and subject, suddenly found themselves in another emerging field of inquiry, well in advance of imagining or discovering the subject themselves. To put a subtle relationship all too crudely, power and money had found their subject first, and shaped fields of inquiry accordingly.

If we began this paper with McGeorge Bundy, it is best to close it with words from one of the few scholars to speak out against the FBI and McCarthyite purge in the early postwar period—and for his efforts, to suffer his due measure of obsessive FBI attention. In 1949 the historian Bernard A. DeVoto wrote words as appropriate to that era as for the "National Security Education Act" today, and implied that the universities must have a corporate integrity separate from, and when need be critical of, the state: "The colleges . . . have got to say: on this campus all books, all expression, all inquiry, all opinions are free. They have got to maintain that position against the government and everyone else. If they don't, they will presently have left nothing that is worth having."[47]

Notes

1. Michel Foucault, *Power/ Knowledge: Selected Interviews and Other Writings, 1972–1977*, ed. Colin Gordon (New York: Pantheon Books, 1980), p.96

2. See Arif Dirlik, "The Asia-Pacific Idea: Reality and Representation in the Invention of a Regional Structure," Duke University (conference paper February 1991).

3. Ezra F. Vogel, *Japan as Number One: Lessons for America* (Cambridge, Mass.: Harvard University Press, 1979).

4. Bundy's 1964 speech at Johns Hopkins, quoted in Sigmund Diamond, *Compromised Campus: The Collaboration of Universities with the Intelligence Community* (New York: Oxford University Press, 1992), p. 10.

5. I presented some of the ideas in this paper at the Association for Asian Studies (AAS) in 1993, on a panel held in honor of the 25th anniversary of the *Bulletin of Concerned Asian Scholars*. I then presented a much-revised version at the 1996 meetings of the Association for Asian Studies, and another version with different emphasis appeared in *The Bulletin of Concerned Asian Scholars* in its spring 1997 issue. For their helpful comments I would like to thank Arif Dirlik, Bill and Nancy Doub, Harry Harootunian, Richard

Odaka, Moss Roberts, Mark Selden, Chris Simpson, Marilyn Young, Masao Miyoshi, and Stefan Tanaka. Obviously I am responsible for the views presented herein.

6. William Nelson Fenton, *Area Studies in American Universities: For the Commission on Implications of Armed Services Educational Programs* (Washington, D.C.: American Council on Education, 1947), paraphrased in Ravi Arvind Palat, "Building Castles on Crumbling Foundations: Excavating the Future of Area Studies in a Post-American World" (University of Hawaii, February 1993). (I am grateful to Dr. Palat for sending me his paper.) Robert B. Hall's seminal study done for the SSRC in 1947 still makes for interesting reading, but Hall, of course, would not have had access to classified intelligence documentation on the government's relationship to area studies. (Hall, *Area Studies with Special Reference to Their Application for Research in the Social Sciences* (New York: Social Science Research Council, 1947).

7. Barry Katz, *Foreign Intelligence: Research and Analysis in the Office of Strategic Services, 1942–1945* (Cambridge: Harvard University Press, 1989), p. 160. Professor Katz has written an informative, well-researched book on academics in the OSS; nonetheless he barely scratches the surface in examining the problems inherent in professors doing intelligence work; furthermore he ends his story in the late 1940s.

8. *Ibid.*; also Palat, "Building Castles on Crumbling Foundations;" also Richard Lambert et. al., *Beyond Growth: The Next Stage in Language and Area Studies* (Washington, D.C.: Association of American Universities, 1984), pp. 8–9.

9. See Betty Abrahamson Dessants, "The Silent Partner: The Academic Community, Intelligence, and the Development of Cold War Ideology, 1944–1946," Organization of American Historians annual meeting (March 28–31, 1996). Katz (*Foreign Intelligence*, pp. 57–60) argues for a break between the anti-fascist politics of theOSS and the anti-communist politics of the CIA, but a close reading of his text suggests many continuities into the postwar period, in the persons of Alex Inkeles, Philip Mosely, W. W. Rostow, and many others; an alternative reading would be that the anti-fascists, many of them left-liberals, were either weeded out or fell by the wayside, distressed at the turn taken by American Cold War policies after 1947.

10. The letter is dated Oct. 28, 1948. Those who wish to pursue this matter can find extensive documentation in the William Donovan Papers, Carlisle Military Institute, box 73a. Others included in this effort were Evron Kirkpatrick, Robert Lovett, and Richard Scammon, among many others. Christopher Simpson terms this same operation "the Eurasian Institute," listing it is a special project of Kennan and Davies,

in which Kirkpatrick participated. See *Blowback: America's
Recruitment of Nazis and Its
Effects on the Cold War* (New
York: Weidenfeld & Nicolson,
1988), p. 115n; Diamond also
has useful information on this
matter in *Compromised Campus*, pp. 103–105.

11. Diamond, *Compromised Campus*, chap. 3 and 4.

12. Boston FBI to FBI Director, Feb.
9, 1949, quoted in Diamond,
Compromised Campus, p. 47;
see also pp. 109–10.

13. For example, the Sigmund Diamond Papers (at Columbia University) contain an enormous
file on Raymond A. Bauer's inability to get a security clearance to consult with the CIA in
1952–54, because he had once
been an acquaintance of William Remington, whom the FBI
thought was a communist (see
box 22).

14. Diamond Papers, box 15.

15. Memo from SAC Boston to J.
Edgar Hoover, Mar. 7, 1949,
Diamond Papers, box 13.

16. Boston FBI report of Feb. 2,
1949, ibid.

17. Boston FBI report of Nov. 1,
1950, ibid., box 14, also has an
extensive file on Robert Lee
Wolff's security check before he
became a consultant to the CIA
in 1951.

18. I refer, for example, to the
"Studies in Political Development" series, sponsored by the
Committee on Comparative
Politics of the Social Science
Research Council, which, by my
count yielded seven books, all
published by Princeton University Press in the mid-1960s and

all of which became required
reading in the political science
subfield of comparative politics:
Lucian W. Pye, ed., *Communications and Political Development*;
Joseph LaPalombara, ed., *Bureaucracy and Political Development*; Robert E. Ward and
Dankwart A. Rustow, eds., *Political Modernization in Japan
and Turkey*; James S. Coleman,
ed., *Education and Political Development*; Joseph LaPalombara
and Myron Weiner, eds., *Political Parties and Political Development*; Lucian W. Pye and Sidney
Verba, eds., *Political Culture and
Political Development*; and Le-
onard Binder (along with Pye,
Coleman, Verba, LaPalombara,
and Weiner), eds., *Crises and
Sequences in Political Development*.

Gabriel Almond and James S.
Coleman authored the ur-text in
this literature, *The Politics of the
Developing Areas* (Princeton:
Princeton University Press,
1960).

Almond also was an aca-
demic participant in intelligence projects. Documents in
the Max Millikan Papers show
that Almond was a member of
a classified "Working Committee on Attitudes Toward Unconventional Weapons" in 1958–
61, along with air force Gen.
Curtis LeMay, Harvard academic Thomas Schelling, and
MIT's de Sola Pool among others. The committee studied "a
variety of types of unconventional weapons, nuclear, biological, and chemical, for use in
limited war." The social scientists were expected to find ways

of "minimizing" unfortunate reactions by target peoples to the use of such weapons—or, as Millikan put it in his letter to Almond inviting him to join the committee, the committee would discuss measures to be taken that "might reduce to tolerable levels the political disadvantages of the use of a variety of such weapons," and how to use weapons of mass destruction and still have "the limitability of limited conflict." (Millikan to Almond, Nov. 3, 1958, Max Millikan Papers, box 8.) Millikan's long memorandum of Jan. 10, 1961, to the committee stated clearly that use of such weapons might include crop-destroying agents that would cause general famine; the covert use of this and other unconventional weapons would be accompanied by overt denial that the U.S. had used them. The key case he mentioned would be use of such weapons against a conventional Chinese attack on a country in Southeast Asia (Millikan Papers, box 8).

19. Mosely's files show that he worked with the Operations Research Office of Johns Hopkins on classified projects in 1949; that he had a top secret clearance for CIA work in 1951 and 1954; that in 1957 he had CIA contracts and was a member of the "National Defense Executive Reserve" assigned to the "Central Intelligence Agency Unit," and that he renewed his contracts and status in 1958; that he worked on an unnamed project for the Special Opera-

tions Research Office of American University in 1958; that he was cleared for top secret work by the Institute for Defense Analysis in 1961; and that in the same year he kept Abbot Smith of the CIA informed about his travel to the USSR in connection with ACLS/SSRC work on academic exchanges with that country. See Philip Mosely Papers, University of Illinois, box 13, Operations Research Office to Mosely, Feb. 28, 1949, and Nov. 2, 1949 (the latter memo refers to "the optimum use of the social sciences in operations research"); also "National Defense Executive Reserve, Statement of Understanding," signed by Mosely Dec. 19, 1957 and renewed, June 6, 1958 (the latter memo also refers to a "contract" that Mosely has with the CIA, separate from his activities in the "Executive Reserve"); also Mosely to Abbot Smith, Mar. 10, 1961. (Mosely begins the letter to Smith, "In accordance with the present custom I want to report my forthcoming travel plans." Smith, an important CIA official and colleague of Ray Cline and William Bundy among others, is not here identified as a CIA man. But he is so in Ludwell Lee Montague, *General Walter Bedell Smith as Director of Central Intelligence* [University Park: Pennsylvania State University Press, 1992], pp. 138–39, where information on Abbot Smith's CIA work can be found.) In 1961 Mosely worked with the IDA on a secret project on "Communist China and Nuclear Warfare" (S.

F. Giffin, Institute for Defense Analyses, to Mosely, Nov. 24, 1961, and Mosely to Giffin, Dec. 6, 1961). See also various memoranda in box two, including a record of Mosely's security clearances.

20. Ibid., box 4, letter from Walt W. Rostow, MIT, to Mosely, Oct. 6, 1952.
21. Ibid., Frederick Barghoorn (Yale University) to Mosely, Jan. 17, 1952.
22. Ibid., Whitman to Mosely, Oct. 5, 1955; Mosely to Whitman, Oct. 10, 1955.
23. Ibid., box 13, Nathan B. Lenvin, U.S. Department of Justice, to Mosely, Apr. 20, 1953.
24. Ibid., box 18, Paul F. Langer to Mosely, May 11, 1953.
25. Ibid., Paul F. Langer to Mosely, Carl Spaeth and Cleon O. Swayze, May 17, 1953.
26. "Report Submitted by Paul F. Langer to the Director of Research, Board on Overseas Training and Research, the Ford Foundation," April 15, 1953, ibid. The books Pye later authored were *Guerrilla Communism in Malaya, Its Social and Political Meaning* (Princeton, NJ: Princeton University Press, 1956); and *The Spirit of Burmese Politics* (Cambridge, MA: MIT, Center for International Studies [CIS, or CENIS], 1959). One could also include in this group Daniel Lerner's *The Passing of Traditional Society* (New York: The Free Press, 1958), another central text in comparative politics; Lerner had worked with Pye, Ithiel de Sola Pool, and other political scientists at MIT's Center for International Studies on projects dealing with communications and society, insights that were later used in the CIA's Phoenix program in Vietnam. Much of this research was funded under CIA or government contracts for psychological warfare. On this see Christopher Simpson, "U.S. Mass Communication Research and Counterinsurgency after 1945: An Investigation of the Construction of Scientific 'Reality,'" in William S. Solomon and Robert W. McChesney, eds., *Ruthless Criticism: New Perspectives in U.S. Communication History* (Minneapolis, MN: University of Minnesota Press, 1993).

27. The conference was held October 9–10, 1953. See the list of those who attended, Mosely Papers, box 18.
28. Ibid, box 18. As Diamond shows, such considerations extended to Carnegie's acknowledged policy of excluding scholars who were "way to the left," which at one point led to worries about Dirk Bodde and Arthur Schlesinger Jr. and major fretting about Gunnar Myrdal; however, these cases paled before Carnegie's concerns about the Institute for Pacific Relations and Owen Lattimore (*Compromised Campus*, pp. 299–301.)
29. Mosely Papers, box 18, George B. Baldwin to Mosely, Dec. 21, 1954.
30. Ibid., Swayze to Mosely, Oct. 21, 1954; Langer said he was involved in developing Chinese studies in Langer to Mosely,

Spaeth, and Swayze, May 17, 1953.

31. Simpson, "U.S. Mass Communication Research and Counterinsurgency," p. 316, 330. Simpson has long lists of social scientists who worked for the OSS and other intelligence agencies. During the war, they included: Harold Lasswell, Hadley Cantril, Daniel Lerner, Nathan Leites, Heinz Eulau, Elmo Roper, Wilbur Schramm, Clyde Kluckhohn, Edward Shils, Morris Janowitz, Alex Inkeles, Herbert Marcuse, and many others. After the war, "a remarkably tight circle of men and women" continued to work for the state, including Lasswell and Lerner, Cantril, Janowitz, Kluckhohn, Eulau, and others.

32. box 13, Smith to Mosely, Feb. 28, 1961; see also notations on Mosely to Smith, Mar. 10, 1961.

33. Ibid., Mosely to Smith, March 16, 1961. In 1962 Mosely told James E. King of the Institute for Defense Analyses (IDA, a major academic arm of government security agencies), who had proposed a three-year program of some sort to Ford, that, "of the major foundations, only Ford has shown a willingness to mingle its money with government money, and even it is rather reluctant to do so." Mosely also counseled King that "the question of 'end-use,' i.e., whether classified or publishable, is important to the foundation" (ibid., Mosely to King, Apr. 17, 1962).

34. JCCC, "Report on the Conference on the Status of Studies of Modern and Contemporary China" (SSRC, New York, March 1968), quoted in Diamond, *Compromise Camps*, p. 98.

35. This transcript was brought to my attention by Kai Bird; it was found by David Armstrong, who is writing a dissertation on the Rostow brothers. The first few pages are missing, so some of the participants are hard to identify; furthermore, their statements were truncated and paraphrased by the transcriber. The meeting was held on May 18, 1959. (All quotations in the text come from this transcript.) Millikan was an assistant director of the CIA in 1951–52, and the director of CENIS from 1952–69, the year in which he died. In the guide to his papers at MIT, it says that the Center for International Studies grew out of "Project Troy," begun by the State Department in 1950 "to explore international information and communication patterns." It later broadened its agenda to "social science inquiry on international affairs" (Max Franklin Millikan Papers, MIT).

36. Ibid.

37. The summary is by Anne Betteridge, executive officer of the Middle East Studies Association, and is to be found in *Asian Studies Newsletter* (June–July 1992), pp. 3–4.

38. *Asian Studies Newsletter* (June–July 1992), pp. 4–5.

39. "The National Security Education Program," *SSRC Items* 46, nos. 2–3, (June–September 1992), pp. 17–23.

40. Ibid., p. 19.

41. "Area scholars are extremely sensitive to the damage that can be done to their personal reputations and to their ability to conduct scholarship abroad when they come to be perceived as involved with intelligence or defense agencies of the U.S. government" (Ibid., p. 22).

42. Mark Selden, James K. Boyce, and the BCAS editors, "National Security and the Future of Asian Studies," *Bulletin of Concerned Asian Scholars* 24, no. 2 (April–June 1992), pp. 84–98. See also the updated information in *Bulletin of Concerned Asian Scholars* 24, no. 3 (July–September 1992), pp. 52–53.

43. I have seen drafts of the restructuring plan and some of the various joint committees' responses, all dated in late 1995 and early 1996, but cannot cite the documents under the terms of their provision to me; this is not because of secrecy, so much as the provisional and evolving nature of the restructuring itself, as SSRC administrators respond to suggestions and complaints about their new plans.

44. Stanley J. Heginbotham, "Rethinking International Scholarship: The Challenge of Transition from the Cold War Era," *SSRC Items* (June–September 1994).

45. Robert T. Huber, Blair A. Ruble, and Peter J. Stavrakis, "Post–Cold War 'International' Scholarship: A Brave New World or the Triumph of Form Over Substance?," SSRC *Items* (March–April 1995).

46. Heginbotham wrote: "those who shaped the emerging institutions of international scholarship in the early years of the Cold War should have been more attentive to a range of issues involving the autonomy and integrity of scholars and scholarly institutions." Equally hypocritical is the response of Huber, Ruble, and Stavrakis, asking Heginbotham to name names: "Which individuals were inattentive to scholarly autonomy and integrity?" they ask, since such people should have "an opportunity to defend themselves."

47. Quoted in Diamond, *Compromised Campus,* p. 43.

(Slava Gerovitch)

Writing History in the Present Tense:

Cold War–era Discursive Strategies of Soviet Historians of Science and Technology

The study of Soviet discourse is a fascinating journey through multiple layers of meaning, exquisite rhetorical feats, and intentional paradoxes. Soviet leaders fairly early arrived at the idea of supplementing direct political censorship with more subtle ideological controls over disciplinary discourses. However, their attempts to supervise and homogenize public discourse simply did not reach its goals. The fragmented and unstable reality of Soviet discourse was a far cry from the (purported) perfect orderliness of totalitarian discourse, so vividly imagined in George Orwell's *1984* and in various Orwell-inspired studies.[1]

Only recently have scholars begun to explore the tensions, inconsistencies, and uncertainties of Soviet discursive practices. Studies of political discourse provided a few illustrative examples of the complexities involved. Michael Gorham, for instance, has pointed to an essential conflict in Soviet political discourse: The more colloquial a tone Soviet propaganda assumed, the less it was capable of conveying abstract ideas and political symbols of the central state. When sophisticated political language was employed, it often caused frustration, distrust, and alienation on the part of peasants and workers.[2] In another study, Rachel Walker identified a "linguistic paradox" in Soviet political discourse, which stemmed from the necessity for Soviet leaders to maintain the appearance of continuity with the teachings of Marx and Lenin, and at the same time "creatively develop" Marxist-Leninist doctrine.[3]

An even more complex picture emerges when we turn from political texts to various disciplinary discourses characteristic of the Soviet academic community. The Soviet state both tried to control professionals and needed their expertise, and this resulted in a tangled and paradoxical structure of discourse. State and party officials promoted those practices that fit the contemporary political agenda, while professionals sought legitimation and support from those in power. Tensions within both official political discourse and professional discourses produced a considerable room for maneuver and negotiation.

Rather than portraying professional discourses as mere servants of the state or victims of totalitarian oppression, it may be more productive to speak of *discursive strategies* developed by professionals themselves in attempt to adapt their knowledge to the current political, socioeconomic, and cultural situation, and to influence this situation at the same time. Such discursive strategies had to be flexible enough to take advantage of the tensions within public discourse. On the other hand, in order to keep up with sociopolitical changes, professionals would have to frequently modify these strategies.

In this article, I will argue that Soviet historians of science and technology have developed a number of such discursive strategies and that these have shaped the face of their discipline as a whole, as well as influenced those historians' individual research agendas and methods. I will examine how Soviet historians of science and technology shifted their discursive strategies in parallel with the political and social evolution of Soviet society. I will attempt to place Soviet historical research in an institutional context, focusing on the role of the Academy of Sciences. In the conclusion, I will compare the discursive strategies that American and Soviet scholars developed in the context of the Cold War.

Early Soviet Years:
Two Academies Contend for the Past

The Soviet Union was the first country in the world to institutionalize the study of the history of science and technology.[4] On the initiative of the prominent geochemist and mineralogist Vladimir Vernadskii, the Russian Academy of Sciences set up the Commission on the History of Knowledge in May 1921.[5] The commission, he hoped, would help raise the prestige of national science and remind the Bolshevik authorities (like the tsarist authorities before them) of the necessity to support academic research, particularly in view of proposals to close the academy down that were circulating at the time.

Vernadskii ascribed a primary role in the advancement of science to the periodic "clustering" of individual geniuses, which he viewed as a natural phenomenon subject to quantitative regularities. At the same time, however, he stressed the importance of favorable social and economic conditions—which was to say, adequate financial and political support—for great "explosions" of scientific thought. "As a professor under tsarism [Vernadskii] had witnessed the blighting effects of politics and inadequate funding on science, and he hoped for better conditions under the Soviet government," the American historian of Russian science Loren Graham has noted.[6]

Militant Marxists scientists of the day downplayed the achievements of national science in their attempt to undermine the prestige of the Academy of Sciences, in which many saw a stronghold of the old regime and a rival to a recently founded Communist Academy.[7] Many regarded Tsarist Russia as an oppressive regime under which nothing, science included, could possibly have prospered.[8] Vernadskii's commission, in contrast, chose to capitalize on Russia's prerevolutionary scientific heritage and take advantage of Marx and Lenin's vision of scientific advancement as integral to socialism as an effective discursive strategy for political protection of the Academy of Sciences under Bolshevik rule.

Probably the most famous manifestation (in the West) of the discursive style of the Marxist-oriented Soviet historians of science and technology during this period was Boris Hessen's paper "The Social and Economic Roots of Newton's *Principia*," which created a furor at the Second International Congress of the History of Science in London in 1931. Elaborating on the Marxist thesis of the primacy of productive forces in the development of knowledge, Hessen contended that Newton's scientific activity was in essence a response to the social and economic needs of contemporary England—building new machines and weapons, as well as the creation of a new worldview that could reconcile religious dogmas with a new social and economic order. "Newton," Hessen maintained, "was a typical representative of the rising bourgeoisie, and in his philosophy he embodied the characteristic features of his class."[9]

Hessen, a prominent physicist and historian of science, had himself come under fire inside the Soviet Union when he attempted to defend Einsteinian physics, which was viewed by militant Marxist critics with considerable suspicion. Hessen's analysis of Newton became in part a means for him to challenge his opponents with their own weapon—a Marxist analysis of science—taken to the extreme. Hessen subjected Newton to the same kind of class-based criticism as his opponents were directing against Einstein. "Hessen was illustrating that Marxists should simultaneously recognize the value of Newton's physics, even though it developed in mercantilist England and was used as a tool to support religion, and the value of Einstein's and Bohr's physics, while acknowledging that they arose in imperialist Europe and are often used to counter Marxism," as historian Loren Graham has written.[10]

Hessen's discursive "ju-jitsu" strategy produced a piece of scholarship that was taken quite seriously in the West.[11] According to the *Dictionary of the History of Science*, Hessen's paper has become instrumental in establishing the "externalist" methodological approach to historical studies, which emphasizes the role of broad social and economic forces in defining the content and evolution of scientific knowledge.[12]

By the early 1930s, the Bolshevik Party established its strong political influence in the Academy of Sciences and trusted the latter with virtual monopoly over fundamental research.[13] As the academy was gaining political respectability, study of the history of science obtained new legitimacy and influence. In 1932, the Academy of Sciences established the Institute for the History of Science and Technology under the direction of the prominent Bolshevik Nikolai Bukharin.[14] On becoming the institute's director, he encouraged a broad range of historical studies, not necessarily Marxist. Unfortunately, Bukharin's political career was already in decline when he became the Institute's director, and soon an association with him cast a deep shadow on the entire field of the history of science and technology. Bukharin was arrested and accused of treason, which led to the denunciation and closure of the institute in February 1938. Many independent-minded Marxist scholars including Hessen and Bukharin, fell victims to the Great Terror.

The crackdown on prominent, yet independent Marxist scholars "signaled the demise of systematic efforts to apply classical Marxist theory to the study of the history of science," the American historian of Russian science Alexander Vucinich has written.[15] This is not to say that the number of reverential quotations from Marx and Marxist sounding terms to any degree decreased in academic writings; on the contrary, such signs of loyalty were being packed into historians' works more densely than ever. The new scholarship, however, was not Marxist, but rather "Marxy," that is, imitating Marxist language with little real correlation with Marx's method or teachings. Being a language with little theoretical substance, "Marxyism" had almost unlimited malleability, which allowed it to be shaped to the political requirements of any given moment. Serious Marxist research was no longer a successful discursive strategy and could in fact be dangerous. The display of "partyness" (loyalty to the party line) became the order of the day.

Ideological controls were relaxed somewhat in the harsh conditions of the Great Patriotic War that followed the Nazi invasion of the Soviet Union in 1941. Many in the academy chose the genre of commemorative events to revive history of science studies. The "great men of (Russian) science" type of discourse fit the prevailing patriotic mood, underscored the value of scientific traditions for the state, and unobtrusively reminded the authorities of the necessity to support science. Between 1941 and 1945, Soviet historians of science and technology held numerous meetings to celebrate anniversaries of various scientific discoveries, institutions, and great Russian and foreign scientists.[16] The message finally reached Stalin's ears. With his personal approval, the Academy of Sciences established the Institute for the History of Natural Science in 1945.

War-time cooperation with the Western Allies brought significant changes for the Soviet scientific community. For a short time after 1943, Soviet scholars were again allowed to publish their papers in American and British journals. Historical studies of Russian science as an integral part of world science were now encouraged.[17] At the 1945 academy session devoted to the celebration of the 220th anniversary of the Academy of Sciences, Soviet foreign minister Vyacheslav M. Molotov spoke of closer ties between Soviet science and the global scientific community. This session was the first Soviet scientific meeting to which foreign guests were invited since 1937. Similarly, one of the leading party ideologues, Georgii F. Aleksandrov, published a fundamental textbook on the history of Western philosophy; and throughout the book, Russian scholars' debt to the great Western thinkers was clearly acknowledged.

The Cold War Discourse for Internal Use

The situation for scientists and particularly for historians of science and technology changed dramatically with the erosion of East-West relations from early 1946 on. The tone of the Soviet official discourse produced by Agitprop—the Department of Agitation and Propaganda of the Party Central Committee—grew much more hostile and became widely employed for internal use in a series of campaigns against "cosmopolitanism" and "servility to the West."[18] Beginning with party resolutions on literary journals, theater, movies, and music, this wave quickly spread into science. In 1946, Agitprop's mouthpiece *Culture and Life* (*Kul'tura i zhizn'*) reprimanded academy institutes for their uncritical attitude toward the economics and politics of the United States and Britain. Just a few months earlier, those institutes' activities had perfectly followed the party line, but now the line had turned, and scholarship was expected to turn along with it. In early 1947, two Soviet medical researchers were put on trial by a special "court of honor" for sharing scientific information with their American colleagues—an act now regarded as highly unpatriotic and equivalent to divulging a state secret.[19] By 1947, Georgii F. Aleksandrov's 1946 text *History of Western Philosophy* (*Istoriia zapadnoi filosofii*) was accused of distorting Marxism and inappropriately exaggerating the role of Western philosophy in the development of Russian thought.[20]

This highly publicized affair sent a clear message to the history of science community, and the point was well taken. In May 1948, historians convened a conference on the history of Russian chemistry in Moscow, with the announced goal of defending "the scientific priorities of Russian scientists in important discoveries and inventions often attributed to scientists or pseudoscientists from capitalist countries."[21]

"The struggle for establishing national priorities in science is part of the war against cosmopolitanism," wrote one campaign activist. "The cosmopolitan conception of world science is theoretically unfounded and politically reactionary. World science is not nonnational; it does not grow apart from specific historical forms. Any science, like any culture in general, is national in form and class-oriented in content."[22]

The history of science again found itself at the center of political tension. Its arguments became a widely used resource for criticizing an opponent or legitimizing one's own position within the scientific community.[23] One of Trofim Lysenko's favorite rhetorical arguments was linking his opponents—Soviet geneti-cists—with the Western "Mendel-Morgan" tradition.[24] He legitimized his own approach, in turn, by referring to the indig-enous "Michurinist" tradition in biology. In another academic storm over the content of physiology, rival biographies of the late Russian Nobel Prize laureate Ivan Pavlov, each written by his disciples, lay conflicting claims to his heritage. The infamous 1950 "Pavlovian" joint session of the Academy of Sciences and the Academy of Medical Sciences turned into a contest over rights to the genuine Pavlovian tradition. Those who failed to prove the purity of their scientific genealogy, lost their positions. These debates had little to do with serious historical questions; the actual links between Pavlov's theory and the contestants' views were much less important than the contestants' position in the then-current academic and political rivalries. In this debate as in others, the history of science did not decide contemporary issues; on the contrary, historical questions were claimed re-solved depending on the outcome of current power struggles.

Governmental actions underscored the political importance of historical studies. Between 1947 and 1952, for example, six books on the history of science and technology were awarded the highly prestigious Stalin Prize, which instantly made them an object of eager imitation. The most notorious among them was Victor Da-nilevskii's *Russkaia tekhnika* (*Russian Technology*), which called for repulsion of "all those who infringe on Russian primogeniture in great deeds."[25] In January 1949, the Academy of Sciences held a special session on the history of national science, thus putting historical questions on the top of the current agenda for the So-viet scientific establishment.[26]

Just as the Soviet Union was competing with the West in the political arena, Soviet historians fought their Cold War on the discursive fields of the past. They gave the credit for the discovery of the law of the conservation of mass, research on atmospheric electricity, and the theory of atomism to the "father of Russian science" Mikhail Lomonosov, proclaimed Alexander Butlerov the founder of structural chemistry and Alexander Popov the inventor of the radio. To meet the high quotas of priority claims, some Soviet historians began to manufacture evidence for such claims. A senior Soviet historian later confessed that "the deeply rooted tradition of work aimed solely at quantitative output led to the promotion of publications based on volume and filled with sets of assembled 'facts' which, at best, were linked together in a chain by their time coordinates. It was even sometimes the case that these historical 'facts' detailed in our history of science literature never actually took place."[27] Among such imaginary "facts" were a balloon flight in 1731, the invention of a submarine in 1829, and the invention of a bicycle in 1801.[28]

While employing the language of the official nationalist discourse, some Soviet scholars were able to use flexible strategies to advance their own causes, which were not necessarily consistent with the dominant scientific interpretation. A rhetorical appeal to the authority of a long-dead "great Russian scientist" could well serve the defenders of an ideologically suspect contemporary theory. For example, Soviet physicists quickly moved to establish links between Nikolai Lobachevskii's non-Euclidean geometry and Einstein's theory of relativity.[29] An association with Lobachevskii, the famous nineteenth-century Russian mathematician, who had been represented in a recent biography as an exemplary scientist by Stalinist standards,[30] substantially shored up the shaky ideological foundations of Einstein's born-in-the-West theory of physics.

Paradoxically, this ideologically inspired search for the lost and forgotten Russian discoveries and inventions moved Soviet historians to explore central and regional archives more thoroughly, and eventually greatly enhanced general knowledge of the history of national science. The then-president of the Academy of Sciences, Sergei Vavilov, gave great praise to the pre-revolutionary achievements of the St. Petersburg Academy of Sciences and Mikhail Lomonosov.[31] What a remarkable reversal of Vavilov's earlier statement about the total absence of physics in Russia before the twentieth century! While earlier Vavilov had expressed the dominant view of prerevolutionary Russian science as totally oppressed and unworthy, now the academy through its "chief rhetorician" could proudly claim its deep roots in a venerable historical tradition.

Internalist Histories as Opposition to "Marxyism"

The post-Stalin political era in the Soviet Union, known as the "thaw," was marked by significant liberalization of the intellectual sphere. The new regime denounced some of Stalin's crimes and rehabilitated many victims of the Great Terror; the new party leader Nikita Khrushchev attempted to put an end to many aspects of Stalin's isolationist policy. The anticosmopolitanism campaign was over. Soviet scientists gradually began to broaden contacts with their Western colleagues and to develop research in such previously banned or restricted fields as genetics, cybernetics, sociology, and social psychology. Meanwhile, the successes of the Russian atomic weapons and space programs dramatically expanded the prestige and legitimacy of Soviet science, both at home and abroad.

Soviet historians of science and technology took full advantage of the new developments—both institutionally and intellectually. As early as September 1953, the Academy of Sciences set up an Institute for the History of Natural Science and Technology (*Institut istorii estestvoznaniia i tekhniki*, hereafter IIET), which exists to the present day.[32] After the 1956 twentieth Party Congress, where Khrushchev gave his famous anti-Stalinist "secret speech," the changes sped up. The new director of IIET Nikolai A. Figurovskii came out against the previous distortions of the history of Russian science and called for restoring its historical links with world science. He condemned recent works in the field as amateurish, compilatory, and lacking analysis.[33] In 1956, a Soviet delegation attended an International Congress of the History of Science for the first time since 1931.[34] By 1959, the Academy had launched a book series, *Scientific Biography*, in which many prominent Western scientists were given an extensive and favorable treatment for the first time.[35]

Soviet historians who had resented the nationalist fervor of the Stalin era and attempted to free their studies from propaganda clichés frequently turned to what is today termed "internalist" historical narratives as a means of both analyis and self-protection.[36] That is, they tended to isolate their historical subject from its social context and instead emphasized the inner logic of the development of scientific thought. Bonifatii Kedrov—the director of IIET from 1962 to 1974—justified this change of discursive strategy by citing the example of prerevolutionary Russia as an argument *against* socioeconomic determinism: despite its successes in science (which had been acknowledged during the Stalinist/nationalist campaigns), tsarist Russia was hardly more advanced socially, economically, or technologically than the Western nations. Thus, it could not be seen as supplying better external factors for the development of science and technology. That meant, then, that the history of science should emphasize internalist explanations and the disciplinary context, rather than the socioeconomic context.[37] Thus, the earlier degeneration of Soviet historical studies into "Marxyism" had ended up facilitating a shift from Marxist socioeconomic explanations to a self-consciously apolitical, "logical" form of historical discourse.

When Soviet historians of science and technology began to gravitate toward an internalist approach, their main concern became "objectivity," meaning an effort to ground their narrative in hard facts rather than in purely ideological or speculative interpretations. For this reason, Soviet historians took to filling their works with "factological" material and made little or no attempt to analyze and interpret it. This strategy was politically safe, and at the same time the author could demonstrate some personal intellectual independence by disregarding "Marxyist" interpretative clichés. The ideological censors of the day could not point to "bias" in a paper in which there was no explicit analysis and facts "spoke for themselves." An attentive reader, however, could find the author's "subjectivity" transferred from the analytical to the factological level, revealed in the selection of evidence and construction of historical narrative.[38]

The historians' focus on the "inner logic" of scientific development had an important connection with the scientists' own preferred vision of science as an essentially self-driven enterprise.
For example, the prominent mathematician and rector of Leningrad University, Alexandr Alexandrov, asserted in his 1970 article:
"Guided by the inherent regularity in the growth of scientific
thought, the scientists concern themselves primarily with problems generated within their disciplines. . . . The most significant achievements of modern technology have been produced by
scientific research guided by a quest for pure knowledge rather
than by practical tasks."[39] The internalist history of science
shored up scientists' appeals for greater autonomy in setting
their current research priorities and elaborating long-term plans.

Internalism had a lasting effect on Soviet historical research;
the appeal (and the effect) of this discursive strategy went beyond its immediate utility as a rhetorical device that historians
could use to sidestep ideological watchdogs. By defining some
type of questions as appropriate for study and excluding others,
the internalist method and strategy of discourse affected the historians' own mode of thinking. The generation that had adopted
this approach in the 1960s, as will be seen in a moment, had
great difficulty overcoming its limitations even decades later.
Within such discourse, many historical problems necessarily
seemed unsolvable, because their answers lay outside the accepted terrain of internalist analysis. And with the field of study
so narrow, academic criticism sometimes degenerated into a list
of misprints, rather than a discussion of substance.[40] Thus
emerged what the American sociologist of Russian science Linda
Lubrano has mildly called a "nonpolemical, academic style."[41]

In the community of Soviet historians, criticism or disagreement was often perceived as an attempt to brand an opponent
and to revive the tradition of politically motivated attacks of the
1930s and 40s. Instead, a common object of criticism was Western scholarship—yet this was often offered not to degrade it but
rather to introduce it to the Soviet reader. Titles like "The Critique
of the Bourgeois Concepts of X" served more than once as an

umbrella for discussion of scholarly ideas that would otherwise be inaccessible in printed form in the USSR. This particularly paradoxical discursive strategy permitted Soviet historians to mask their disagreement (with one another) by the lack of criticism, while downplaying their accord (with some Western colleagues) by the presence of criticism. This made Soviet historical scholarship look rather cryptic to most Western observers, who were occasionally deluded by "Marxyist" rhetoric and pro forma criticism. Among Soviet readers, however, the meanings that lay between the lines were usually clear enough.

The Brezhnev-era Communist Party in the USSR—which is to say, from the mid 1960s through the early 1980s—usually focused its efforts at ideological control of the social sciences and humanities. Not surprisingly, most Soviet historians of science clearly preferred to explore the inner mechanisms of the development of knowledge rather than study science as a social phenomenon. The choice of "apolitical" scientific knowledge instead of social processes as the subject of study made the historians less vulnerable to ideological control. Nevertheless, some historians soon managed to incorporate sociology into their studies without submitting to the official "Marxyist" social theory. The discursive technique that opened this door was treating the development of science as a "natural process" subject to quantitative regularities which (purportedly) could be studied by the exact methods of natural science.[42]

Soviet science studies (the "science of science," or *naukovedenie*) thus attempted to constitute themselves as an exact science, whose vocabulary and methods were distinct from the calcified dogmas of Marxyist-style historical materialism. This was presented as a "science of science" rather than one of the social sciences, as the name "sociology of science" would have suggested.[43] One of the most important arguments in support of *naukovedenie* was its promise to optimize national science policy in an era of intense international competition. A popular literary magazine wrote in 1968: "The race for scientific and technological superiority gives a momentum to *naukovedenie*. The scientific study of scientific activity thereby becomes an essential condition of success in the struggle of the two political systems for supremacy in the scientific community."[44]

This Soviet "science of science" was created by a diverse group of scholars—historians, philosophers, sociologists, specialists in cybernetics, psychology, systems approach, and so on. They put forward a variety of logical, sociological, and informational models of science.[45] Nevertheless, "there was no standard format for Soviet studies of science, no single set of issues constituting the subject of research, and no unified theory underlying it all," as Linda Lubrano has observed.[46] What was common for most of these studies, however, was their view of science from scientists' *own* perspective, which put the questions of increasing "scientific productivity" and improving conditions for the scientific community to the forefront, and pushed examination of the social role of science to the background.

Soviet specialists in *naukovedenie* played an important role in turning the formula from the Communist Party Program about science becoming a "direct productive force" to the advantage of the scientific community. The historian Yakov Rabkin explained the issue at stake as follows: "At least two opposed interpretations of the formula have been made by officials engaged in science policy. One is that science has to be brought 'back to production,' reduced to applied research and development and thus to become a 'real productive force.' The other interpretation advocates that pure and basic research should be fostered on the grounds that 'science' as such is a 'productive force' which leads in the course of time to important technological and economic benefits."[47]

Expressing the opinion prevalent in the research-oriented academy, science studies specialists usually advocated the second view and turned this ambiguous ideological pronouncement into a powerful rhetorical argument for state support of basic research.

Soon Soviet science studies became a field contested by both party and government officials (the State Committee for Science and Technology was a major patron of *naukovedenie*) and Soviet scientists. The authorities wanted to have a tool to monitor and manage the scientific community, while the scientists needed convincing-sounding quantitative data to lobby for more state support. The direction of science studies was thus an outcome of combined pressures from the two groups.

Perestroika: From Black-and-White to White-and-Black History

Perestroika, a great social reconstruction of Soviet society, ended with the disappearance of the reconstructed object—the Soviet Union—in December 1991. Something else, however, was reconstructed: people's thinking, their attitude to socialism, to their history, and to themselves. Remarkable changes also emerged in Soviet research on the history of science and technology, both reshaping the thematic profile and altering the discursive strategies.

In 1985, Mikhail Gorbachev, the new general secretary of the Central Committee of the Communist Party, launched *perestroika* and announced the policy of openness (*glasnost*) in many areas of public concern that had been previously closed to discussion. For historians, this shift meant the weakening of ideological censorship and access to newly opened archives.[48] Up to that point, Soviet censorship had two major consequences—one direct, the other indirect. The direct was an unwritten prohibition on exploring certain topics, such as Lenin's attack on "bourgeois" intelligentsia in the 1920s or the impact of Stalinist purges on the Soviet scientific community in the 1930s. The indirect effect was a particular Soviet style of historical narrative—internalist, factological, and discussion-avoiding. When censorship was to a large degree eliminated, the direct consequences, naturally, were the first to share the same fate. The indirect effects, however, appeared much more difficult to overcome.

Among the first, most obvious, signs of *perestroika* in the history of science and technology were publications of previously censored or forbidden works. For example, all the passages from Vladimir Vernadskii's *Scientific Thought as a Global Phenomenon* (1938) which had been cut out earlier by censors were published for the first time.[49] It also became possible to study the nature and impact of Stalinist purges and ideological campaigns in physics,[50] cybernetics,[51] genetics,[52] and physiology.[53] Before *perestroika*, the historian A. A. Berzin could not publish his study of the northern railroads, built between 1947 and 1953 by Gulag prisoners; now it came out under the title, "A Road to Nowhere."[54] Berzin even managed to get access to KGB archives and publish materials concerning engineer prisoners of the Gulag, who built a new engine for passenger trains, later named *JS*, after Joseph Stalin.[55]

Another conspicuous sign of change was a sharp reduction in the number of ritual references to Marx and Lenin in scholarly articles appearing in IIET's academic journal, *Voprosy istorii estestvoznaniia i tekhniki* (hereafter *VIET*). At the outset of perestroika in 1986, about one-third of *VIET* publications appealed at least once to the authority of the "classics." By 1991, however, only one in twenty-five *VIET* articles contained *any* direct reference to Marxism. Indeed, the strong wave of criticism of Marxist political theory at that time rendered it very awkward to make any positive mention of Marxist methodology at all. If the ideological climate of pre-*perestroika* years had often forced historians to declare themselves Marxists when they were not, *perestroika* had the opposite effect, wiping any surface signs of Marxism from historical discourse.

As *perestroika* opened formerly forbidden areas for exploration and discussion, a remarkable thematic shift followed that now stressed creating a social history of Soviet science, particularly that of the Stalinist era. That shift in turn has been accompanied by corresponding changes in the geographic and temporal patterns of research with the general trend in the direction of "closer in time, nearer in space."[56] That is, historical discourse gravitated toward twentieth-century Russia. Since 1986, Soviet research published in *VIET* has concentrated more and more on modern history of Russian science and technology, reaching a peak of some 80 percent of the articles published in 1991. New opportunities for study in previously inaccessible archives and concern that this chance might soon be lost to yet another shift in party policy spurred researchers to work intensely with new historical material and to publish old studies that had previously been censored.

Political debates of the *perestroika* period over the future of the Soviet Union drew heavily on historical discourse about the communist past. Liberal-minded intellectuals often chose denunciation of Stalinism (and later, Leninism) as a powerful argument for a radical reform that would make a "return to the past" impossible. Scientists, historians of science, and journalists searching for evidence of party interference with scholarship began to systematically explore newly accessible Communist Party archives, KGB files, and the archives of various academic societies of the Soviet period. Not surprisingly, the materials they uncovered strongly suggested that the development of science and technology in the Soviet Union had not been a self-determined or "natural" process. Instead, it had been strongly affected by the political and ideological context of the time, as well as by the party apparatus and various governmental agencies.

New archival findings, however, were often regarded simply as a source for new facts, rather than the catalyst of new interpretations. Those who understood the recovery from enforced amnesia as merely adding new facts effectively perpetuated the factological approach that had been serving Soviet historians since at least the mid-1950s. This approach presumed a model of history in which the general picture had already been drawn (in this case, it was the image of the communist regime oppressing scientific thought); only some "dark spots" were left. As historians discovered forgotten facts, the dark spots would disappear, and the picture would finally become clear and complete. This view of history required recollection, not reinterpretation.

As in previous historical periods, the various interpretations of the past became weapons in contemporary political struggles, and the political struggles in turn exerted some measure of influence on the content of historical debates. Today's "gold rush" atmosphere in archival research in the former USSR is more than simply a matter of entrepreneurship it also has a distinctly political character. In the intense process of restructuring the field of power/knowledge relationships, any new interpretation of the role of scientists and engineers in decisive moments of Soviet history is a statement laden with political values.

For example, in the summer of 1992 *VIET* sparked a major controversy when it published a number of historical documents concerning the history of the Soviet atomic project.[57] Among the documents uncovered by a former KGB officer were two memoranda revealing that Soviet nuclear physicists in the 1940s had access to Soviet intelligence information on certain details of the Manhattan Project as well as to the design of the first American plutonium bomb. The key issue where historical interpretation converged with political campaigns of the 1990s was the evaluation of the degree to which the Soviet atomic project actually depended on the intelligence information about its American counterpart.

After an issue of *VIET* containing this article was already in print, prominent Soviet physicists made every possible effort to stop publication. They warned that some data contained in these 1940s documents might prove useful to those who were trying to build a bomb now, in the 1990s. Moreover, it turned out that the materials in question had been declassified by the KGB but not by the Ministry of Atomic Energy. Although many copies of the journal had already been sent to subscribers, all remaining copies were immediately confiscated.[58]

In the dispute that followed, the well-known Russian scientist Roald Sagdeev contended that the KGB had selectively disclosed the valuable archives in order to present KGB officers as the true "heroes of the Soviet nuclear miracle,"[59] As for the physicists, one reason for their objection to publication was a desire to prevent the devaluation of their own, more strictly scientific, contribution. The journalist Sergei Leskov suggested that "the reason for the ban on publishing the intelligence record on the bomb program [in *VIET*] is part of the struggle for a place on the Mount Olympus of history rather than a concern with nuclear nonproliferation. Experts who saw the banned text told me that even Edward Teller and Andrei Sakharov would not have been able to build a bomb based on the information it contained."[60]

Taking credit for the Soviet atomic bomb was not just a matter of the reputation of two professional groups, the physicists and the intelligence officers. It became instead part of a larger political dispute among the Russian democratic movement, communists, and Russian nationalists. For many communists, it was particularly important to give the credit for major scientific and technological accomplishments of the former Soviet Union not to the scientists and engineers with their liberal, pro-Western views, but instead to the Soviet intelligence officers, who were presented as "patriots" and "dedicated communists." Nationalists, on the other hand, were more willing to give credit for the Soviet atomic project to Russian science, rather than to its Western counterpart. Liberal journalists meanwhile tried to turn both interpretations to the advantage of further criticism of Stalin's government. Among journalists, some claimed that Soviet scientists achieved their goal independently, despite the intrigues on the part of the intrusive secret police. Others preferred the version of the "stolen bomb," thus depriving Stalinism of one of its proudest accomplishments.

Later the ban on the issue of *VIET* in question was lifted, and the journal is now available. Nevertheless, Russian historians of science frequently confront debates over the political meaning of their research. While Brezhnev-era internalist histories could pose as "apolitical," today's analysis of science and technology in a social context cannot, and that in turn raises complex questions for Russian and other students of the history of science and technology.

The historian Joseph Agassi once warned that the "approach of the up-to-date textbook worshipper paints all events in the history of science as either black or white, correct or incorrect."[61]

When internalist scholars applied this approach, they tended to evaluate scientists according to their attitude toward whatever theory was thought to be correct at the moment. The same usually was true of Soviet official histories of science and technology. Before *perestroika*, for example, Soviet historiography traditionally ascribed major scientific contributions to "progressive" scientists, while portraying those who were politically "imperfect" as scientists whose research was in error. This was an integral part of the general ideological framework in which good science could only be done by scientists with dialectical materialist views on both nature and society. Changes in the assessment of the scientific merits of a given scholar typically could be made only if a corresponding political reconsideration took place. In such a case, the consequences for the history of science and technology followed the political decision, rather than the other way around.

After his posthumous rehabilitation in 1988, Nikolai Bukharin—a prominent Bolshevik, one of the organizers of the study of the history of science and technology in the Soviet Union, and long labeled a "black"—instantly became a "white." *VIET* published a highly laudatory article about him and reprinted the text of one of his 1936 speeches.[62] There were even suggestions to rename IIET in his honor.[63]

Similarly, Nikolai Vavilov, a famous Russian geneticist who perished in a Stalinist prison, became for many historians a symbol of Stalinist intrusion in science. Vavilov's scientific merits were generously complemented by the image of good citizenship; the historian V. M. Surinov portrayed him as pristinely "white", writing that, "In every situation [Vavilov] displayed himself as a statesmanly leader, as a scientist citizen."[64] In another prominent case, the theoretical physicist Leonid Mandel'shtam had been severely criticized on ideological grounds in the 1940s and 1950s. Now, historians of science have quite properly exposed these notorious accusations as another example of political pressure on science, then gone on to idealize Mandel'shtam as a perfect scientist: he is said to have been "almost absolutely unable to make mistakes on questions of physics."[65]

Thus, the old heroic history has been supplanted by a new form that is sometimes disturbingly similar. Today's (revised) "true" heroes are still giants, not living people with complex lives. We have been given an updated textbook of political history in which the previous black-and-white history of science and technology often becomes white-and-black.

From Science in a Vacuum to Science in Context

When *perestroika* reduced ideological barriers and opened the social context of science and technology for study, that certainly implied changes in the thematic discourse of Soviet historians. It took some additional time, however, for historians to realize that not only themes, but also research methodologies, ought to change.

In early 1987, the editorial board of *VIET* was changed, and in an editorial in the first issue of that year one can find a promise "to extend the publication of materials that relate to the social history of science—such an intensively growing and problematic field and one that has provoked sharp discussions."[66] Nevertheless, the new board at *VIET* still considered social history to be problematic, standing apart from the main path of development of the history of science. The examination of sociocultural context was relegated to the special (that is, problematic) field of social history, while nonproblematic traditional history was encouraged to develop within the tried-and-true internalist paradigm.[67]

Soon, however, the drastic methodological shifts then underway among historians significantly altered the terrain of the history of science and technology in the Soviet Union. The share of internalist articles in *VIET* sharply declined from 57 percent in 1986 to 16 percent in 1991. The internalist tradition was now being challenged by those historians who began to put more emphasis on the cultural and political context of science and technology.

In May 1989 in Leningrad, young scholars organized a conference called "Sociocultural Aspects of the Development of Soviet Science." When the science-state relationship was discussed, the sharpest debates focused on the question: Which external factor influenced the formation of the cognitive agenda of the scientific community more—the dominant ideology or the direct administration of political power? The participants divided into two groups, which observers named "statists" and "ideologists."[68] The "statists" insisted on preserving the image of science as a system of knowledge with its cognitive traditions largely isolated from society. In this view, all external influences are reduced to administrative state measures–either support and funding, or interference and oppression. The "ideologists," on the contrary, envisioned science as an integral part of the sociocultural continuum and maintained that although the "virus of ideology" does not always infect the scientific community from above, ideology nonetheless inevitably penetrates scientists' consciousness.

Interestingly enough, this argument became possible only after historians of science had begun to examine the *negative* aspects of the state's relationship with the scientific community, particularly during the Stalinist purges. Now it became possible to consider scientists as independent-thinking individuals whose views could differ from the official ideology, and there emerged a tension between science and the state. The "good Soviet state, good ideology, good science" model had not permitted any distance between the "good state" and "good science." The relationship between the two was not conceived of in terms of influence, acceptance, or resistance. Good Soviet scientists developed the only possible Soviet science, and that was, of course, good. In this scenario, scientists' internal motives never contradicted external ones, either as individuals or as members of a group. But when *perestroika* led to the reevaluation of the former Soviet regime as totalitarian, in which the state imposed "bad ideology" on science, a significant gap suddenly appeared between science and the "bad state." The statists chose a model "bad state, good science." The ideologists argued for a more

subtle picture, where the actual operation of power in Soviet society was not simply a top-down process, where political and
ideological controversies could emerge under certain conditions
within a scientific community, and where ideology served as a
language of negotiation among various groups of scientists and
bureaucrats.

Two historians from St. Petersburg, Daniel Alexandrov and
Nikolai Krementsov, developed the views of the "ideologists" further in "An Experimental Guide to an Unknown Land: A Preliminary Outline of a Social History of Soviet Science from 1917 to the
1950s."[69] They maintained that the Soviet scientific community
was not separated from the rest of society; the established model
of power in science was to a large extent supported by scientists
themselves. Alexandrov and Krementsov described Soviet scientists' striving for the monopolization of power in science and the
use of political arguments in scientific discussions as examples
of scientists' internalization of state ideology. The portraits of
scientists who were formerly considered black, then white, now
became a bit gray. Alexandrov and Krementsov emphasized, for
example, that the concentration of power in the hands of a few
top administrators (among them such heroes of historical narratives as Nikolai Vavilov or Leon Orbeli) effectively intensified
power struggles within the scientific community and paved the
way to the top for such individuals as Trofim Lysenko.[70]

Generations Come and Methodologies Go

In May 1990, a second conference on the social history of Soviet
science was held in Moscow. Here, the division between the proponents and the critics of new methodological approaches increasingly resembled a generational conflict. The elder
generation, long compelled to keep silent about the state's negative impact on science, at last obtained a chance to tell more of
the truth as *perestroika* developed. Such truth-telling was the aim
of most contributors to the published collection *Science Repressed*, which exemplified the new "white-and-black" history.[71]

The younger generation, on the other hand, had developed an

approach they called "social history." The historian Alexei Kojevnikov wrote, "This term [social history] implies a certain disagreement with an approach that dominates in publications during *perestroika* and may be conventionally characterized by the term 'science repressed.' Instead of considering the science-power relationship solely in a passive voice, in terms of violence, with a stress on its most notable forms—repression and ideological interference—we would like to make a more sober and integrated representation of the highly specific mode of the existence of science in our society, a mode that determines its successes and failures. We would like to attach great significance to sociological, institutional, and cultural factors. The scientific community in this process is believed to play a highly active and ambiguous role."[72] Thus, as Loren Graham has commented, "the coming generation of historians of science in the former Soviet Union go beyond the mere identification of heroes and villains and instead look for institutional and social reasons for the emergence of such individuals."[73]

The manifesto of the younger generation, Alexandrov and Krementsov's "Experimental Guide to an Unknown Land," was met by senior scholars with distrust and skepticism, and labeled "vulgar sociologism." Many supporters of the "statist" analysis perceived ideology as something inherently alien to the science enterprise.[74]

There emerged a pronounced conceptual and linguistic gap between the two generations.[75] In its first issue of 1990, *VIET* published an article by the American historian of science Paul Forman in which he criticized the tendency to look for a rational reconstruction of scientific discovery and argued for greater attention to the external factors of scientific development.[76] In his response, the retired former director of IIET, Semen Mikulinskii, called Forman's approach an "extreme externalism" and continued: "We must say that a crude externalist interpretation of social influences on science is not a harmless thing. It leads to the blurring over and even erasing the boundary between science and ideology, and this predetermines the end of science and makes it possible to conceive of scientists as proponents of alien ideology, resulting in grave consequences."[77] In this way, many of the elder generation of Soviet historians of science and technology rejected the externalist methodology on what might be termed moral rather than cognitive grounds. Science, they maintained, had suffered so much because of the Soviet state, why must it suffer once again today because of social history? One result has been that, in 1993, *VIET* opened a regular rubric or section on the social history of Russian science and technology, thus reserving a space for this approach while remarkably separating it from "normal" history of science and technology.

As *perestroika* made it possible to travel to the West for scholarly meetings and research, Soviet historians vastly broadened the contacts with their Western colleagues. If before the academy authorities appointed the members of Soviet delegations to international conferences and granted permission for publication abroad, now such contacts became largely the result of individual efforts. The younger researchers, more mobile and proficient in foreign languages, took a greater advantage of this opportunity. Aimed at publishing in the West,[78] their discursive strategy has been shaped by the necessity to fit in the current trends in Western scholarship, for writing grant proposals and preparing papers for publication are among the best-known means to internalize the norms of the dominant discourse. The younger generation began to shift their attention from analyses of the science-state relationship to some more popular in Western historiographical approaches, such as social constructivism, historical anthropology, studies of laboratory culture, informal social networks, rhetoric, visual representations, scientists' games, rituals, and so on. The collapse of the old system of state support for science spurred their interest in various forms of science patronage—from both historical and contemporary perspectives.[79]

History of Science, Discourse, and Structure

Another important factor in understanding the development of science and technology—and by extension the intellectual his-

tory of science and technology—is the institutional or administrative structure of the discipline under review. In his detailed
study of the evolution of the Soviet-era Institute of Experimental
Biology, the American historian of Russian science Mark Adams
argued that, "Ideology has played a less significant role than we
have tended to assume, and . . . structure played a more significant role. Ideological shifts without structural alterations produced very little effect on the character of the scientific work
done; structural changes without ideological concomitants have
played a much greater role."[80]

The implications of Adams's insight can only be touched on
here. Nevertheless, it is worth noting that Soviet research in the
history of science and technology has been institutionalized
within the Academy of Sciences in a somewhat similar manner to
that documented in Adams's study—namely, as a separate
institute—so it is reasonable to suspect that here, too, the disciplinary and administrative structure of the field might have
played an important role in the content of studies. Indeed, IIET is
built around disciplinary departments (history of physics, mathematics, chemistry, biology, aerospace technology, shipbuilding
technology, and so on), while the Science Studies Department
(sociology of science, social psychology of science, complex
problems of the scientific-technological revolution, and so on)
exists as a separate unit. This institutional structure itself suggests that the social context is to be studied by sociologists and
the psychological subtext by psychologists, while historians of
science and technology are to do little more than "collect
facts."[81] Like specialization in science itself, internalist specialization in the history of science has erected conceptual barriers
among historians of different disciplines. "What do historians of
mathematics have in common with historians of biology, if they
both honestly follow the internalist tradition?," as Daniel Alexandrov has queried. "In this case, there is no common language or
common problems. Internalist history of science divides and
thereby conquers."[82]

Can we then, following Adams, conclude that in our story, too, structure has played a more significant role than ideology? First, we have to clarify the meaning of "ideology" here, and that is always a vexed process. Adams builds his case upon the separation of "science" ("the actual experimental and theoretical work") from "ideology" ("statements about the scientific enterprise"—"not only what government or party officials say about science in approved statements, but also what the Academy as a whole, and individual influential scientists, say about science").[83] Ideology in this vision serves "as a flexible language of justification, the legitimizing 'glue' between the scientific institution and its political patron."[84]

Given that history of science discourse is nothing other than the production of "statements about the scientific enterprise," it therefore should have been called "ideology" in its entirety, at least in Adams' terms. In the history of science and technology one can hardly separate scholarship from ideology,[85] for, as I have attempted to show, discursive strategies of Soviet historians of science and technology have been tightly connected with the role of historical knowledge in the discourses of politicians, bureaucrats, and scientists. Whether construing a heroic historical tradition of national science, emphasizing the class roots of a particular scientific theory, focusing on the logic and beauty of ideas, or arguing that greater funding would increase scientific productivity, Soviet historians of science and technology shaped their research agenda both in response to the current political and cultural situation and in attempt to influence it.

The structure of Soviet research in the history of science and technology was itself formed as an institutional support for a particular kind of discourse. The Institute for the History of Natural Science was founded as a center for the study of national traditions in various scientific disciplines; later on, basically the same structure supported internalist studies. Less orthodox trends in science studies found (or produced) their own microstructures: informal seminars, summer schools, and an oral culture of discussion.[86] When *perestroika* changed a general political climate in the country, the old IIET structure proved unable to contain new trends in the discourse. Although the structure of IIET remains much the same even now, the discursive terrain of the history of science and technology has completely changed.

Thus, the role of structure in this case *is* important, yet it is but one of a larger mix of forces. Structural factors such as departmental divisions, patterns of education for specialists, and control of key academic publications, for example, each channeled the discourse and fostered some discursive strategies over others. For the moment—and a "moment" could last forty years—structure has emerged as the embodiment of power relations of the dominant discourse. But during sharp sociopolitical and ideological changes in the broader society, the determinative authority of institutional structure can erode rather quickly. Further study of the evolution of both administrative structures and discursive strategies may help us better understand the constraints imposed by structure, and the reasons for its change.

Conclusion: Is the Soviet Case Unique?

In this article, I have examined several of the discursive strategies that Soviet historians developed over the past eighty years in their attempt to make history respond to contemporary concerns. Instead of portraying Soviet scholarship as driven by a single set of ideological assumptions or theoretical presuppositions, I focused on the ways historians varied their narrative strategies, rhetorical techniques, and patterns of criticism, while they worked to adapt their discourse to the changing sociopolitical situation. Whether praising or denying the achievements of prerevolutionary Russian science, integrating national traditions with world science, or isolating them from it, portraying science as a purely intellectual enterprise, or emphasizing its role as a "direct productive force," Soviet historians employed flexible discursive strategies to convey the desired meaning without violating the constraints of the then politically acceptable language. I argued that rather than being a mere servant of political authorities or victim of ideological pressure, Soviet discourse on the history of science and technology played an active role in advancing contemporary agendas through historical narrative.

In the *perestroika* years, and especially in the post-Soviet period, historical questions have loomed large in current political debates. The history of science and technology became a contested field for critics and defenders of the Communist regime. Different generations of Soviet historians have chosen different strategies: while much of the elder generation advanced the image of science as purely cognitive activity to condemn totalitarian pressures on science, many of the younger generation began to emphasize socioeconomic and cultural aspects of scientific developments.

Soviet historians' tendency to construct a historical image of science with an eye on contemporary debates is hardly unique. Throughout the Cold War, many American historians of Soviet science focused their attention on social environment of Soviet research. As the historian Susan Gross Solomon has argued, in the 1950s, American specialists developed "different rules for the study of Western and non-Western science. Whereas emphasis on the societal environment of science was taboo in the study of American or British science, stress on the societal setting of foreign science was broadly accepted."[87] Their depiction of Soviet science largely as a victim of political intrusion shored up the totalitarian model of Soviet society, which was one of the cornerstones of the intellectual basis for American foreign policy of the day. At the same time, this double standard in science studies marginalized the issue of the relations between science and politics in the West, thereby contributing to the image of an "objective," "unbiased" Western science. Soviet science was thus portrayed as "deviant" compared to its Western counterpart.

By the early 1960s, however, after Sputnik and other notable successes of Soviet science and technology, the tone of American discourse on Soviet developments had changed. The Soviet case was now seen as a strong argument in favor of greater governmental support for science. In the flood of literature on Soviet science policy that followed, "the [Soviet] government was no longer portrayed as an intruder in science; instead, it was treated as the agent responsible for shaping, engineering, and even facilitating scientific development."[88] American specialists no longer described the Soviet case as "deviant," but rather "normal" and in some respect even instructive for Western policymakers concerned with science. Thus, the various images of Soviet science, whether "deviant" or "normal," served specific discursive strategies, which American scholars developed in the changing sociopolitical contexts of American intellectual life.

In this essay, I have attempted to present academic discourse not as a container of a particular ideology or theory, but rather as a mechanism for advancing a certain agenda via disciplinary knowledge. Many ideological beliefs and theoretical concepts can be viewed as the result of conscious attempts to explicate and rationalize discursive norms, in much the same way that grammatical rules are evoked to describe and prescribe linguistic practices. Instead of depicting the Cold War solely as a clash of ideologies, it may be more productive to examine the discursive strategies that were employed to shape the image of the opponent and to build up "our" ideology against "theirs." In both American and Soviet academic discourses, at various moments in history, evaluation of the "academic other" ranged from total negation (with the use of such labels as "bourgeois pseudoscience" or "dogmatic and servile scholarship") to its elevation as an exemplar to be imitated ("innovative and dynamic" or "rationally planned and organized"). Soviet historians actively developed various discursive strategies to appropriate the image of the opponent to the needs of the current situation.

The American sociopolitical situation differed in many ways, of course, but nevertheless frequently was more closely related to its Soviet counterpart than most observers preferred to admit. Academics in both countries ingeniously shifted the focus of their analysis from the differences between the two countries to the similarities, and vice versa, depending on a larger political agenda. American and Soviet scholars often employed similar discursive mechanisms for similar goals, for example, by choos-

ing an internalist methodology to retreat to politically safe fo-
rums, or by creating disciplinary structures that damped out
conceptual and methodological challenges to the status quo.
One could compare scholarship in the two countries to the two
faces of the same coin, for the Soviet Union and the United
States viewed each other and to a certain extent defined themselves against the background of the Cold War. Although on the
surface their Cold War–era ideologies seemed totally incompat-
ible, the discursive mechanisms that constructed those ideologies have been very similar for some decades, and remain so
today.

Notes

1. Such studies touch only the surface of Soviet discourse. See, for example, N. A. Kupina, *Totalitarnyi iazyk: Slovar' i rechevye reaktsii* (Ekaterinburg—Perm': Izdatel'stvo Ural'skogo universiteta, 1995); Françoise Thom, *Newspeak: The Language of Soviet Communism*, trans. Ken Connelly (London: The Claridge Press, 1989).

2. Michael Gorham, "Tongue-tied Writers: The *Rabsel'kor* Movement and the Voice of the 'New Intelligentsia' in Early Soviet Russia," *Russian Review* 55 (July 1996), p. 414.

3. Rachel Walker, "Marxism-Leninism as Discourse: The Politics of the Empty Signifier and the Double Bind," *British Journal of Political Science* 19 (1989), p. 179–80.

4. On the history of science and technology studies in the Soviet Union, see Loren R. Graham, *Science in Russia and the Soviet Union: A Short History* (Cambridge, England: Cambridge University Press, 1993), esp. pp. 137–55; Irina Gouzevitch, "The History of Technology in Today's Russia," *SHOT Newsletter* No. 72 (June 1996), pp. 13–16; David Joravsky, "Soviet Views on the History of Science," *Isis* 46 (1955), pp. 3–13; Linda L. Lubrano, *Soviet Sociology of Science* (Columbus, Ohio: AAASS, 1976); Yakov Rabkin, "'Naukovedenie': The Study of Scientific Research in the Soviet Union," *Minerva* 14 (1976), pp. 61–78; Alexander Vucinich, *Empire of Knowledge: The Academy of Sciences (1917–1970)* (Berkeley: University of California Press, 1984); Alexander Vucinich, "Soviet Marxism and the History of Science," *Russian Review* 41 (1982), pp. 123–42; Maria S. Bastrakova, "Iz istorii razvitiia istoriko-nauchnykh issledovanii," *VIET* 61–63 (1978), pp. 34–47; Simon S. Ilizarov, *Materialy k istoriografii istorii nauki i tekhniki: Khronika: 1917–1988 gg.* (Moscow:

Nauka, 1989); Vladimir S. Kirsanov, "Vozvratit'sia k istokam? Zametki ob Institute Istorii Nauki i Tekhniki AN SSSR, 1932–1938 gg." *VIET* (1994), no. 1, pp. 3–19; Alessandro Mongili, "Prikliucheniia naukovedeniia: sluchai Instituta istorii estestvoznaniia i tekhniki," *VIET* (1995), no. 1, pp. 116–137 (a summary of A. Mongili's doctoral dissertation "Sociologues et sociologie des sciences en U.R.S.S.: Le cas de l'Institut d'Histoire des Sciences Naturelles et de la Technologie de Moscou" defended in Paris in 1993).

5. This paper will focus on the historical research done at the Academy of Sciences, rather than in Soviet universities. This is because throughout the Soviet era, the Academy of Sciences (now a network of hundreds of institutes with tens of thousands of full-time researchers) conducted the lion's share of fundamental research, while the institutions of higher education (the universities and technical institutes) fulfilled mostly pedagogical functions. True, some universities maintained strong traditions of research in mathematics, physics, and biology, but in the field of the history of science and technology the divorce of research and teaching was nearly complete. For Vernadskii's biography, see Kendall Bailes, *Science and Russian Culture in an Age of Revolutions : V. I. Vernadsky and His Scientific School, 1863–1945* (Bloomington: Indiana University Press, 1990).

6. Graham, p. 138.

7. In 1918, the Bolsheviks founded the Socialist (later Communist) Academy as a center of Marxist studies and a counterweight to the traditional Academy of Sciences.

8. Prominent Soviet physicist Sergei Vavilov, for example, claimed that "up to the 20th century there was really no physics in Russia."

9. Boris Hessen, "The Social and Economic Roots of Newton's *Principia*," in *Science at the Crossroads* [1931], ed. Nikolai I. Bukharin et al., reprint ed. (London: Frank Cass, 1971), p. 182.

10. Graham, p. 149. For an example of criticism of Einstein's physics, see Arkadii K. Timiriazev, "Teoriia otnositel'nosti Einshteina i dialekticheskii materializm," *Pod znamenem marksizma* (1924), no. 8–9, pp. 142–57; no. 10–11, pp. 92–114. In the late 1920s, Hessen attempted to argue that relativity theory was fully compatible with dialectical materialism in his *Osnovnye idei teorii otnositel'nosti* (Moscow, 1928).

11. In the Soviet Union, Hessen's work was immediately criticized for establishing mere "mechanical" and "formal" links between Newton's ideas and the societal needs (Matvei A. Gukovskii, "Tseli i zadachi istorii nauki," *Vestnik AN SSSR* (1934), no. 1, p. 39).

12. *Dictionary of the History of Science*, eds. William F. Bynum, E. Janet Browne, and Roy Porter (Princeton, N.J.: Princeton University Press, 1981), pp. 145–46.

13. On the "Sovietization" of the Academy of Sciences, see Loren R. Graham, *The Soviet Academy of Sciences and the Communist Party, 1927–1932* (Princeton, N.J.: Princeton University Press, 1967); and Feliks F. Perchenok, "Akademiia Nauk na velikom perelome," in *Zven'ia*, vol. 1 (1991), pp. 163–238. The Communist Academy lost its autonomous status and was incorporated into the Academy of Sciences in 1936.

14. For a standard biographic source on Bukharin, see Stephen Cohen, *Bukharin and the Bolshevik Revolution: A Political Biography, 1888–1938* (New York: Knopf, 1973).

15. Vucinich, "Soviet Marxism and the History of Science," p. 130.

16. The wide celebration of Newton's tercentennial anniversary in 1943 was politically significant as a friendly gesture toward the British allies.

17. Some Soviet historians' discursive strategy was flexible enough in this context to implement what amounted to a hidden agenda. The "great men of science" discourse with its strong emphasis on moral virtue, could well be used for implicit criticism of the current regime. The historian of antiquity S. Ia. Lur'e, for example, opened his 1945 book *Archimedes* with what was seen even at the time as a thinly veiled attack on Stalin's rule: "Tyranny is a horrible and vile disaster which owes its origin to only one cause: people no longer feel the necessity for the law and justice that would be one and the same for everyone" (quoted in Ilizarov, *Materialy*, pp. 24–25).

18. The question whether the Cold War prompted the anticosmopolitanism campaigns, or they had a different origin (in the struggle within Soviet leadership, for example) and simply utilized the Cold War rhetoric as a convenient language, is too complex to deal with here. In any case, the Cold War in international politics and anticosmopolitanism in the domestic sphere soon began to reinforce each other, and so the origins question became irrelevant.

19. See Nikolai Krementsov, "The 'KR Affair': Soviet Science on the Threshold of the Cold War," *History and Philosophy of the Life Sciences* 17 (1995), pp. 419–46.

20. See Vladimir D. Esakov, "Kistorii filosofskoi diskussii 1947 goda," *Voprosy filosofii* (1993), no. 2, pp. 83–106.

21. *Materialy po istorii otechestvennoi khimii: sbornik dokladov na Pervom Vsesoiuznom soveshchanii po istorii otechestvennoi khimii, 12–15 maia 1948 g.* (Moscow and Leningrad: AN SSSR, 1950), p. 4.

22. Ivan I. Potekhin, "Kosmopolitizm v amerikanskoi etnografii," in *Anglo-amerikanskaia etnografiia na sluzhbe imperializma*, ed. Ivan I. Potekhin (Moscow: AN SSSR, 1951), pp. 36–37.

23. On Soviet science under Stalin, see Loren R. Graham, *Science, Philosophy, and Human Behavior in the Soviet Union* (New York: Columbia University

Press, 1987); Nikolai Krementsov, *Stalinist Science* (Princeton, N.J.: Princeton University Press, 1997); and Vucinich, *Empire of Knowledge.*

24. This argument was reinforced by Stalin in his personal editing of Lysenko's 1948 speech. See Kirill Rossianov, "Editing Nature: Joseph Stalin and the 'New' Soviet Biology," *Isis* 84, no. 4 (December 1993), pp. 728–45.

25. Victor V. Danilevskii, *Russkaia tekhnika*, 2nd ed. (Leningrad: Lenizdat, 1948), p. 468.

26. See the proceedings of this meeting in *Voprosy istorii otechestvennoi nauki: Obshchee sobranie AN SSSR, posviashchennoe istorii otechestvennoi nauki, 5–11 ianvaria 1949 g.* (Moscow and Leningrad: AN SSSR, 1949).

27. Vladimir I. Kuznetsov, "Ob osnovnykh napravleniiakh issledovanii v oblasti istorii estestvoznaniia i tekhniki i naukovedeniia," *VIET* (1987), no. 1, p. 12.

28. See Vitalii I. Dovgopol, "O velosipede Artamonova'" *VIET* no. 1 (1989), pp. 149–50; Leonid E. Maistrov and N. L. Vilinova, "O velosipede Artamonova," *VIET* no. 1 (1983), pp. 89–96; Victor S. Virginskii et al., "Kak tvoriatsia mify v istorii tekhniki," *VIET* no. 1 (1989), pp. 150–57.

29. Vucinich, *Empire of Knowledge*, p. 236.

30. Sofia Ia. Ianovskaia, *Peredovye idei N. I. Lobachevskogo – orudie bor'by protiv idealizma v matematike* (Moscow and Leningrad, 1950).

31. Alexei Kojevnikov, "President of Stalin's Academy: The Mask and Responsibility of Sergei Vavilov," *Isis* 87 (March 1996), no. 1, p. 35.

32. In the late 1980s, IIET employed some two hundred full-time researchers. For a survey of the Institute's activities, see *Institute of the History of Natural Sciences and Technology*, ed. Nikolai D. Ustinov (Moscow: Nauka, 1989). Between 1954 and 1962, the Institute published forty-five volumes of its *Transactions,* which was then succeeded by the series *Problems in the History of Science and Technology* (68 volumes); the latter in 1980 was turned into a quarterly journal under the same title (*Voprosy istorii estestvoznaniia i tekhniki, VIET*). For a brief, but informative review of *VIET*, see Paul R. Josephson, review of *Voprosy Istorii Estestvoznaniia i Tekhniki Isis* 82 (1991), pp. 298–300.

33. Nikolai A. Figurovskii, "Zadachi issledovanii po istorii nauki," *Vestnik AN SSSR* (1959), no. 11, p. 31.

34. A report filed by this delegation on their return, is preserved at the archive of the Central Committee of the Communist Party (Center for the Preservation of Contemporary Documents (TsKhSD), f. 5, op. 35, d. 30, ll. 57–61).

35. To the present, more than 400 biographies have been published. See a guide to this series: Zoia K. Sokolovskaia, *400 biografii uchenykh* (Moscow: Nauka, 1988).

36. In 1968, the American historian

of science Thomas Kuhn distinguished "internalist" and "externalist" approaches to historical studies in the West this way: "The still dominant form, often called the 'internalist approach,' is concerned with the substance of science as knowledge. Its newer rival, often called the 'externalist approach,' is concerned with the activity of scientists as a social group within a larger culture." Kuhn saw "putting the two together" as "the greatest challenge" for the historian of science (Thomas Kuhn, "The History of Science," *International Encyclopedia of the Social Sciences*, ed. D. L. Sills, vol. 14 (New York: Macmillan, 1968), p. 76). The American historian of technology John Staudenmaier later classified articles on the history of technology in a similar way: "[T]hose focused on the data of technical design alone ('internalist history'), those focused on contextual evidence alone ('externalist history'), and those attempting to integrate both types of evidence ('contextual history')." (John Staudenmaier, *Technology's Storytellers: Reweaving the Human Fabric* (Cambridge, Mass.: MIT Press, 1985), p. 25).

37. For discussion of this argument, see Bonifatii M. Kedrov, *O marksistskoi istorii estestvoznaniia* (Moscow: Nauka, 1968), pp. 20–21. Kedrov's own work provides a brilliant example of logical reconstruction of a scientific discovery; see B. M. Kedrov, *Den' odnogo velikogo otkrytiia* (Moscow: Izdatel'stvo

sotsial'no-ekonomicheskoi literatury, 1958).

38. Under Stalin, such strategy would have been labeled "objectivism," for it placed "impartial facts" over loyalty to ideological dogmas (see Vucinich, *Empire of Knowledge*, p. 235). In the post-Stalin period, avoidance of explicit historical interpretation was allowed, and it often meant implicit disagreement with the offical viewpoint.

39. Aleksandr D. Alexandrov, "Raz uzh zagovorili o nauke," *Novyi mir* (1970), no. 10, p. 210.

40. In one particularly absurd example, a senior Soviet historian of mathematics reviewed a 1987 book noting, for instance, "the incorrect position of letters in the first table on p. 76 and the loss of a bracket on p. 163, in the second paragraph from the top" (Fedor A. Medvedev, review of *Metodologicheskie problemy intuitsionistskoi matematiki*, by Mikhail I. Panov, *VIET* (1987), no. 1, p. 151).

41. Lubrano, p. 6.

42. To avoid potential accusations of reductionism, Soviet scholars, of course, acknowledged that quantitative data must be complemented by qualitative analysis. Then they simply stated that calculating three parameters—scientific discoveries, tests of existing theories, and new theories proposed—would provide a quantitative measure for qualitative change in science (Semen R. Mikulinskii and Naum I. Rodnyi, "Nauka kak predmet spetsial'nogo issledovaniia,"

Voprosy filosofii (1966), no. 5, pp. 31–32).

43. This made Soviet science studies less susceptible to "Marxyist" rhetoric. According to Yakov Rabkin's data, articles in the leading science studies journal in the late 1960s and early 1970s contained on average ten times fewer references to official ideological documents than comparable journals in philosophy, history, or economics (Rabkin, p. 77).

44. M. Petrov and A. Potemkin, "Nauka poznaet sebia," *Novyi mir* (1968), no. 6, p. 250.

45. See Vladislav Zh. Kelle, "Stanovlenie v SSSR sotsiologicheskikh issledovanii v poslevoennyi period," *VIET* (1995), no. 2, pp. 41–48.

46. Lubrano, p. 13.

47. Rabkin, p. 77.

48. In 1938, the state archives were transferred under the secret service's oversight, and thereafter Soviet historians had very limited access to the government archives; only party members with special clearance could work in local party archives, and the records of the KGB and the Party Central Committee were completely closed to researchers. For updated information on newly opened Russian archives, see *Archives in Russia, 1993: A Brief Directory*, ed. Patricia K. Grimsted, (Washington, D.C.: IREX, 1993); Vitaly Chernetsky, "On the Russian Archives: An Interview with Sergei V. Mironenko," *Slavic Review* 52 (Winter 1993), pp. 839–46; J. Arch Getty and Oleg V. Naumov, eds., *Research*

Guide to the Russian Center for the Preservation and Study of Documents of Contemporary History (Moscow, 1993); Gordon M. Hahn, "Researching Perestroika in the Archive of the TsK KPSS (Soviet Communist Party Central Committee archive, Center for the Preservation of Contemporary Documents)," *Russian Review* 53 (July 1994), pp. 419–23; David L. Hoffman, "A first glimpse into the Moscow Party Archives," *Russian Review* 50 (October 1991), pp. 484–86; Nikolai Krementsov, "Footprints of a Vanished Science: Russian Archival Sources for the History of Soviet Genetics," *Mendel Newsletter* no. 4 (1994), pp. 2–4.

49. See Vladimir I. Vernadskii, "Nauchnaia mysl' kak planetnoe iavlenie (1938 g.) (Neopublikovannye fragmenty)," *VIET* (1988), no. 1, pp. 71–79.

50. Gennadii E. Gorelik, "Obsuzhdenie 'naturfilosofskikh ustanovok sovremennoi fiziki' v Akademii nauk SSSR v 1937–1938 godakh," *VIET* (1990), no. 4, pp. 17–31; Vladimir P. Vizgin, "Martovskaia (1936 g.) sessiia AN SSSR: sovetskaia fizika v fokuse," *VIET* (1990), no. 1, pp. 63–84; (1991), no 3, pp. 36–55.

51. Ilia B. Novik, "Normal'naia Izhenauka," *VIET* (1990), no. 4, pp. 3–16.

52. Stranitsy istorii sovetskoi genetiki v literature poslednikh let," *VIET* (1987), no. 4, pp. 113-124; (1988), no. 1, pp. 121–31; (1988), no. 2, pp. 91–112.

53. "'Pavlovskaia sessia' 1950 g. i sud'by sovetskoi fiziologii,"

VIET (1988), no. 3, pp. 129–41; (1988), no. 4, pp. 147–56; (1989), no. 1, pp. 94–108.

54. A. A. Berzin, "Doroga v nikuda. Materialy o stroitel'stve zheleznoi dorogi Salekhard-Igarka. 1947–1953," VIET (1990), no. 1, pp. 38–49.

55. A. A. Berzin, "Parovozy za koliuchei provolokoi: Novye materialy o sovetskom parovozostroenii iz arkhivov KGB," VIET (1991), no. 4, pp. 35–38.

56. Here I draw upon my quantitative analysis of the changes in the methodological, thematic, temporal, geographic, and disciplinary patterns of Soviet historians' research as reflected in VIET articles during the perestroika period, 1986–91. The details of that study, and a comparison with the results of John Staudenmaier's similar analysis based on the content of the journal of American historians of technology, Technology and Culture, from 1959 to 1980 (see Staudenmaier, Technology's), can be found in my "Perestroika of the History of Technology and Science in the USSR: Changes in the Discourse," Technology and Culture 37, no. 1 (January 1996), pp. 102–34.

57. "U istokov sovetskogo iadernogo proekta: rol' razvedki, 1941–1945 gg.," VIET (1992), no. 3, pp. 103–34.

58. See Gennadii E. Gorelik, "Iadernaia istoriia i zloba dnia," VIET (1993), no. 2, pp. 159–61.

59. Roald Sagdeev, "Russian Scientists Save American Secrets,"

The Bulletin of the Atomic Scientists 49 (1993), p. 32.

60. Sergei Leskov, "Dividing the Glory of the Fathers," The Bulletin of the Atomic Scientists 49 (1993), p. 38.

61. Joseph Agassi, Toward an Historiography of Science (Gravenhage: Mouton, 1963), p. 2.

62. See Mikhail Ia. Gefter, "V preddverii gibeli," VIET (1988), no. 4, pp. 4–10; Nikolai I. Bukharin, "Osnovnye problemy sovremennoi kul'tury," VIET (1988), no. 4, pp. 10–31.

63. Later, when criticism of the Communist regime deepened and reached the Lenin generation (to which Bukharin belonged), Bukharin again became a controversial figure—not just a victim of Stalinism, but perhaps a guilty party himself. The plans to give his name to IIET were abandoned, and the institute was renamed in the honor of the former academy president Sergei Vavilov, an acceptable candidate for both Communists and democrats.

64. V. M. Surinov, "N. I. Vavilov kak organizator nauchnykh issledovanii," VIET (1988), no. 1, p. 45.

65. Sergei M. Rytov, "Ideinoe nasledie L. I. Mandel'shtama i ego dal'neishee razvitie," VIET (1988), no. 3, p. 45.

66. Zadachi zhurnala v usloviiakh perestroiki," VIET (1987), no. 1, p. 6.

67. In an article on the history of computing in the USSR, for example, the section on the background of the topic was entitled, "On Some Technical

and Mathematical Problems of the 1930s," and included nothing about the social context. The article left the reader with the impression that under Stalin's regime in the 1930s, the only problems relevant to the history of computing were technical and mathematical ones. See Andrei N. Tikhonov et al., "Integrator Luk'ianova v istorii vychislitel'noi tekhniki," VIET (1990), no. 1, pp. 49–57.

68. Daniel A. Alexandrov and N. L. Krementsov, "Sotsiokul'turnye aspekty razvitiia sovetskoi nauki v 1920-1930 gg.," VIET (1990), no. 1, pp. 166–68.

69. Daniel A. Alexandrov, N. L. Krementsov, "Opyt putevoditelia po neizvedannoi zemle. Predvaritel'nyi ocherk sotsial'noi istorii sovetskoi nauki (1917-1950-e gody)," VIET (1989), no. 4, pp. 67–80.

70. A somewhat parallel methodological controversy was meanwhile taking shape among historians of Soviet technology. One senior researcher, G. N. Alekseev, presented a manifesto entitled "The Subject, Method, and Foundations of the Concept of the Development of History of Technology (and Natural Sciences) as an Independent, Complex Scientific Discipline." In his theoretical framework, technology was depicted as a direct derivative of science: "The activity of technical specialists is as follows: (1) scientists transform natural sciences' knowledge into scientific-technological knowledge; (2) designers, engineers, inventors, etc., materialize

scientific-technological knowledge into various technical objects. [Thus,] the subject of the history of technology as a scientific discipline . . . ought to be exposing causal links and qualitative-quantitative complex regularities of the development of technical objects and creating on this basis a picture of their [the objects'] historical development along with the assessment of prospects and prognostic orientation." (Georgii N. Alekseev, "Predmet, metod i osnovy kontseptsii razvitiia istorii tekhniki (i estestvoznaniia) kak samostoiatel'noi kompleksnoi nauchnoi distsipliny," VIET (1989), no. 3, p. 111). Alekseev's manifesto culminated in a proposal for a mathematical formula which "fully expresses" a general state of the development of the natural sciences and technology at any given moment.

The most surprising aspect of the debate around Alekseev's article was not that he presented the old internalist doctrine as a revelation, but rather that this tactic was not seriously questioned. His colleagues confined their criticism to the discussion of the limits of formalization and the role of prognosis in a historical study.

71. Repressirovannaia nauka, ed. Mikhail G. Iaroshevskii, 2 vols. (Leningrad [St. Petersburg]: Nauka, 1991–94).

72. Alexei B. Kojevnikov, "Vtoraia konferentsiia po sotsial'noi istorii sovetskoi nauki," VIET (1991), no. 1, p. 154.

73. Graham, *Science in Russia and the Soviet Union*, pp. 154–55.

74. One senior physicist noted, for example, that " in physics such extrascientific factors could not operate . . . because the structure of physical science is much harder"; "in the case of physics, ideologization occurred somewhere in the periphery (the situation was different in the humanities, psychology, and biology), although physicists, of course, had to put a lot of effort in order to preserve the autonomy of scientific research and to guard science from the dangerous intrusions of alien ideological elements," (Vladimir P. Vizgin, "Neskol'ko zamechanii k stat'e D. A. Alexandrova i N. L. Krementsova 'Opyt putevoditelia po neizvedannoi zemle,'" *VIET* (1989), no. 4, p. 84).

75. When Daniel Alexandrov used the terms broker and client to describe the relations of science patronage in his paper at a 1994 Russian-American workshop, "New Directions in the History and Sociology of Science and Technology," a senior historian indignantly replied that "great Russian scientists never ever were brokers."

76. Pol Forman [Paul Forman], "K chemu dolzhna stremit'sia istoriia nauki," *VIET* (1990), no. 1, pp. 3–9.

77. Semen R. Mikulinskii, "Po povodu stat'i Pola Formana," *VIET* (1990), no. 2, p. 85.

78. Daniel Alexandrov has noted that this communicative strategy is characteristic of those in relatively lower positions in the academic hierarchy: "The academic establishment is undoubtedly deeply entrenched in the national structure of science and has a vital interest to support and develop further a network of national journals in Russian. Yet those who do not have a firm standing in the power structure of science and do not identify themselves with it, are mostly oriented toward foreign languages and journals published abroad," (Daniel Alexandrov, "Pochemu sovetskie uchenye perestali pechatat'sia za rubezhom," *VIET* (1996), no. 3, p. 22).

79. See Daniel Alexandrov, "The Historical Anthropology of Science in Russia," *Russian Studies in History* 34 (1995), pp. 62–91; a special issue of *Configurations: A Journal of Literature, Science, and Technology* 1 (1993), no. 3, ed. Daniel Alexandrov; essays by Daniel Alexandrov, Mikhail Konashev and Nikolai Krementsov in *The Evolution of Theodosius Dobzhansky: Essays on His Life and Thought in Russia and America*, ed. Mark B. Adams (Princeton, N.J.: Princeton Univ. Press, 1994); Elena A. Gorokhovskaya and Elena L. Zheltova, "Myth of Flight and the Flying Machine," *Phystech Journal* 1 (1994), no. 1, pp. 59–68; Alexei Kojevnikov, "President of Stalin's Academy"; Alexei Kojevnikov, *Games of Soviet Democracy: Ideological Discussions in Sciences Around 1948 Reconsidered* (Max-Planck-Institut f. Wissenschaftsgeschichte, Preprint #37 (1996) (forthcoming in *The Russian*

Review); Nikolai Krementsov, *Stalinist Science*.

80. Mark B. Adams, "Science, Ideology, and Structure: The Kol'tsov Institute, 1900–1970," in *The Social Context of Soviet Science*, eds. Linda L. Lubrano and Susan Gross Solomon (Boulder, Colo.: Westview Press, 1980), p. 198.

81. When in October 1986, Soviet historians held a conference to discuss the "basic directions of *perestroika* within IIET," typical proposals for improvement did not challenge the existing "division of labor" between sociologists and historians, but rather reinforced it: "One department will study a certain field of science from the history of science viewpoint, while another will examine it from the sociocultural context, a third from the context of the structure of science and of the interaction of different sciences, a fourth through the methods of measuring the parameters of science." ("Ob osnovnykh napravleniiakh perestroiki raboty IIET AN SSSR (Materialy nauchno-prakticheskoi konferentsii)," *VIET* (1987), no. 1, p. 25.) Thus, the historian of science may ignore the social context of science—it is the business of people in another department!

82. Daniel Alexandrov, "Istoriia nauki dlia istorikov nauki, ili Slovo o pol'ze obrazovaniia aspirantov," *VIET* (1996), no. 1, p. 94.

83. Adams, pp. 173–74.

84. Ibid., p. 195.

85. Whether this can be done with science itself, is also a question.

86. On the interplay of formal/informal and written/oral culture in Soviet science studies, see Mongili, pp. 130–131.

87. Susan Gross Solomon, "Reflections on Western Studies of Soviet Science," in *The Social Context of Soviet Science*, eds, Linda L. Lubrano and Susan Gross Solomon (Boulder, Colo: Westview Press, 1980), p. 5.

88. Ibid., p. 12.

(**Lawrence Soley**)

The New Corporate Yen for Scholarship

After the United States entered World War II, many parts of the U.S. economy were retooled to assist the war effort. Like other U.S. institutions and professions, universities and professors became engaged in this all-out effort to win. William ("Wild Bill") Donovan's use of the academy to develop the Office of Strategic Services, the predecessor of the Central Intelligence Agency, is legendary. The Office of War Information also drew on universities for personnel and intelligence information. Other agencies did, too. For example, Princeton University's Listening Center, established in 1939 to monitor and study Axis broadcasts, was taken over by the Federal Communications Commission in 1941 and renamed the Foreign Broadcast Intelligence Service.[1] The monitoring service became the Foreign Broadcast Information Service after the war, a de facto CIA project that has been nominally administered by the Department of Commerce.

After World War II ended and the Cold War began, substantial government grants in physics, chemistry, and engineering helped develop computer, ballistics, and communications technologies. In the biomedical fields, government grants underwrote studies of drugs, bacterial weapons, and radioactivity, many of which were ethically questionable, such as exposing mentally retarded students and pregnant women to varying levels of radioactivity in order to study the possible effects of exposure during nuclear war.[2]

Many well-known psychologists and sociologists also solicited grants to conduct psychological warfare studies. Political scientists such as Michigan State University's Wesley Fishel conducted research for the CIA on Cold War "hot spots" such as Indochina, while the federal government poured millions into on-campus research centers such as Harvard University's Center for International Affairs, which researched and taught about national security issues. Civilian agencies, such as the Department of Education, meanwhile provided funding and fellowships for instruction in areas chosen primarily for their usefulness to intelligence and national security agencies, such as Chinese and Russian studies.

One byproduct of this funding was that entire disciplines were created, reshaped, or redirected. In communication studies, for example, "Government psychological warfare programs helped shape mass communication research into a distinct scholarly field, strongly influencing the choice of leaders and determining which of the competing scientific paradigms of communication would get funded, elaborated and encouraged to prosper," according to one recent study.[3]

This sort of overt government funding for research continued well into the mid–Cold War era, as did other forms of direct government support to universities. As college enrollments increased a staggering 122 percent between 1960 and 1970, federal grants and subsidies kept universities prosperous, and expanding, into the 1970s.

However, federal grants to universities were scaled back in the early 1970s as the United States redirected resources to direct military investments and think tanks, rather than university-based social science research. Between 1970 and 1974, for example, federal expenditures on scientific research increased just

2.5 percent, far less than the inflation rate. College enrollment growth also slowed.[4]

Many universities attempted to regear, hoping that corporations could use their idled capacity. The University of Wisconsin convinced firms such as Kimberly-Clark, Kohler, Allen Bradley, and Johnson Controls, for example, to join a consortium in the 1970s that provided support for research in areas "too basic or costly for the companies to conduct themselves."[5]

Universities looked to industry for instructional funding, as well. For example, in the late 1970s, Gannon University in Pennsylvania and Springfield College in Massachusetts started teaching courses in economics for high school teachers which were designed and funded by Hammermill Paper Company. The courses presented economics from a pro-business perspective—a perspective that the firms hoped would then be taught to adolescents.[6] One result of agreements like these is that corporations and a network of their foundations started exerting much the same type of influence on the academy in the 1980s and 1990s as the federal government had done in the 1950s and 1960s.

This influence of corporations is not unique to the academy. As Herbert Schiller points out in *Culture, Inc.,* corporations now wield power within many social and artistic institutions, such as museums, sports teams, and orchestras, where they had previously wielded little—or far less—power. The greater power of corporations is the result of several factors, including the downsizing of the federal government, deregulation, and the growth in the size of corporations, stemming from the mergers and buyouts of the last decade.

Outside Funding for the Creation of 'New' Courses

The House Committee on Standards of Official Conduct, commonly known as the House ethics committee, concluded not long ago that Speaker and historian Newt Gingrich's teaching of a course titled "Renewing American Civilization" at Reinhardt and Kinnesaw State colleges in Georgia violated federal campaign financing laws. Gingrich's purpose was indoctrination rather than instruction, the ethics committee decided, and he had used tax deductible contributions from well-heeled Republicans and corporations to carry out the task.

In a letter soliciting contributions for the course, Gingrich wrote that he was using the lecture series to recruit Republican activists for the 1996 campaign. "Our goal is to have 200,000 committed citizen activists nationwide before we're done," he wrote.

Gingrich used corporate contributors who had paid up, such as Hewlett-Packard and Scientific Atlanta, as models of corporate virtues during lectures. The House Speaker described Hewlett-Packard Corporation as "one of the great companies in American history." In a second lecture, Gingrich described Scientific Atlanta as "a model of the spirit of invention and discovery." Promotional videos and other public relations propaganda from corporate contributors were also shown in class.[7]

Much of the congressional investigation and media coverage of this scandal tacitly suggested that arrangements such as these are unusual within the academy. In reality, though, they are not. Money going into the academy from corporations and corporate foundations for instruction is common, influencing the direction of disciplines in much the same way that government funding influenced disciplines during the Cold War era. For example, the John M. Olin Foundation, founded and funded by a conservative munitions manufacturer, underwrites programs of study in "Law and Economics" at several universities with top-notch law schools, including the University of Chicago, Yale, Stanford, Harvard, Columbia, George Mason, Georgetown, and Duke universities. "Law and Economics" is a judicial philosophy that is consistent with the foundation's ultra-right ideology. In *The Politics of the Rich and Poor*, the Republican analyst Kevin Phillips described "Law and Economics" as a neo-Darwinian "theology" reminiscent of the views of Herbert Spencer and William Graham Sumner. Lamenting its increasing popularity, Phillips wrote that

"Law and Economics" preaches that "commercial selection processes in the marketplace could largely displace government
decision-making."[8]

The "Law and Economics" movement was widely regarded as
an extremist, fringe philosophy even in Republican circles until
the Olin Foundation began underwriting programs at universities The foundation provided generous scholarships to students
who agreed to attend Law and Economics seminars; provided
research funds to selected professors; and sponsored lucrative
awards to students who wrote sympathetic papers on the movement. One result of the Olin Foundation's sponsorship—
together with the Reagan and Bush administrations' aggressive
appointment of judges like former University of Chicago professor Richard Posner—is that Law and Economics is today regarded as a mainstream legal philosophy, accounting for
"roughly 25% of the scholarship in the Yale, Harvard, Chicago,
and Stanford law reviews," according to the *Antitrust and Economic Review*.[9]

The Olin Foundation also underwrites a journalism course at
Boston University titled "Reporting Military Affairs." According to
a former B.U. dean, that course is designed "to make journalists
more sympathetic to the military" rather than train future journalists. At Harvard University, Olin underwrites the hawkish John
M. Olin Institute for Strategic Studies, which "educate[s] and prepare[s] younger scholars in strategy and national security for positions in colleges and universities, research institutes and
government."[10]

Today, numerous corporations and foundations underwrite
substantially similar programs in business, communications, industrial psychology, molecular biology, engineering, and medical
and computer sciences, many of which are offered at well-
respected research institutions. The University of Wisconsin at
Madison's business school houses the A. C. Nielsen Center for
Marketing Research, for example, whose purpose is "scholarly
work and the preparation of graduate students" for the marketing research industry. The center "admits 10 to 20 students per

year" and boasts that it is in "partnership with business." Its advisory board includes executives from AT&T, Coca-Cola, General Motors and Ralston Purina. Coca-Cola funds a similar program in marketing research at the University of Georgia.[11]

Ameritech, the "Baby Bell" of the upper midwest, funds telecommunications programs at Indiana, Northwestern, and Michigan State universities. MSU houses the Ameritech Center for Information Technologies Studies, an instructional and research center filled with Ameritech equipment. Armco Steel, the National Gas Association of America, IBM, and similar blue chip companies underwrite the business journalism program at the University of Missouri–Columbia, while the New York Times Foundation funds studies in communication law at Columbia University. As these examples suggest, corporations and foundations have superceded the federal government as the principal backers of communication studies.[12]

High Deutsche Marks for the Academy

Even foreign governments and industrialists have also discovered that a small contribution can go a long way in garnering influence on college campuses. Beginning in the mid-1970s, when the U.S. government reduced its direct investments in universities, Korean dictators Park Chung Hee and Chun Doo Hwan used grants given by ostensibly private Korean foundations to cultivate goodwill on college campuses. According the House committee investigating Koreagate, "the Korean government attempted to use grants to influence universities for political purposes." The committee concluded that "making or encouraging grants to U.S. universities in support of Korea studies was the most conspicuous and costly measure undertaken by Korea in its attempt to influence American academic opinions."[13]

Although the recipients claimed at the time that Korean grants came without strings, in fact most grants clearly influenced the content of ostensibly independent academic programs. The House committee discovered that a grant to the University of California at Berkeley was given with the understanding that "topics involving Korean politics were to be avoided," thereby silencing critics of the military government's policy. At the University of Washington, a vice provost's request for the Korean government to underwrite the university's Korea studies program secretly promised the military government a veto over appointments to the program, even as other administrators assured faculty that "the money has no strings attached." In return for funding, the vice provost promised to seek "the assistance of the Korean government in helping us select a senior professor from Korea in Korean Language and Literature, who could fill this position."[14]

Korea's attempts to influence universities didn't end with the Park-Hwan dictatorships. Currently, the Korean government, through its Korea Foundation, has been pouring money into U.S. universities for courses, endowed professorships, fellowships, and Korean studies centers. One result is that scholars receiving Korean money generally avoid antagonizing their benefactors and "censor themselves, and that is the most severe form of influence," says Bruce Cumings, the director of Northwestern University's Center for International and Comparative Studies. Cumings's view are shared by the Indiana University professor Michael Robinson, who says that the relationships that the Korea Foundation cultivates "are long-term and reciprocal. . . . So if you want a relationship with the Korean [sic] Foundation, you have a vested interest in pleasing, not offending it."[15]

Taiwanese foundations and business leaders, many of whom are also political leaders, have provided universities with grants, most said to be without strings. However, the grants are often contingent on the recipients' acting in behalf of Taiwan's foreign policy goals. When recipients fail to act in ways that their Taiwanese benefactors had hoped, the grants are quickly withdrawn. By taking back a few grants and making examples of a few universities, Taiwanese donors have shown recipients what is expected of them. In 1996 for example, a Taiwanese foundation withdrew a $450,000 grant from the University of Michigan soon after a prominent Michigan professor signed a document supporting the United States' "one China policy." Taiwan accused the professor of failing to "promote our national cause." Two years earlier, Harvard University was forced to return $40,000 to Taiwan when the government objected to the university's choice of a speaker for a major public lecture. Before that, a $400,000 grant to Columbia University was withdrawn after Taiwanese officials claimed that dissidents from Taiwan were accorded too much prominence at a Columbia-sponsored academic conference. Most universities have been more indulgent of their benefactors' wishes and have thereby retained their funding.[16]

Taiwanese are not the only donors who demand that universities heel or lose funding. A much-publicized example of this is provided by the American tycoon Lee M. Bass, who gave $20 million to Yale University in 1991 to develop and teach a sequence of courses in Western civilization—the largest sum ever given to a university for course development. In 1995, after the university spent four years developing (and arguing over) the courses, Bass informed Yale that he wanted veto power over who would teach the courses. Embarrassed by Bass's demand and the publicity arising from it, Yale administrators reluctantly returned the money.[17]

Similarly, Duke University administrators promised financier Disque Dean that he would have final approval of professors appointed to the "Deane Human Futures Institute" (aka "Institute for the Study of the Human Agenda"), an on-campus research center that was to be established by a $20 million donation from Deane. After Deane's veto power was disclosed and publicized by the student newspaper—two months after Deane's funding for the institute was announced—a number of professors protested. In an effort at spin control, Duke president H. Keith Brodie asked Deane to surrender his veto power, which Deane refused to do because university administrators had already agreed to his terms. In fact, Brodie had agreed to sit with Deane on the oversight committee empowered to veto appointments to the institute.[18] Thereafter, Deane withdrew his offer of support, saying, "I sit here in great surprise . . . that they would alienate someone as wealthy as I am . . . The idiots have plucked a bad chicken."[19]

The U.S.-Japan Foundation, which is funded by Ryoichi Sasakawa, a Japanese businessman, political influence peddler, and ultranationalist who was jailed by the Allies after World War II as a war criminal, has given grants for Japanese studies programs to Duke, the University of Kansas, the University of Arkansas, and other colleges. The author of *Agents of Influence* and 1996 Reform Party vice-presidential candidate, Pat Choate, maintains that this funding promotes pro–Japanese government attitudes at universities, a view shared by several Japanese scholars. York University professor Bob Wakabayashi believes that, if nothing else, Sasakawa is "working hand in glove with the Japanese government to white-wash their war record."[20]

Similarly, Germany and France underwrite German and French studies courses at Harvard, Princeton, Georgetown, and other universities. And the Saudi government has recently given $5 million to Harvard University, which will teach classes in "Islamic Law."[21]

Faustian Contracts

Directly funding programs and courses is just one way that corporations, governments, millionaires, and foundations wield influence at universities. Other ways include contracts and grants, the funding of endowed chairs, and the sponsoring of "research centers."

Contracts are commercial agreements between universities and corporations, whereas grants are tax-deductible contributions given to universities by corporations. Grants are most often given for research in areas of interest to the donor.

Recently, corporations like Coca-Cola, Pepsico, Nike, and Reebock have signed contracts with universities, giving the corporations exclusive licensing or campus marketing rights. Typical of these were the agreement signed by the University of Minnesota and Coca-Cola, and by the University of Wisconsin–Madison and Reebock. The Minnesota-Coke deal, heralded by university officials as "a national model for beverage partnering in higher education," gave Coca-Cola the exclusive rights to sell soft drinks on campus, the use of the University of Minnesota name and logo, and the right to stage promotional events, such as the Diet Coke Volleyball Classic, on campus.[22]

The University of Wisconsin's marketing agreement with Reebock, signed in 1996, gives the manufacturer exclusive rights to produce clothing and athletic shoes bearing the university logo. The terms of the deal were similar to ones signed by Reebock with UCLA and the University of Texas, and by Nike with the University of Michigan and Florida State University. In addition to the usual athletic scholarships, monies for coaches who make promotional appearances for Reebock, and student internships at the manufacturer's headquarters, the University of Wisconsin contract carried a paragraph prohibiting the university and its employees from criticizing Reebock. The "university will not issue any official statement that disparages Reebock," the agreement said, and the "university will promptly take all reasonable steps to address any remark by any university employee, including a coach, that disparages Reebock."[23]

The speech-restriction provisions were not publicly disclosed until long after other details of the contract had been made public and debated, particularly by student activists who protested Reebock's use of low-paid Asian workers to manufacture their athletic shoes. When the censorship provisions finally surfaced, dozens of UW faculty signed a letter expressing their opposition to it. Embarrassed by the flak that the speech-restriction paragraph generated—and their willingness to cast aside First Amendment and academic freedoms for several million dollars—university administrators retreated, asking Reebock to cancel the speech-prohibition paragraph of the contract. Reebock, facing a public relations disaster, soon agreed.[24]

In fact, however, contracts between universities and corporations that contain restrictive speech and publication clauses of this type are common, particularly in the biomedical disciplines. A study published in the New England Journal of Medicine found that the majority of companies entering into research agreements with universities require that any findings be "kept confidential to protect its proprietary value *beyond the time required to file a patent* [emphasis added]."[25] The added time gives the companies a competitive advantage with follow-up research. It also makes it far more difficult for other scientists to replicate the study—thus undercutting basic principles of the scientific method.

According to the National Cancer Institute's Steven Rosenberg, this secrecy is already impeding scientific research. Rosenberg contends that "open discussion among scientists, even about the preliminary results of ongoing experiments, if the preliminary nature of the results is made clear, can play an important part in advancing research." Instead of this taking place, the secrecy agreements have imposed "the ethical and operational rules of business" on scientific researchers.[26]

Some contracts also contain paragraphs giving the corporate contractor the right to determine whether research findings can ever be made public. For example, a British pharmaceutical corporation, the Boots Company, funded research at the University of California–San Francisco that compared the company's Synthroid drug, used by hypothyroid patients, with competing, lower-cost alternatives. The company hoped that the research would demonstrate that Synthroid and the lower-cost competitors were not bioequivalents. The contract was for $250,000 and was conducted by clinical pharmacist Betty Dong.

Instead of demonstrating Synthroid's superiority, however, the study found that the lower-cost drugs and Synthroid were equivalent. The results, if made public, had the potential to save consumers some $356 million annually if they switched from Synthroid to the lower cost alternatives, according to the *Wall Street Journal*, but would have undermined Synthroid's domination of the $600 million synthetic hormone market.[27]

When Boots discovered that Professor Dong intended to publish her findings in the *Journal of the American Medical Association*, which had subjected the study to vigorous blind-review,

Boots barred publication, citing provisions in the research contract. The contract stated that the study results "were not to be published or otherwise released without written consent" of the company. Not only did Boots block the publication of the findings, but it publicly attacked the study the company itself had funded, claiming that the research was severely flawed. Dong was unable to effectively counter these claims because she could not make the study public.

Named Professorships and Research Centers

Another method by which corporations today influence universities is through endowed chairs, also called endowed professorships. Endowed professorships were first established by universities to honor nationally known scholars who taught or graduated from them. For example, Harvard University's Charles Eliot Norton Professorship of Poetry honors the university's first professor of the history of art, who died in 1898. Other professorships are named for deceased alumni, who bequeathed their estates to their alma maters.

Increasingly, however, endowed chairs are funded by and named for corporations, conservative foundations, and wealthy patrons with distinct political and academic agendas. Cal Bradford, a former fellow at the University of Minnesota's Humphrey Institute for Public Policy, criticizes these endowed professorships, saying that such funding determines "what universities will teach and research, what direction the university will take. . . . If universities would decide that they needed an endowed chair in English, and then try to raise the money for it, it would be one thing. But that's not what happens. Corporate donors decide to fund chairs in areas that they want research done. Their decisions determine which topics universities explore and which aren't." Bradford's own contract at the University of Minnesota was not renewed after he criticized university-corporate ties.

Corporate-funded professorships often bear the corporation's name and define the purpose of the professorship. Some examples are the Bell South Professor of Education through Tele-communication (at the University of South Carolina), the Reliance Corp. Professor of Free Enterprise (at the University of Pennsylvania), the Carlson Travel, Tour and Hospitality Chair (at the University of Minnesota), and the Lamar Savings Professor-ship of Finance (at Texas A & M), the last of which was named for a defunct savings and loan whose operators were convicted of embezzling $85 million.

Many endowed professorships come with strings attached. The initial agreement between the University of Pennsylvania and Saul Steinberg, head of the Reliance Corp., stipulated that the Reliance Corp. Professor of Free Enterprise was to be "a spokes-person for the free enterprise system" and engage "twice a year in employee training or another aspect of Reliance operations."[28]

The Carlson Chair at the University of Minnesota was en-dowed by the owner of the Carlson Travel Network, which also serves as the university's travel agency. The endowment provides money for the Carlson Chair to do research on issues of interest to the travel industry. Arnold Hewes, the executive vice president of the Minnesota Restaurant, Hotel and Resort Associations, praised this arrangement, saying, "we'll have data on who comes to Minnesota and why, why people fail to return, and other statis-tics that we need to make decisions about advertising, marketing and promotion."[29]

The University of Memphis, based in Federal Express Corp.'s hometown, houses the Federal Express Chair of Excellence in Information Technology. The Federal Express professor also heads the Federal Express Center for Cycle Time Research, a think tank or research center devoted to studying overnight air delivery.

Research centers such as the Federal Express Center for Cycle Time Research also allow patrons to influence universities. Re-search centers are typically funded by a single corporation or tycoon and often bear the name of their sponsor. The University of Wisconsin—Milwaukee houses the Johnson Controls Institute for Environmental Quality in Architecture, which is funded by

Johnson Controls, Inc., a manufacturer of electrical controls for heating and air conditioning. Johnson Controls provides $200,000 a year to support the center, whose professors work on research projects of interest to the corporation. A company spokesperson said the purpose of the institute is to discover how "workers and students can be more productive when a building's heating, cooling, lighting and sound systems are properly controlled."[30]

Southern Methodist University in Dallas is home to the Maguire Oil and Gas Institute, named for and funded by Cary M. Maguire, the CEO of Maguire Oil Co. The institute's purpose "is to advance productive working relations with key industrial and government leaders, and with academic departments and programs."[31] The institute achieves this goal by producing reports such as "Oil and Environmentalism Do Mix," which laments that "instead of harmonizing oil and gas discoveries with environmental goals, [environmental laws] have resulted in an extravagant amount of federal land being placed off-limits to oil and gas leasing. . . . Experience in Alaska, Michigan and Wyoming show that oil and gas activity, with proper care and supervision, can be compatible with the environment."[32] Such opinionated writings gain an aura of objectivity because they are produced at universities rather than corporate public relations departments.

Most universities have similar centers. The University of Utah is home to the Garn Institute of Finance, which functions as a pseudononymous lobby group for banks and savings and loans, which are its principal funders. The institute is named for former senator Jake Garn, who co-wrote the legislation that deregulated the savings and loans industry, setting the stage for the multibillion dollar frauds and bankruptcies of the 1980s. The Garn Institute's chairman is Richard T. Pratt of Merrill Lynch Mortgage Capital, who, as President Reagan's first head of the Federal Home Loan Bank Board, oversaw the unfolding S & L crisis. In *The Greatest-Ever Bank Robbery*, Martin Mayer wrote that Pratt "had fired the guards and suspended the rules. . . . [I]f you had to pick one individual to blame for what happened to the S & Ls and to hundreds of billions of dollars in taxpayer money, Dick would get the honor without even campaigning."[33]

Foreign corporations, foundations, and governments, especially those in Taiwan, Japan, and Korea, have also funded research centers and endowed professorships. For example, the University of Minnesota houses the China Times Center for Media and Social Studies, which seeks "humbly to promote China's democracy." The center is named for a Taiwan publishing company, which produces Taiwan's largest circulation, pro-government newspaper, owned by a member of the central committee of Taiwan's ruling Kuomintang political party. Funding for the China Times Center comes from a foundation established and controlled by the publisher.[34]

To help Taiwan achieve its objectives of embarrassing and isolating its archenemy, the People's Republic of China, the center sponsors conferences and research critical of China, and its associates pump out articles condemning China's policies. A professor associated with the China Times Center recently returned from a sabbatical leave in Hong Kong, where he wrote numerous articles criticizing China's impending takeover of Hong Kong.[35]

Japanese money underwrites the Fuyo Bank Professorship of Japanese Law at Columbia University, the Nissan Chair of International Economics at Northwestern University, and the Konsuke Matsushita Professorship of International Economics and Policy Analysis at Stanford University. Five Japanese firms, including Nippon Telephone and Telegraph, Kirin Brewery, and Mitsubishi Bank, have endowed chairs at the Massachusetts Institute of Technology.[36]

At Johns Hopkins, Japan has endowed the Yasuhiro Nakasone professorship, provided professors with research money, and funded the Center for East Asian Studies. "We are uninfluenced by Japanese money," contends Vance Packard, the Dean of Johns Hopkins's Nitze School of Advanced International Studies and head of the Center for East Asian Studies. Although Japan's largesse has not influenced him, Packard nevertheless published articles such as "The Japan Bashers Are Poisoning Foreign

Policy" and "The U.S. and Japan: Partners in Prosperity," which extoll the virtues of Japan's trade practices and criticized opponents of these practices. The space in the *Atlantic Monthly* for the latter sixteen-page "article," actually an advertisement, was purchased by the Japanese Chamber of Commerce.[37]

Other countries and interest groups are now investing in the academy with similar goals in mind. Since 1993, Turkey has contributed some $3 million for endowed chairs in Turkish studies at Princeton, Harvard, Georgetown, and the University of Chicago.

Rather than selecting an expert on the Turkish genocide of Armenians or on the repression of Turkish Kurds for its "Ataturk Chair of Turkish Studies," Princeton hired Heath Lowry, who previously served as the executive director of a Turkish-funded lobbying group, the Institute of Turkish Studies. Lowry attracted attention to himself, and the hostility of genocide scholars, by claiming that Turkey did not massacre thousands of Armenians in 1915 and 1916. The deaths were not the result of genocide, Lowry contends, but an unintended outgrowth of wartime deprivation. As Lowry explains it, the Turkish "government's decision to relocate its Armenian citizenry into northern Syria created a situation in which the deportees were subjected to attacks by marauding Kurdish tribesmen, starvation and the ravages of cholera and typhus epidemics." Several bona fide genocide scholars have described Lowry as "an apologist for the Turkish government."[38]

From Federal Grants to Corporate R & D

Corporations and foreign governments have struck up such intimate relations with universities in part for public relations and tax purposes. Corporations receive tax breaks for their contributions, even when the contributions primarily advance the interests of the company. For example, contributions by banks to the Garn Institute at the University of Utah are tax-deductible, since they are given to an ostensibly nonprofit, educational institution. Moreover, research centers such as the Garn Institute and the China Times Center promote the interests of their donors, as previously noted, but have a facade of objectivity that trade and lobbying groups lack.

Another reason why corporations—including foreign-based companies—have provided research funds to universities can be explained by economics: it is cheaper to have research done at university laboratories, built by taxpayers and tuition dollars, than building and equipping comparable corporate laboratories. Universities also employ low-paid graduate students as research assistants, who make far less than their counterparts in the private sector, allowing universities to perform research for less.

An example of universities providing low-cost, high-tech research for companies can be found at the University of Wisconsin–Milwaukee (UWM), which performs studies on latex paint for the Rust-Oleum Corp. Rust-Oleum traditionally tested its paints by exposing painted samples to corrosive conditions but was unable to determine what was leading to early corrosion in one of its latex paints.

To solve the problem, the paint manufacturer turned to UWM's well-equipped, taxpayer-funded laboratories. UMW chemists used electron microscopy and energy dispersive X-ray spectroscopy costing tens of thousands of dollars—equipment which the company would not buy on its own—to determine that a sulphur compound in the pigment was the source of the corrosion. UWM received a few thousand dollars for the studies.[39]

Research like this is subsidized by taxpayers and students, in effect, because they pay for the facilities and researchers' salaries. An audit of the University of Rhode Island's finances by the *Chicago Tribune* found that research costs are passed on to students in the form of higher tuition, which has increased some 232 percent in the past fifteen years. The *Tribune* study concluded that "without the losses research incurs, Rhode Island, in theory, could have cut its $4,404 tuition almost in half." The University of Rhode Island's president disputed the amount that tuition was raised to subsidize research, but nevertheless conceded that a tuition subsidy for research probably exists.[40]

Another reason why corporations have been striking up relationships with universities is the Dole-Bayh Act, passed by Congress in 1980. The act, also known as the University–Small Business Patents Procedures Act, allows universities to sell the results of federally funded research to corporations, often at a fraction of the cost that would be involved if the companies did the studies themselves.

Corporations have learned that they are able to buy federally funded research results by investing modest amounts of money in universities. For example, the Switzerland-based Sandoz Corp. signed an agreement in December 1992 with the Dana-Farber Institute, a Harvard University teaching hospital, that gave Sandoz the rights to research discoveries made at the institute, even if Sandoz did not directly pay for the studies. Sandoz bought the rights to the discoveries of any researcher who accepted any Sandoz funding, even when Sandoz's money went to an unrelated project. In effect, Sandoz can claim the rights to the results of federally funded studies during the ten-year agreement, if the scientists involved had accepted any Sandoz money during the same term.[41]

Finally, corporate contributors can count on universities when they are in a bind. For example, at the University of Texas at Austin, the dean of the College of Communication ordered the chair of the Department of Journalism to not testify in a lawsuit against the owner of the *Dallas News*, the Belo Corp., which donated $300,000 to the University of Texas's College of Communication. The lawsuit charged that the Belo Corp. engaged in unfair business practices that drove the competing *Dallas Times Herald* out of business. The journalism department chair had conducted research showing that the *Dallas News* monopolized popular syndicated features, which contributed to the *Times Herald*'s demise.

To rationalize his order, Dean Robert Jeffrey contended that there "is an unwritten rule in the Department of Journalism, and the college in general, that says a professor should not testify in a trial against a newspaper."[42]

There is another unwritten rule in academe, which explains why universities now generally attend to the interests of their well-heeled patrons, rather than students: it is the old adage "Whoever pays the piper calls the tune."

Notes

1. Bradley F. Smith, *The Shadow Warriors* (New York: Basic Books, 1983), pp. 360–361. Lawrence C. Soley, *Radio Warfare* (New York: Praeger, 1989), p. 59. Allan Winkler, *The Politics of Propaganda* (New Haven: Yale University Press, 1978). Hadley Cantril, *The Human Dimension* (New Brunswick, N.J.: Rutgers University Press, 1967), pp. 31–34. The Listening Center was initially funded by the Rockefeller Foundation.

2. Stephen Budiansky, Erica Goode, and Tod Geste, "The Cold War Experiments," *U.S. News & World Report,* January 24, 1994. Keith Schneider, "Nuclear Scientists Irradiated People in Secret Research," *New York Times,* Dec. 17, 1993.

3. Christopher Simpson, *Science of Coercion* (New York: Oxford University Press, 1994), p. 3.

4. National Science Foundation, "Table B-2: Federal Obligations for Science and Engineering Going to Colleges and Universities by Type of Activity and Agency: Fiscal Years 1963–1993," http://www.nsf.gov/srs. (1996)

5. Millard Johnson, "Majoring in Technology Transfer," *Corporate Report Wisconsin,* September 1994, p. 8.

6. Ronald Alsop, "Capitalism 101: Programs to Teach Free Enterprise Sprout on College Campuses," *Wall Street Journal,* May 10, 1978.

7. Peter Applebome, "In Gingrich's College Course, Critics Find a Wealth of Ethical Concerns," *New York Times,* Feb. 20, 1995.

8. Kevin Phillips, *The Politics of the Rich and Poor* (New York: Random House, 1990), pp. 84–85.

9. Nan Aron, Barbara Moulten and Chris Owens, "Economics, Academia, and Corporate Money in American," *Antitrust and Economic Review* (1993), pp. 27–42.

10. *John M. Olin Institute for Strategic Studies* (Cambridge, Mass.: Harvard University Center for International Affairs, n.d.), p. 1. Charles Claffey, "Separating Myth from Maître," *Boston Globe,* July 12, 1991.

11. *The New Face of Marketing Research* (Madison: University of Wisconsin, n.d.), p. 8. "Coke Gives $1 Million to University of Georgia," UPI, Feb. 23, 1983, BC cycle.

12. "MSU Department of Telecommunication and Michigan Bell Dedicate New Information Technologies and Services Lab," *PR Newswire,* Apr. 21, 1989. "Ameritech Grants," *PR Newswire,* Apr. 30, 1987. Chris

Welles, "Fit or Unfit Business News," in William McPhatter, ed., *The Business Beat* (Indianapolis: Bobbs-Merrill, 1980), pp. 33–34.

13. Subcommittee on International Organizations, International Relations Committee, U.S. House of Representatives, *Investigation of Korean-American Relations* (Washington, D.C.: USGPO, Oct. 31, 1978), p. 280.

14. Quoted in Bruce Cumings, *South Korea's Academic Lobby*, JPRI Occasional Paper No. 7 (Cardiff, Calif.: Japan Policy Research Institute, May 1996), p. 3.

15. Amy Magaro Rubin, "South Korean Support for U.S. Scholars Raises Fears of Undue Influence," *Chronicle of Higher Education*, Oct. 4, 1996, A10–A11.

16. Peter S. Goodman, "Foreign Funding Can Be Problematic for U.S. Academics," *Washington Post*, Nov. 29, 1996.

17. Jacques Steinberg, "Yale Returns $20 Million to an Unhappy Patron," *New York Times*, Mar. 15, 1995.

18. Michael Milstein et al., "When the Price Is to High," *Newsweek on Campus*, Nov. 1987.

19. Kevin O'Brien, "The $20 Million Question: Did Financier Renege on Duke University Gift?," *Charlotte Observer*, Feb. 6, 1990.

20. Karen Grassmuck, "Japanese Businessman's Background Stirs Debate Over Whether Colleges Should Accept his Gifts," *Chronicle of Higher Education*, May 2, 1990. Walter Shapiro, "Is Washington in Japan's Pocket?," *Time* Oct. 1, 1990.

21. Ken Brown, "Fearing Shrunken Stature, France Endows a Fund," *New York Times*, Feb. 23, 1994. "Saudi Gift Sets Up Islamic Law Center," *New York Times*, June 11, 1993.

22. "U of M Signs Agreement with Coca-Cola," University of Minnesota press release, undated; F.J. Gallagher, "U Gets Ready for Coke Deal," *Minnesota Daily*, January 10, 1996.

23. "Campus Fight Leads Reebock to Modify a Shoe Contract," *New York Times*, June 28, 1996.

24. Robert McChesney and Linda Gordon, "UW Faculty, Staff Say the Reebock Deal Should be Reversed," *Capital Times*, July 1, 1996.

25. David Blumenthal et al., "Relationships Between Academic Institutions and Industry in the Life Sciences—An Industry Survey," *New England Journal of Medicine*, Feb. 8, 1996.

26. Steven A. Rosenberg, "Secrecy in Medical Research," *New England Journal of Medicine*, Feb. 8, 1996.

27. Ralph T. King Jr., "How a Drug Firm Paid for a University Study, Then Undermined It," *Wall Street Journal*, Apr. 25, 1996.

28. "Documents Relating to the Endowment of the Reliance Professorship/Dean," *Almanac* (University of Pennsylvania publication), Jan. 27, 1981.

29. Maura Lerner, "Endowed Chair for Tourism at 'U' May Be a First," *Minneapolis Star Tribune*, Feb. 28, 1991, p. B3.

30. Johnson Controls, "Business-Education Partnership Creates Mecca for Study of More Pro-

ductive Buildings," Sept. 17, 1993 (news release). Interviews, Sept. 17, 1993.

31. *Graduate Bulletin of Southern Methodist University* (Dallas: Southern Methodist University, 1992), pp. 101–102.

32. "Oil and Environmentalism Do Mix," *Chicago Tribune,* June 21, 1986, p. 9.

33. Martin Mayer, *The Greatest-Ever Bank Robbery* (New York: Charles Scribner's Sons, 1990), 61.

34. "Director's Forward," *Messenger* (Report of the China Times Center for Media and Social Studies), Aug. 1, 1990.

35. Jon Lundgren, "Chang Studies Press Freedom in Hong Kong," *The Murphy Reporter* (University of Minnesota publication), summer 1995.

36. Barbara Durr, "Japanese Strategy to Win Friends," *Financial Times,* Apr. 17, 1990.

37. George R. Packard, "The Japan-Bashers Are Poisoning Foreign Policy," *Washington Post,* Oct. 8, 1989, p. C4. George R. Packard, "The U.S. and Japan: Partners in Prosperity," *Atlantic Monthly,* February 1989, pp. A1–A16.

38. William H. Honan, "Princeton Is Accused of Fronting for the Turkish Government," *New York Times,* May 20, 1996, p. B6. John Yemma, "Turkish Largesse Raises Questions," *Boston Globe,* Nov. 25, 1995, p. 1.

39. Mark Ward, "UWM Lab Digs Beneath the Surface," *Milwaukee Journal Sentinel,* July 28, 1995, p. 2B.

40. Ron Grossman and Charles Leroux, "Research Grants Actually Add to Tuition Costs, Study Reveals," *Chicago Tribune,* Jan. 28, 1996, pp. A1 and A19. Robert L. Carothers, "University Research Not a 'Loss,'" *Chicago Tribune,* Feb. 24, 1996, p. 20.

41. Julie Nicklin, " University Deal With Drug Company Raises Concern over Autonomy, Secrecy," *Chronicle of Higher Education,* Mar. 24, 1993, pp. A24–A25.

42. "UT Dean May Be Subpoenaed in Newspaper Dispute," *United Press International* (regional news), Apr. 5, 1990, BC cycle.

Index

Page references followed by "n." or "nn." refer to information in notes.

About the Authors

Franz Boas is widely regarded as a founder of modern anthropology. He was among the first to bring scientific techniques to the discipline, articulated many basic principles for the interpretation of human culture, pioneered much of the modern anthropological curriculum, and exhaustively documented the beliefs and customs of indigenous peoples of the Pacific northwest. Boas was among the most outspoken opponents of racism and Nazism of his generation. He died in 1942.

Bruce Cumings is professor of international history and East Asian economy at the University of Chicago. He is the author or co-author of eight books, including the two-volume *Origins of the Korean War* (1981, 1990), *War and Television* (1992), and *Korea's Place in the Sun: A Modern History* (1997).

Kevin Gaines is an associate professor of history and African American studies at the University of Texas, Austin. He is the author of *Uplifting the Race: Black Leadership, Politics, and Culture During the Twentieth Century* (1996). He is presently writing a book on African American expatriates in Ghana and the impact on the early civil rights movement of the Cold War and U.S. foreign policy toward Africa.

Irene L. Gendzier is a professor of political science at Boston University and works in the areas of U.S. foreign policy, North African and Middle East studies, and problems of development and maldevelopment. Among her recent books are *Development Against Democracy* (1995) and *Notes from the Minefield: U.S. Intervention in Lebanon and the Middle East* (1997).

Slava Gerovitch earned his Ph.D. in the history and philosophy of science from the Russian Academy of Sciences in 1992. He is currently working on his second doctorate in the Science,

Technology, and Society program at MIT. Gerovitch is also a research associate at the Institute for the History of Natural Science and Technology of the Russian Academy of Sciences. His specialties include the history of Soviet cybernetics and cross-cultural scientific communication.

Ellen Herman is the author of *The Romance of American Psychology: Political Culture in the Age of Experts* (1995) and *Psychiatry, Psychology, and Homosexuality* (1995). She is an assistant professor of history at the University of Oregon and has also taught at Harvard University and the University of Massachusetts. She is interested in norms and normalizing technologies, the professionalization of help, and the problem of knowability in the human sciences. Portions of her essay in this collection appeared in somewhat different form in *The Romance of American Psychology*.

Max Franklin Millikan served as the chief of economic intelligence for Europe at the U.S. Department of State shortly after World War II, assistant director of the Central Intelligence Agency during 1951–52, then director of the Center for International Studies at MIT from 1952 until his death in 1969. Millikan also served as president of the World Peace Foundation (1956–69) and trustee of the Carnegie Endowment for International Peace (1964–69).

Allan A. Needell is a curator in the Space History Department of the Smithsonian Institution's National Air and Space Museum. He is responsible, among his collecting areas, for the museum's manned space flight collections (Mercury, Gemini, and Apollo). He has published on the history of physics, the origins of American national laboratories, science and national security, and government-science relations. He is currently working on a biography of the American science administrator Lloyd V. Berkner.

Walt W. Rostow is a professor emeritus of economics and history at the University of Texas at Austin. Rostow is the author of more than a dozen books, including *The Dynamics of Soviet Society* (1953), *Prospects for Communist China* (1953), and *The Stages of Economic Growth: A Non-Communist Manifesto* (1960). Professor Rostow is perhaps best known as author of the "Rostow thesis" concerning U.S. strategy in Vietnam and other emerging nations during the 1960s, which outlined "a combined physical and psychological assault" to deter support for insurgents who might otherwise challenge U.S. interests.

Christopher Simpson is the author of four books concerning the history and politics of mass media and Cold War and national security agencies, including *Blowback* (1987), *The Splendid Blond Beast* (1993), *Science of Coercion* (1994), and *National Security Directives of the Reagan and Bush Administrations* (1995), as well as numerous articles for journals and professional publications. His work has won many awards, including the National Jewish Book Award for historical writing concerning the Holocaust and the Investigative Reporters and Editors Prize for books. He teaches in the School of Communication at American University in Washington, D.C.

Lawrence Soley holds the Colnick Chair of Communication at Marquette University in Milwaukee. He is the author of *Leasing the Ivory Tower* (1995), *The News Shapers* (1992), *Radio Warfare* (1989), and *Clandestine Radio Broadcasting* (with J. Nichols, 1987). Soley and *Nation* reporter Marc Cooper shared the 1991 Sigma Delta Chi Award for reporting on political pundits.